The New Silk Road and the Innovation Economy in China

This book provides deep insight into the emergent Chinese innovation economy, as we head towards the Fourth Industrial Revolution. It describes, discusses and analyses the period from China's opening up to foreign investment in the 1980s until the New Silk Road project, from 2013 onwards. The developments are assessed from a systemic thinking and evolutionary economic standpoint.

The book presents the latest research findings on the direction and achievements of the Belt and Road Initiative and the results both for China, the countries along the new Silk Road as well as for Europe and the United States are brought to light. The author asserts that the phenomenon of the New Silk Road as an innovation generator can be understood and explained through the effects of various social mechanisms. He labels these five social mechanisms as: the locomotive force; the explosive force of the butterfly effect; the force of co-creation; the force of expectation; and the force of competence.

The book presents 20 cases to substantiate the descriptions, analysis, theoretical reflections and the practical utility of the questions examined in each chapter. It utilizes economic history research methods, scenario thinking, futures research and conceptual generalization to offer different views on the research problem under investigation. Further, the book offers policy suggestions, which include promoting effective macroeconomic policies and extending microeconomic cooperation schemes related to the innovation economy.

The book will appeal to academics, researchers and graduate students concerned with Chinese economic expansion, Chinese foreign policy and US– and Europe–China relations, as well as policymakers and political advisors.

Jon-Arild Johannessen is Full Professor at Kristiania University College, Oslo, Norway.

Routledge Studies in the Economics of Innovation

The *Routledge Studies in the Economics of Innovation* series is our home for comprehensive yet accessible texts on the current thinking in the field. These cutting-edge, upper-level scholarly studies and edited collections bring together robust theories from a wide range of individual disciplines and provide in-depth studies of existing and emerging approaches to innovation, and the implications of such for the global economy.

The Dynamics of the Innovation Divide between China and Europe
National and Regional Dimensions
Edited by Arkadiusz Michal Kowalski

A Systemic Approach to Continuous Change in the Innovation Economy
Jon-Arild Johannessen

Industrial Revolution 4.0
Economic Foundations and Practical Implications
Edited by Stanisław Mazur

Global Innovation, Finance, and International Commerce
F. John Mathis and Raja M. Almarzoqi

Philosophy of Digital Currencies
A Theory of Monetising Time
Ugochukwu Chigoziem Ikpeazu

The New Silk Road and the Innovation Economy in China
Jon-Arild Johannessen

For more information about this series, please visit: www.routledge.com/Routledge-Studies-in-the-Economics-of-Innovation/book-series/ECONINN

The New Silk Road and the Innovation Economy in China

Jon-Arild Johannessen

Routledge
Taylor & Francis Group
LONDON AND NEW YORK

First published 2023
by Informa Law from Routledge
4 Park Square, Milton Park, Abingdon, Oxon OX14 4RN

and by Informa Law from Routledge
605 Third Avenue, New York, NY 10158

Informa Law from Routledge is an imprint of the Taylor & Francis Group, an informa business

British Library Cataloguing-in-Publication Data
A catalogue record for this book is available from the British Library

Library of Congress Cataloging-in-Publication Data
Names: Johannessen, Jon-Arild, author.
Title: The new silk road and the innovation economy in China / Jon-Arild Johannessen.
Description: Milton Park, Abingdon, Oxon ; New York, NY : Routledge, 2023. | Includes bibliographical references and index.
Identifiers: LCCN 2022040545 (print) | LCCN 2022040546 (ebook) | ISBN 9781032328362 (hardback) | ISBN 9781032328379 (paperback) | ISBN 9781003316978 (ebook)
Subjects: LCSH: Technological innovations--Economic aspects--China. | Economic development--China. | China--Commerce. | Yi dai yi lu (Initiative : China)
Classification: LCC HC430.T4 J65 2023 (print) | LCC HC430.T4 (ebook) | DDC 338/.0640951--dc23/eng/20220914
LC record available at https://lccn.loc.gov/2022040545
LC ebook record available at https://lccn.loc.gov/2022040546

ISBN: 978-1-032-32836-2 (hbk)
ISBN: 978-1-032-32837-9 (pbk)
ISBN: 978-1-003-31697-8 (ebk)

DOI: 10.4324/9781003316978

Typeset in Bembo
by SPi Technologies India Pvt Ltd (Straive)

Contents

Figures

Foreword

The book's focus is on innovation processes linked to the New Silk Road. The ancient Silk Road was a trade route for silk that was established at the beginning of the Han Dynasty (second century BC). The Silk Road became an important factor in the development and growth of China, Korea and Japan.[1] The Silk Road refers to both land and sea trade routes connecting Europe, the Middle East, India and Africa. The New Silk Road has something of the same purpose: connecting the countries along the New Silk Road so that the countries can cooperate, reduce tensions and develop value creation in and between the nations along the route.

The old Silk Road was not only a trading route.[2] "The Silk Road" may also be viewed as a generalized concept that included trade, infrastructure, info-structure,[3] cultural cooperation projects, etc. Among other things, Chinese innovations were exported to Europe, such as the compass, gunpowder, paper-making and printing techniques. In addition to these innovations, goods were exported along this route, such as silk, porcelain, tea, rice, millet, cinnamon, ginger, musk, etc. There were also many goods that were exported east along the old Silk Road to China, such as walnuts, melons, black pepper, carrots, etc. (Zou, 2018: 2).

The New Silk Road as a concept was originally announced by Xi Jinping in September 2013, during an official visit to Kazakhstan.[4] Among other things, the purpose of the initiative is to develop and implement innovations along the New Silk Road. These innovations will to a great extent be linked to artificial intelligence, intelligent robots and all the new technology that is expected to emerge during the Fourth Industrial Revolution (Angang, 2014; Batzhan et al., 2020). Moreover, one of the major economic consequences of the New Silk Road could be that millions of unskilled workers will find employment in the thousands of projects and infrastructure projects. This will create an economic multiplier effect for many of the countries that have not developed expertise in the development and maintenance of new technology. In this way, the New Silk Road will also function as an economic stimulus for many of the countries that are struggling to find employment for unskilled workers. This can create a "locomotive-effect"[5] for industrialization and especially the dispersal and development of technological innovations in these countries. At the same time, the New Silk Road can act as a two-way circular economic generator for these countries. This means that the countries will be able to develop a stable national economy where there is strong domestic demand, while at the same time benefiting from the economic development that follows from the cooperation projects along the New Silk Road.

The New Silk Road was first intended as an infrastructure initiative.[6] However, in recent years many other projects that go far beyond infrastructure development have also become part of the New Silk Road initiative. The intention was and is a mutual-cooperation or co-creation effect,[7] where the countries along the New Silk Road reap the benefits of synergy effects and win–win projects and situations. The economic ties between the countries that are part of the New Silk Road, along both the land and sea routes, such as countries in Africa like Namibia, have become more closely knit. The development of such economic ties is evident in many of the projects found along the maritime New Silk Road in Africa in general (French, 2015), and in Namibia in particular.[8] The development of the projects along the New Silk Road, along the land and sea routes, is intended to bring about positive transformations for the economies of the countries involved. We refer to this effect here as an economic and social type of "butterfly-effect".[9] The co-creation effects and the butterfly-effects lead to a new effect which we refer to here as the "feedforward-effect".[10] This refers to the expectations regarding national sub-production and national participation in the development of the technological innovations that are expected to result from the development of projects along the New Silk Road. This was also made clear in the speech mentioned above, where Xi Jinping announced the New Silk Road initiative.[11]

Notes

1 https://en.wikipedia.org/wiki/Silk_Road.

2 There were four main trade routes than ran west from China: the original "Oasis Route"; the sea route to India, the Middle East and Africa; the route that went over the Steppes of Asia to the west; and the south-western route (Zou, 2018: 2).

3 Information structure (info-structure) is the development of all information and communication processes, which are not related to the infrastructure "matter / energy processes".

4 https://en.wikipedia.org/wiki/Belt_and_Road_Initiative.

5 Locomotive-effect: This refers to something that generates and then reinforces an activity or development.

6 https://en.wikipedia.org/wiki/Belt_and_Road_Initiative.

7 Co-creation: Co-creation involves working together to promote knowledge processes and innovation. If knowledge processes and innovation are essential for value creation in the knowledge society, co-creation is an important social mechanism for initiating, maintaining and strengthening these processes. The balance between competition and cooperation, embodied in the concept of co-creation, leads to constructive criticism and the necessary scope of knowledge that exists in the network so as to promote creativity and the innovative. Instead of a zero-sum situation, a positive-sum situation will be developed where everyone wins.

8 https://www.chinadaily.com.cn/a/202010/28/WS5f98b8a8a31024ad0ba8164d.html.

9 **Butterfly-effect**: Small, often haphazard and improbable variables potentially capable of having large-scale consequences for social systems and nature.

10 **Feedforward**: Feedforward is regarded here as an expectation mechanism. It seems reasonable to assume that our expectations influence our behaviour in the present. It is therefore important that we make explicit to ourselves the expectations we have of a situation. By making expectations explicit, we have a greater opportunity to learn from our experiences and thus improve our performance. (https://en.wikipedia.org/wiki/Feedforward).

11 https://en.wikipedia.org/wiki/Belt_and_Road_Initiative.

References

Angang, H. (2014). Silk Road economic belt: Strategic considerations, positioning and implementation routes. *Journal of Xinjiang Normal University*, 2: 1–10.

Batzhan, A., Alpysbayeva, S., & Kapsalyamova, Z. (2020). The Belt and Road initiative: Case of Kazakhstan. In Wah, C.Y., Menkhoff, T., & Low, L. (Eds.), *Chinas Belt and Road initiative: Understanding the dynamics of a global transformation*, World Scientific, London. pp. 71–97.

French, H.W. (2015). *Chinas second continent*, Random House, London.

Zou, L. (2018). *The political economy of China's belt and road initiative*, World Scientific, London.

1 The New Silk Road as an innovation generator

Key points in this chapter (and this book)

The phenomenon of the New Silk Road as an innovation generator can be understood and explained through the effects of various forces. The five forces are as follows: the locomotive force; the explosive force from a butterfly; the force of co-creation; the force of expectation; and the force of competence.

General findings

- The New Silk Road is not only an institutional innovation, but it is also an innovation generator for the countries affected by the various OBOR[1] projects.
- What has happened from China's opening up to foreign investment in the 1980s up until China's New Silk Road project, from 2013 onwards, is metaphorically a process where information has flooded into the country, where it has been transformed into knowledge, and then this knowledge has been exported as technological projects to large parts of the world through, among other things, the OBOR project.
- It would be a strategic blunder if China were to decide to escalate military tensions in the South China Sea because this would provide the United States and its ideological allies with an argument for isolating China from the international community.
- If the United States manages to create a conflict in the South China Sea involving China, their naval presence in the region will have achieved positive strategic results from an American perspective; namely, setting up barriers and building walls along the New Silk Road, isolating China, and providing the United States with the opportunity to take the leading global role as we enter the Fourth Industrial Revolution.

The Locomotive-effect

- American superprofits fuelled the Chinese technological and economic locomotive up the steep mountain slopes towards the West.

DOI: 10.4324/9781003316978-1

- If the New Silk Road and the various OBOR projects are viewed by observers in the EU and the United States as China's new expansion strategy, then the New Silk Road will be impeded by new East–West barriers, long before the road is fully constructed.
- If the EU erects barriers, there is much to suggest that the New Silk Road will turn even more towards Asia, Russia, Turkey, the Middle East and the African continent.
- From a long-term perspective, it may be Europe rather than China that has the most to lose from erecting barriers against China.

The butterfly-effect

- The United States is increasing military tensions in the South China Sea and East China Sea with the aim of portraying China as the aggressor to all those countries participating in the New Silk Road project.
- The United States' growing military build-up in the South and East China Seas is really a struggle to be the leader in the new technology because the country that is at the forefront of artificial intelligence development will also become the world leader as we enter the Fourth Industrial Revolution.
- If the United States manages to create a conflict in the South China Sea involving China, their naval presence in the region will have achieved positive strategic results from an American perspective; namely, setting up barriers and building walls along the New Silk Road, isolating China, and providing the United States with the opportunity to take the leading global role as we enter the Fourth Industrial Revolution.

The co-creation effect

- By "systemic involvement", we mean here that the countries that are most likely to succeed are those countries involved in projects from the beginning to the end. The hypothesis is that the greater the degree of systemic involvement, the greater the probability of project success.
- Economic growth and prosperity are the strategic intentions. China is not building a new Great Wall of China or an Iron Curtain along these economic corridors, but rather a bridge that binds together people who have more in common than what separates them. This bridge has been called the Eurasian Land Bridge by a leading institute in Berlin, which studies the relations between China and Germany.
- If the New Silk Road in Europe can promote the integration of the EU and those countries in Europe that aspire to EU membership, then the New Silk Road will have acquired a new function for the European continent.
- It may very well be the case that the US's involvement in the South China Sea does not have a military intention, but rather the oblique intention of breaking down the economic, political, and diplomatic ties that the New Silk Road (the Eurasian Land Bridge) will create with regard to the Europe–China relationship.

- In its consequences, the US military actions could slow down the development of the New Silk Road as an innovation generator for Europe.
- With the development of the New Silk Road, China has taken the step from being an export-driven economy to becoming an innovation-driven economy.

The feedforward effect

- There are two social mechanisms that can counteract the United States' attempt to exclude Chinese technology companies: (1) Cooperation takes precedence over competition. (2) A new globalization based on a high-tech innovation economy.
- What has happened from China's opening to foreign investment in the 1980s, up until China's Silk Road project from 2013 onwards, is metaphorically a process where information has flooded into the country, where it has been transformed into knowledge, and then this knowledge has been exported as technological projects to large parts of the world.
- Paradoxically, China's national security is linked to the security of all the countries participating in the projects linked to the New Silk Road, in Asia, the Middle East, Africa, and Europe. In other words, an economic attack on one of the countries included in the New Silk Road will represent an attack on all the countries because it will negatively impact the win–win projects.
- A significant point of the feedforward effect is the transition from the old globalization to the new globalization.
- The new globalization is characterized by innovative green economic growth, driven forward by high-technology, artificial intelligence and intelligent robots.
- It is the competence differentials not wage differentials that constitute the central social mechanism of the new globalization.
- Furthermore, the feedforward effect is based on a transition from an old mindset to a new mindset. The old mindset was driven by competition and win–lose thinking. The new mindset is driven by a collaborative philosophy and win–win thinking.

Introduction

An important consequence of the four above-mentioned "effects" of the New Silk Road, the "locomotive-effect", the "butterfly-effect", the "co-creation effect" and the "feedforward effect", is the development of what we refer to here as the "competence-network effect". This is the competence that is created by the collaborative networks that are developed through thousands of sub-projects that are being initiated along the New Silk Road. These competence networks may be divided into political, social, economic, technological and cultural patterns. It is when these five patterns interact that one may perceive the overall pattern. In the global knowledge economy, it seems reasonable to assume that those who control this pattern set the conditions for economic development. These global competence networks will most likely make an impact on organizations and companies competing for this kind of expertise in national markets. The purpose of competence networks is the development, dissemination and use of new ideas that promote wealth creation.

There is much to suggest that a greater degree of integration and cooperation between private and public sectors at the national and regional levels is an important prerequisite for initiating the innovative locomotive-effect. The competence networks are metaphorically the energy source that sustains the motion of this locomotive. It would be counterproductive to replace the locomotive once in motion. Conversely, the individual carriages of the locomotive (read: organizational level) can be changed depending on their competitive position. The individual passengers on the train create ideas and knowledge through the processes that may be called *creative chaos*. In this way, we will arrive at a tripartite of the prerequisites for competence networks. At the individual level, creative chaos occurs. At the organizational level, there will be creative destruction. At the social and global levels, creative collaboration takes place. These three processes create innovation and economic growth as an emergent, not as a *future perfectum*, i.e. a planned process with given results.

In this book, we will examine what role the New Silk Road will have in the development of new technology, artificial intelligence and intelligent robots. We will investigate the following research problem: What social mechanisms are promoting the New Silk Road as an innovation generator?

In order to address the research problem, we have formulated five research questions:

RQ1: How does the locomotive-effect promote the New Silk Road as an innovation generator?
RQ2: How does the butterfly-effect promote the New Silk Road as an innovation generator?
RQ3: How does the co-creation effect promote the New Silk Road as an innovation generator?
RQ4: How does the feedforward effect promote the New Silk Road as an innovation generator?
RQ5: How does the networks-of-competence effect promote the New Silk Road as an innovation generator?

The purpose of this chapter, and this book, is to provide inputs to, and perspectives on, the emergent Chinese innovation economy and Chinese strategic awareness as we head towards the Fourth Industrial Revolution.

The knowledge basis we apply is systemic thinking.

In this book, we use the following methods: economic history research methods; scenario thinking; future research; and conceptual generalization. The point of using these various methods is to offer different perspectives on the problem, the research problem, and the research questions under investigation.

Conceptual generalization uses the empirical findings of other researchers, which is then conceptualized and abstracted, and by means of frameworks, models and mini-theories an attempt is made to show possible future scenarios. This is not so much a prediction of the future, but more a way of using history and the present to understand how certain social mechanisms can influence behaviour in the here and now. Conceptual generalization is closely related to what Georg Henrik von Wright terms "time-diagnostics", and which he describes as follows:

> My way of working can be briefly described as follows: First, I focus on features and tendencies that occur to me as being typical of our time. I then investigate their origins and the historical dynamics that have driven them. And finally, I try to project the trends on what I call the 'screen of the future', in that I assume that it will largely remain unchanged. The image that appears on the screen can then give rise to considerations about the possibility and desirability of influencing tendencies.
>
> (Wright, 1996: 174)

Similar to von Wright's method, in this book, we will also examine how technological developments may affect individuals, organizations and societies in the future.

In this chapter, and in this book, we will investigate how five phenomena are related to central social mechanisms that will promote the New Silk Road as an innovation generator. When referring to the New Silk Road, other writers also use the names BRI (Belt and Road Initiative) and OBOR (One Belt One Road).[2] The five phenomena are as follows:

The locomotive-effect: This effect focuses on the emergence of innovations along the New Silk Road.

The butterfly-effect: This effect focuses on the development of the many positive connections for the countries along the New Silk Road.

The co-creation effect: This effect focuses on synergy consequences for the countries along the New Silk Road.

The feedforward effect: This effect focuses on the expectations regarding national sub-production for the countries along the New Silk Road.

The networks-of-competence effect: This effect focuses on the impact that collaborative networks will have on competence development along the New Silk Road.

The five research questions above focus on how these five effects promote the New Silk Road as an innovation generator.

Figure 1.1 shows how this chapter is organized, and it also shows how the rest of the book is organized. In other words, this chapter will first examine the elements in Figure 1.1. The remaining chapters will focus on the same elements but in more detail.

High-technological competence

In this section, we will examine the following questions: How does the locomotive-effect promote the New Silk Road as an innovation generator?

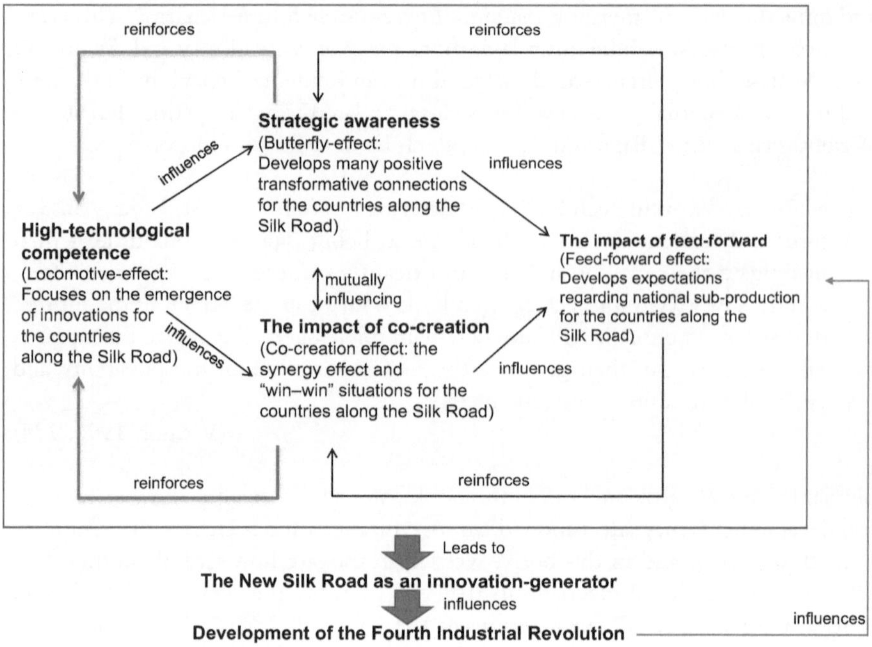

Figure 1.1 The New Silk Road as an innovation generator.

The New Silk Road is both metaphorical and concrete; although Xi Jinping has emphasized that it should not be understood metaphorically but as something real and concrete.[3] Nevertheless, it is metaphorical in the sense that it refers back to the historically well-known old Silk Road that had its beginnings more than 2,000 years ago. It is also metaphorical in the sense that it is not something that will be used to specifically trade "silk" and the other types of goods that were transported along the old Silk Road. On the other hand, it is real and concrete in the sense that it already produces major economic ripple effects for the countries that are involved in "Silk Road" projects (Beeson & Li, 2016; Macaes, 2020).

Narratives related to high technological competence

Case letter 1: The locomotive's end station – The Fourth Industrial Revolution

The development of a new type of technology, artificial intelligence and intelligent robots, which will permeate the economies of most countries worldwide, will inevitably disrupt the prevailing world order. After the fall of the Soviet Union, the old world order was dominated by the United States as sole economic and military superpower. The United States had superiority because it had been one of the leading players in bringing about the Second and the Third Industrial Revolutions. The United States also played an important role in bringing World War II to an end, allowing us to avoid life under an authoritarian regime. This world order is now under threat. It is threatened by the emergence of China as a new economic and military superpower. The locomotive-effect that we referred to above will drag more wagons along behind it and build the New Silk Road for regions that were previously dominated by the United States. These actions will not go unnoticed, regardless who is resident in the White House. Obviously, the New Silk Road does not need to result in a military confrontation between the United States and China, but there is a high likelihood that the United States, in one way or another, will attempt to derail a locomotive that is attempting to enter areas that the Americans consider to be within their own sphere of economic interests.

Tensions and military build-up in the South China Sea, China's new pressure on Taiwan, and a growing interest in the East China Sea are just some of the areas of conflict that have already emerged. The United States has also strengthened its connections to some of the countries along the maritime New Silk Road, such as Sri Lanka, where the Chinese have been involved in the construction of port facilities.[4] Perhaps the best way to understand what is happening in the leading circles in the United States in relation to a growing Chinese dominance along the New Silk Road is to read what Henry Kissinger (2015) writes in his book *World Order*, about how the new world order after World War II was built and maintained by the United States. In his book, Kissinger describes the legitimacy he and many others believe the United States had to assume the leadership of the new world order established after World War II. Even if no armed conflicts develop between the United States and China in the future, the conflicts between these two alpha males will lead to a new division of the world, and a new world order will emerge, not from the ashes of the Phoenix bird, but due to the locomotive-effect that the New Silk Road will have for the world economy. Like all locomotives that stop at stations along the line, this locomotive also has an end station: the Fourth Industrial Revolution.

Description of high technological competence

The locomotive-effect has technological innovation as its focus, and especially artificial intelligence. On the other hand, it will be crucial for the countries in the region, which have signed OBOR projects, that they achieve dual economic circulation. In concrete terms, dual economic circulation means that the countries involved in OBOR projects will increase their domestic growth, while also benefitting from economic growth in the other countries involved in the projects. In order for the countries participating in OBOR projects to achieve economic growth resulting from increased domestic demand, as well as receiving external support through demand for strategically important goods and services, it will be important for the respective governmental authorities to strategically intervene by steering investments towards new technologies. Both the public and private sectors will be involved in developing both infrastructure and info-structure projects along the New Silk Road. Infrastructure projects largely demand unskilled and semi-skilled labour, which will reduce unemployment among this category of workers. The info-structure projects will be concerned with all the information and communication processes in the public and private sectors. These projects will require higher competence than the infrastructure projects, that is, employees with higher education. In this way, the locomotive-effect will attract different categories of labour, which will be very beneficial in the regions where the New Silk Road is established, along both the land and maritime routes. The New Silk Road will most probably meet opposition from many quarters, both internally in the various countries involved in the OBOR initiative, and not least from those countries that are not part of the initiative, or do not wish to be part of the initiative. In this context, it is most probable that the United States will pose the greatest opposition. This can be explained by the fact that the global position of the United States will be threatened by this gigantic Chinese initiative that will come to dominate the economies, technologies, and diplomatic and cultural relations of the countries involved in the OBOR initiative (Yuan, 2019).

From 2013 onwards, OBOR has been expanded from its original plan of being an Asian initiative to becoming a Chinese initiative that is being implemented over large parts of the world, not only Asia but also areas such as Europe, Africa and South America (Xing, 2019). The US opposition to the OBOR initiative is perhaps to be expected when one considers how the initiative has expanded since its launch in 2013. The New Silk Road now extends far beyond the bounds of the old Silk Road. From when the idea was launched in 2013 up until 2021, it has manifested itself in Egypt, Kazakhstan, Pakistan, Sri Lanka, Myanmar, Indonesia, Russia and in many other countries around the world. The New Silk Road may be a metaphor, but it is something that has become very real, and also something that anyone interested in economics, trade, technology, diplomacy and relations between countries should take seriously because the initiative will come to have great geo-economic and geo-political consequences (Figure 1.2).

Analysis of high technological competence

The New Silk Road can be understood as an international collaborative project aimed at creating multiplier effects in China and the countries involved in the initiative. However, China may have underestimated the resistance this initiative may meet in the future; for instance, resistance from the United States, whose international position is being threatened. One might suggest that China will be confronted with the so-called "Law of Jante" at an international level. The Law of Jante (Danish: *Janteloven*) was formulated by the Danish-Norwegian author Aksel Sandemose in his novel *A Fugitive Crosses His Tracks*.[5] In short, this law requires that "you're not to think that you're better than us". In other words, don't try to get ahead because someone will only knock you back down; that is, the punishment for transgressing the Law of Jante is that others will do their best to make sure you do not try to rise above them.

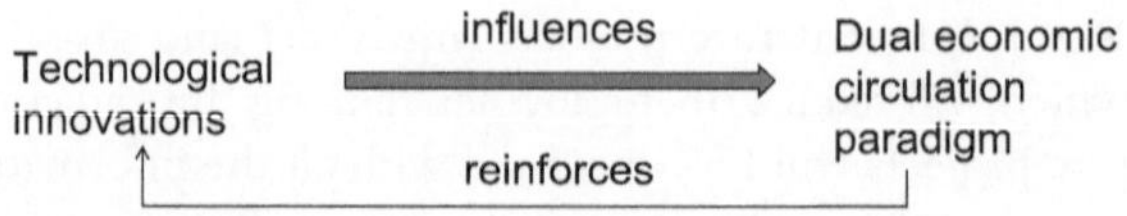

Figure 1.2 Elements included in the locomotive-effect.

China's most recent five-year plan from 2020 to 2025 and its plans towards 2035 are to downplay the specific goals for technology and economic growth.[6] In this way, it is perhaps attempting to appear less ambitious, while tolerating American assertiveness in the South China Sea, and the NATO discussions concerning the rise of China.

Regardless of whether China has taken seriously the opposition it has faced internationally regarding its growing strength, both during the Obama and the Trump administrations, Xi Jinping has stated that it is crucial that China makes rapid breakthroughs in important technological projects, i.e. technology related to artificial intelligence and intelligent robots.[7]

China has developed a two-sided strategy in relation to the locomotive-effect, and especially regarding technological innovations. First, breakthroughs in key technological projects are crucial. Second, these breakthroughs will benefit the OBOR partner countries. In this way, they are attempting to avoid direct competition with American technology projects so that they will not trigger the punitive consequences of transgressing the "Law of Jante"; that is, China has become more reserved about stating its explicit goals so that the external world does not become that much aware of Chinese expansion, already in the planning phase. At the same time, the Chinese technological locomotive is running unhindered towards its end station in 2035, i.e. global leadership in the Fourth Industrial Revolution.

International cooperation and regional development are the key words for understanding both the latest Chinese five-year plan and the launch of the New Silk Road in 2013. The origin of the New Silk Road was based on technological partnerships. However, this strategy received a shot across the broadsides, when the United States, during the Trump presidency, prevented Chinese technology from competing on an equal footing with American technology. Or more specifically, when Huawei was excluded from the American market and also excluded from the markets of many European countries. The US government has explained this exclusion is due to the so-called security concerns regarding Huawei's operations. However, the US government has been unable to provide concrete evidence in this matter. It has been pointed out that Huawei could be required to hand over data to the Chinese government if the government required it because of Chinese national security laws. Yet, such laws also exist in most Western countries, including the United States.[8] It is more probable that the reason given for Huawei's exclusion, that is, because of a threat to national security, is no more than a false argument. The real reason is that the United States intends to put all possible obstacles in the way of China's technological innovative growth because such growth could threaten the position of the United States in the long run. This is nothing new. We have seen such protectionist measures adopted by nations in the previous industrial revolutions (Billington, 2020).

The Chinese economic growth, which has been huge since the 1980s, is viewed as a threat by the United States. This is made clear in Hillary Clinton's article "America's Pacific century" in the *Foreign Policy* magazine (2011), where Clinton writes about the future need of the United States to have an assertive Asia-Pacific regional strategy in order to deal with China's rise and re-establish America's regional hegemony. In other words, the US "conflict" with China did not emerge as a consequence of Trump's "America First" policy, or because of Trump's trade war against China, but started long before this, during the Obama administration (Clinton, 2011). From the 1980s to 2011, American governments were all in favour of investments in China because this served the interests of the US companies. On the other hand, it did not necessarily serve the interests of the American working class because millions of industrial jobs were "exported" to China. This was also evident in the election of Donald Trump as president in 2017. The question for the American working class, which amounts to approximately 45% of the population, was why should they vote for Clinton and the Democrats, when it was believed by many that the Democrats were guilty of implementing policies that encouraged shipping jobs overseas (Frank, 2020; Sandel, 2020).

Theoretical points related to high technological competence

Once the locomotive-effect is set in motion, it pulls the technological innovations up the steepest slopes, both in China and along the maritime and land-based Silk Road routes. Metaphorically, one can say that the locomotive has already traversed the large mountain ranges, and even though it is being impeded by the United States and some countries in Europe, it has gained so much speed under its own momentum that it cannot be stopped. Neither the US trade war, nor Hillary Clinton's tough approach to China as mapped out in her article in *Foreign Policy* (2011), has managed to put a brake on the runaway Chinese economic train. In this context, it is worth remembering that it was not China that started and provided fuel for this locomotive, but the United States. It was the United States that outsourced and invested in China from the 1980s up until around 2016–2020; that is, it was American superprofits that fuelled the Chinese technological and economic locomotive up the steep mountain slopes towards the West. The economic and technological locomotive has now gained so much momentum that attempts by the United States to put a brake on its progress have little effect.

In the current situation between China and the United States, as well as between China and some European countries, given the complications that Chinese technology has run into, e.g. Huawei, it seems that the Silk Road initiative has encountered some fortuitous but nevertheless predictable obstacles. From a Chinese perspective, the opposition has been difficult to understand, but it is highly understandable from a Western perspective. This opposition is primarily due to China's immense economic and technological progress over the past 40 years, and not other factors; despite the Western rhetoric about human rights abuses, such as the reported Chinese abuses against the Hui Muslims in Xinjiang province, or the Communist Party's surveillance of the people of Hong Kong and the rest of China. From being a poor and backward country with little expertise in advanced technology, China has become a leading country both economically, technologically and educationally. This is perceived by the United States and many European countries as a threat, especially at a time when we are moving towards the Fourth Industrial Revolution. The envisioned nightmare scenario for the United States is that China will become the leading nation in the high-tech industrial race. The United States is well aware of the fact that if China takes the lead technologically and economically in the new industrial revolution, this will mean that they will also set the terms for new developments and also topple the United States from its leading global position, a position it has held since World War II (cf. Clinton (2011).

We have developed a typology for the locomotive-effect in Figure 1.3.

Proposition: The greater the degree of technological innovation, and the greater the degree of dual economic circulation that takes place along the Silk Road, the greater the probability of innovative gravitational fields emerging in the countries included in the OBOR initiative.

Proposition: The greater the degree of technological innovation, and the smaller the degree of dual economic circulation that takes place along the Silk Road, the greater the probability of opposition to the Silk Road initiative in the countries included in the OBOR project.

Proposition: The smaller the degree of the technological innovation, and the greater the degree of dual economic circulation that takes place along the Silk Road, the greater the probability that governmental authorities will initiate traditional infrastructure projects to develop innovative multiplier effects.

Proposition: The smaller the degree of technological innovation, and the smaller the degree of dual economic circulation that takes place along the Silk Road, the greater the probability of innovative sparsity in the countries included in the OBOR initiative.

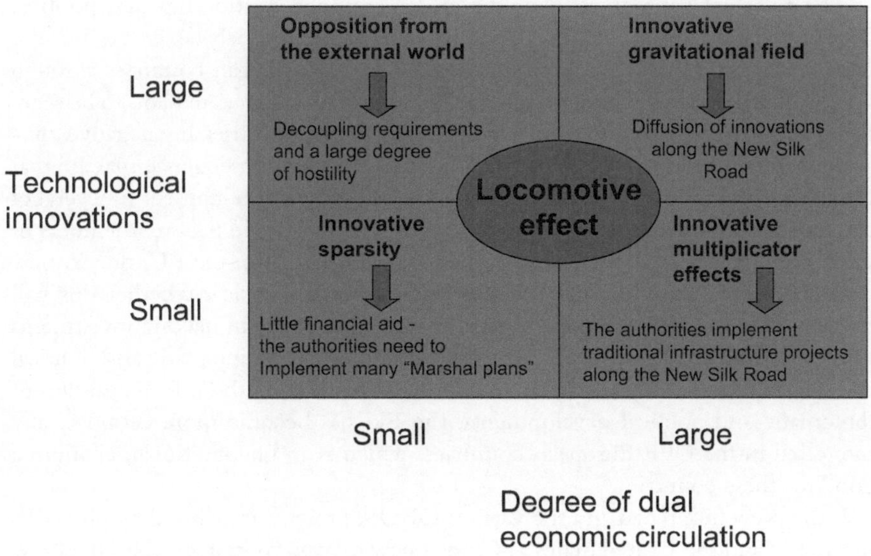

Figure 1.3 The locomotive-effect.

Practical utility related to high technological competence

The global economy, and all its institutions built up after World War II, has come under scrutiny; that is to say, the global economy has experienced various crises, both small and large in recent years, especially from 2016 to 2020 during the Trump presidency. Many countries have re-evaluated their relationship with the old world economic order with the United States in the lead. However, as of 2021, there is no "new" world economic order. On the other hand, there have been many innovation projects, both in Asia and Europe, which have connected parts of the international economy (Xing, 2019). For instance, this has occurred in Central Europe and in Eastern Europe (Pavlicevic, 2019: 249–278). Moreover, various transport, energy and infrastructure projects are being developed between China and several countries in Europe.

OBOR connections to Europe go through several Central and Eastern European countries, referred to as CEE[9] and include 16 European countries. This concerns projects that are linked to financial integration, infrastructure, people-to-people exchange, policy coordination and trade development (Pavlicevic, 2019: 249). Several of the European countries that are part of the OBOR initiative have already signed declarations that support the intentions of the main initiative. When the United States, during the Trump presidency, halted negotiations regarding the Transatlantic Trade and Investment Partnership (TTIP),[10] this further opened up the possibility of trade relations between China and several European countries. Moreover, the Trump administration initiated a trade conflict with Europe, imposing tariffs on certain European goods; this act further opened up Chinese-European trade relations. In practice, this meant that the United States, through its trade policy with Europe under Trump, dealt the Chinese a good hand enabling them to further develop the OBOR initiative towards Europe, and especially CEE.

The financial consequences of the aforementioned relationships are positive. The political consequences, on the other hand, are more debatable. It is beyond doubt that China will gain a greater influence on European countries through CEE. Whether this will have positive or negative consequences remains to be seen. If the alternative is economic emaciation, then this might offset any negative consequences of a political affiliation with China. Another consequence may be that the EU project may be weakened because the economic development in several of the member countries, as well as several countries in Europe that are members of CEE but not part of the EU, may have a negative effect on the EU, due to new connections to China through OBOR projects. It is not clear whether this will have the effect of increasing EU's efforts to be more active in making investments in these countries, or whether there will be an increasing diplomatic and political opposition between the EU and the countries associated with CEE. Regardless of diplomatic and political developments, the EU has become more economically interested in the CEE European countries, which is an unconditional, economic good for these countries.

If the New Silk Road and the various OBOR projects are viewed by observers in the EU and the United States as China's new expansion strategy, then the New Silk Road will be impeded by new East–West barriers, long before the road is fully constructed. We could observe the contours of this strategy not only during the Trump administration, but as far back as 2011 in the strategic ideas proposed in the article "America's Pacific century" in the Foreign Policy magazine written by the former Secretary of State, Hillary Clinton. In other words, the US government was attempting to put the brakes on Chinese development long before the trade war that Trump launched against China. If the Chinese government fuel this view among the American leaders, then it is probable that this will only contribute to erecting barriers along the Silk Road, at least as far as the routes into Europe are concerned.

If the EU erects barriers, there is much to suggest that the New Silk Road will turn even more towards Asia, Russia, Turkey, the Middle East and the African continent. From a longer term perspective, it may be Europe that loses the most from erecting barriers and not China. On the other hand, it seems reasonable to assume that innovations will increase in strength both in the East and the West, if the border barriers are completely removed along the New Silk Road.

For the countries along the New Silk Road, economic development and sustainability are the main arguments. If the OBOR projects can reduce unemployment, promote skills development internally in the countries and increase domestic demand, then the OBOR projects will be considered in a positive light.

Sub-conclusion for high technological competence

In this section, we have addressed the following research question: How does the locomotive-effect promote the New Silk Road as an innovation generator?

The short answer is that the countries involved in the OBOR initiative will be able to develop major technological innovations that they can use in the projects along the New Silk Road, while those who manage the main projects will be able to ensure that the countries involved develop strong domestic markets and strong growth impulses from the other countries along the New Silk Road.

Strategic awareness: how the butterfly-effect promotes the New Silk Road as an innovation generator

In this section, we will examine the following question: How does the butterfly-effect promote the New Silk Road as an innovation generator?

"In chaos theory, the butterfly-effect is the sensitive dependence on initial conditions in which a small change in one state of a deterministic nonlinear system can result in large differences in a later state."[11] The butterfly-effect refers to the small, often haphazard and improbable variables potentially capable of having large-scale consequences for social systems and nature. It is against this background that we are examining OBOR and the consequences the various projects may have along the New Silk Road. It is for this reason that we have chosen the "butterfly-effect" from chaos theory as a metaphor for the New Silk Road because the various projects are simple yet at the same time complicated. These projects will be both traditional and modern; for instance, using future technological solutions and collaboration regarding infrastructure projects and artificial intelligence in info-structure projects.[12] It is also the case that very small disturbances or political opposition to OBOR projects at one place along the Silk Road, e.g. border barriers erected by the EU, may have very large consequences elsewhere along the Silk Road, and possibly also very large negative consequences for innovation development in the EU. This is analogous to the Lorenz system in chaos theory, which gave rise to the idea of the butterfly-effect (Gleick, 1997). The idea that small events can have major consequences is also found in systems theory, more specifically in the cybernetics of the mathematician and philosopher Norbert Wiener.[13] An effective illustration of the butterfly-effect is that what was initially considered to be a seemingly harmless virus, which originated in the city of Wuhan in China, would at a later point in time cause the city of New York to lockdown.

Narratives for strategic awareness

Case letter 1: The butterfly-effect in Africa

China has financed and built a large port in Djibouti, a country located in the Horn of Africa, which provides the maritime New Silk Road with access to the Red Sea, the Suez Canal and the Mediterranean. Moreover, millions of Chinese emigrants are building a new life for themselves in Africa and contributing to the future development of the continent (French, 2015).

What is happening in Africa may be viewed metaphorically as an economic and technological larva that is transforming into a butterfly. It is when this butterfly begins to fly that we will see what we here term as the butterfly-effect. Exactly when this will happen no one knows. However, the multiplier effects of China's investments in Africa can already be seen. Chinese entrepreneurs have built factories and been involved in developing infrastructure projects in many African countries, e.g. Nigeria, Zambia, Senegal, Djibouti, Mozambique, Liberia, Ghana, Tanzania, Congo, Mali, Namibia, Guinea, Sierra Leone to name a few of the countries where China has made major investments in mineral extraction and infrastructure projects (French, 2015).

The view that China is the 'world's factory' and that global leadership, as well as the centres of innovation, are only to be found in the West, is outdated. This may have been true in the past, but great changes have occurred in the last 20 years to challenge this view. Not least, this is evident with regard to technological expertise in China, which has now been for some considerable time on a par with the United States and has even surpassed the United States in several areas. This increase in technological competence has been made possible by the development of higher education in China in recent years. In 2017, there were 2,914 universities and colleges in China, with 20 million students enrolled; the private universities accounted for approximately 6% of the student body.[14] In 2008, approximately 6 million students graduated from Chinese universities. It is this education industry, which constitutes the input into the innovation economy in China (Linehan, 2018: 128–143). It is also largely these graduates who are responsible for the development of new businesses based on artificial intelligence and other new technologies that characterize the Fourth Industrial Revolution. The nine universities in China that go by the name C9 League are ranked among the top 200 universities in the world.[15]

We have focused on the development of expertise in China and the development in Africa, precisely to show that China is no longer merely the "world's factory" but has long since emerged as the country that has taken the lead in the Fourth Industrial Revolution, after the United States imploded due to various internal and external problems at different levels. Developments in China and China's investments abroad provide a good example of the butterfly-effect. However, this is not so much a random butterfly-effect but rather one that has been developed for strategic intentions.

Description of strategic awareness

The New Silk Road is such a powerful metaphor that it can become a reality. It is first and foremost the strategic awareness of the Chinese leaders that gives the metaphor the driving force it has acquired along the entire New Silk Road, as well as in some countries in Europe (Beeson & Li, 2016; Macaes, 2020). A metaphor that becomes reality by its own strength shows that the butterfly-effect can also become a reality for China and the countries participating in OBOR.

The strategic awareness of the Chinese leaders mainly concerns economic expansion. This is reflected in the whole concept of the New Silk Road, along both the land and sea routes. We can observe this specifically in China's economic expansion in Africa (French, 2015) and many other countries that are part of OBOR (Mahbubani, 2020; Pavlicevic, 2019). In other words, economic expansion is definitely a key element in the economic butterfly-effect because it has the potential to transform many countries along the New Silk Road into modern economies.

This economic expansion not only influences but is also influenced by, the "Chinese Dream", which stands in stark contrast to the "American Dream" (Johannessen, 2021). However, it is crucial that the "Chinese Dream" does not become a "nightmare" for the other countries included in the New Silk Road. Therefore, it is crucial that the strategic awareness of the Chinese leaders takes into account the dreams, visions and strategic intentions of the other countries along the New Silk Road. In other words, to avoid the economic butterfly-effect becoming an economic nightmare, cooperation, reciprocity and win–win scenarios are needed.

Last but not least, with regard to the butterfly-effect, it is crucial that both China and many of the countries along the New Silk Road move upwards along the value chain. For some countries, economic progress and success may mean increasing output at a relatively low level in the value chain. For other countries, such as China, it will be crucial to be at the forefront of the Fourth Industrial Revolution; this will involve delivering technological innovations and products that are at the very top of the value chain. In practice, this means that China will have a considerable focus on creating innovations in the fields of artificial intelligence and intelligent robots.

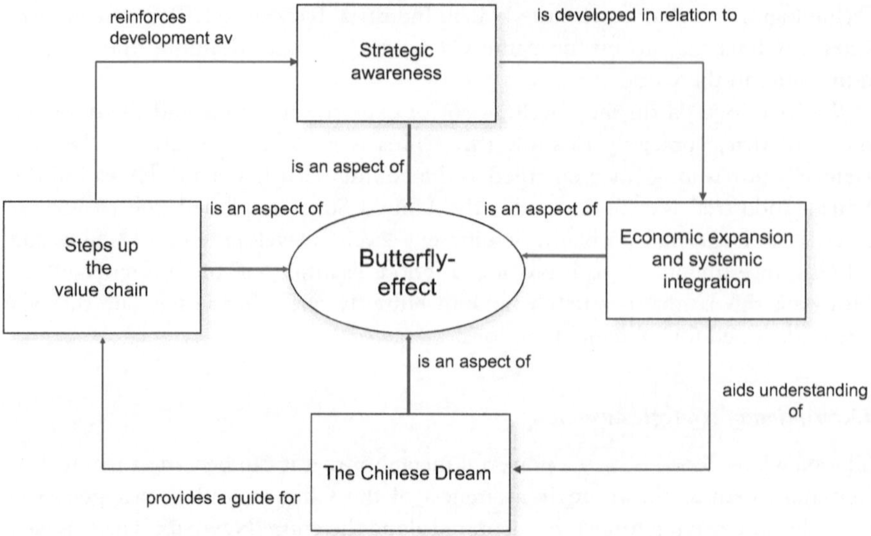

Figure 1.4 The butterfly-effect.

Although China is the world's second largest economy and has approximately 400 million inhabitants at the middle-income level, the country still faces several challenges, according to Liu Qiao, the Dean of the Guanghua School of Management at Peking University.[16] In short, these challenges can be said to be linked to the Chinese innovation economy (Johannessen, 2021). One of the key challenges, pointed out by both Johannessen (2021) and Liu Qiao, is how to raise China's position in the global value chain, while the country's innovation system does not overlook the importance of the consumer market.

Figure 1.4 shows the five elements described above. In this chapter, they have only been described and analysed at a general level. However, we will examine the elements more thoroughly in Chapter 3.

Analysis of strategic awareness

The developments we see unfolding in China, with regard to artificial intelligence, intelligent robots and applications connected to 5-G networks, are creating ripple effects, not only in China but also in Europe and the United States. The United States is taking these effects so seriously that they are flexing their military muscles in the South China Sea, as well as launching a trade war against China in 2018. This is not the first time butterfly-effects from China have transformed the European economy.

Four Chinese innovations that were brought into use during the European Renaissance around the 15th and 16th centuries[17] helped to transform European civilization. These innovations were paper-making, the printing press,[18] gunpowder and the compass.

The production of paper and the art of printing helped to disseminate new ideas, both religious and non-religious, throughout Europe. Gunpowder also became very important for the art of war. The compass became essential for navigation and later was indispensable for the ships that sailed to and from the New World.

These Chinese innovations were introduced into Europe by means of the old Silk Road. The New Silk Road will most probably result in similar butterfly-effects for all the countries involved in the various OBOR projects, including some countries in Europe. In this way, the New Silk Road, like the old Silk Road, can function as an innovation generator for the countries participating in the OBOR projects.

The old Silk Road went not only over land routes but also along sea routes. For instance, the Romans used the maritime Silk Road to China (Robert, 2005), which went from Rome, via Alexandria, then through canals to the Red Sea, via the Arabian Peninsula, India, the Straits of Malacca and then to Changán. It has also been documented that the Silk Road from China followed a route via the Mozambique Channel to South Africa (Jianglin, 2020: vii–viii). The Chinese Admiral Zheng He carried out several expeditions to the areas around the east coast of Africa, including Kenya, in the early 15th century.[19] Consequently, the maritime Silk Road expanded trade between China and the countries along the maritime route, as well as contributing to a development of diplomatic relations (Hudson, 1961).

The point being made here is that the Silk Road is not just a metaphor for the distribution of innovations, goods and services but is also a reality, both historically, when the old Silk Road transformed much of the economic system, as well as now in the New Silk Road with its OBOR projects.

The Silk Road as an innovation generator can point back historically to the impact it made on the European and African economies; while the New Silk Road has the potential in the future to be an innovation generator for European countries, Asian countries, the Middle East, and several countries in Africa.

The development of diplomacy, economies, cultures and innovations can be understood as consequences of the butterfly-effect along the New Silk Road. Diplomacy can expand and strengthen relations between countries. Economic development provides a basis for material security. The development of cultures deepens and strengthens the understanding of the diversity that exists; all these factors contribute to the understanding that material well-being constitutes the basis for peace and security between the various countries. New innovations create the expectation of a better future for the countries participating in the many Silk Road projects. To integrate the four factors of diplomacy, economies, cultures and innovation, a large degree of strategic awareness is presupposed, where the vision is that economic cooperation takes place through systemic integration.

Theoretical points related to strategic awareness

It is essential to be aware of the distinction between the short-term and long-term goals of the New Silk Road. The short-term goals are economic expansion, that is, the development and economic growth of all the countries participating in the various OBOR projects. On the other hand, the long-term goals are economic cooperation, innovation development, integration and increased prosperity (Jianglin, 2020). However, the short-term and long-term goals can in some cases conflict with each other because economic expansion does not necessarily promote innovation development. Innovation development presupposes long-term competence building, especially in complex systems. Applying an innovation also presupposes a certain level of competence in the countries that will adopt the new innovation (Billington, 2020). On the other hand, economic development is not always linked to the development of innovations in the short term. Therefore, it is conceivable that the governmental authorities in some countries are mainly interested in short-term economic growth and do not invest in the necessary expertise to develop and apply innovations in the longer term perspective. However, the conflict that can arise between the short-term perspective and the long-term perspective can be resolved by focusing on strategic awareness. The greater the strategic awareness, the more probable it is that there will be a focus on both short-term economic expansion as well as on economic cooperation, innovation development, integration and long-term prosperity.

It would appear naive to believe that China is launching OBOR to help the world, and more specifically the countries that are part of OBOR. However, it is this view that is expressed by Wang Linggui (2020: v) in his foreword to Jianglin's book *21st-century Maritime Silk Road Initiative: Aims and Objectives, Implementation Strategies and Policy Recommendations* (2020) when he says that "it (OBOR) is aimed at helping today's China to contribute to the world".

It seems more reasonable to apply a pragmatic and "help to self-help" perspective towards the OBOR initiative. Such a pragmatic and "help to self-help" perspective also emerges in the "Chinese Dream", as expressed by Xi Jinping. We find support for this perspective in the work and writings of many researchers and authors who have examined the Chinese strategy regarding OBOR.[20] The strategic awareness of the Chinese leaders focuses on economic growth and economic cooperation regarding help to self-help and in relation to the countries participating in the Silk Road initiative; this involves cooperation, innovation development and economic integration, not only within the individual countries but also between the countries (Macaes, 2020; Pavlicevic, 2019).

Figure 1.5 shows a typology of how the butterfly-effect influences the countries participating in the New Silk Road initiative.

Proposition: The larger the degree of strategic awareness, and the greater the focus on economic cooperation and systemic integration, the greater the likelihood that innovation development will be integrated and benefit all the countries participating in the New Silk Road initiative.

Proposition: The larger the degree of strategic awareness, and the greater the focus on economic expansion, the greater the likelihood will be of economic growth that is unsustainable over time.

Proposition: The smaller the degree of strategic awareness, and the greater the focus on economic cooperation and systemic integration, the greater the likelihood that innovations will emerge randomly.

Proposition: The smaller the degree of strategic awareness, and the greater the focus on economic expansion, the greater the likelihood that competition will develop without cooperation, which will prevent the diffusion of innovations and will be potentially detrimental in the longer term perspective to those involved.

Practical utility for strategic awareness

If one looks at the map of the world in relation to the New Silk Road, then the following routes will be evident: the maritime New Silk Road begins in China, goes via Vietnam, Indonesia, Malaysia, Sri Lanka, to the port of Gwadar in Pakistan and through the Strait of Hormuz and into the Gulf states. Furthermore, the maritime New Silk Road runs to Djibouti in Africa into the Red Sea and through the Suez Canal to Greece and Italy. Another route also goes from Djibouti to the port of Lamu in Kenya.

The land-based New Silk Road has several points of departure from China, for instance, via Kazakhstan, with a northern route to Moscow and from there to Berlin. A southern route goes via Ukraine and into Europe with the destination Duisburg in Germany. An even more southerly route runs from the northern route and then south to Kashgar in China, and then through former Soviet republics into Turkey with Istanbul as the destination (Yuan, 2019: 93).

This infrastructure will be an important social mechanism for creating a butterfly-effect with regard to economic expansion and innovation development for the many countries involved in the various OBOR projects along the New Silk Road,

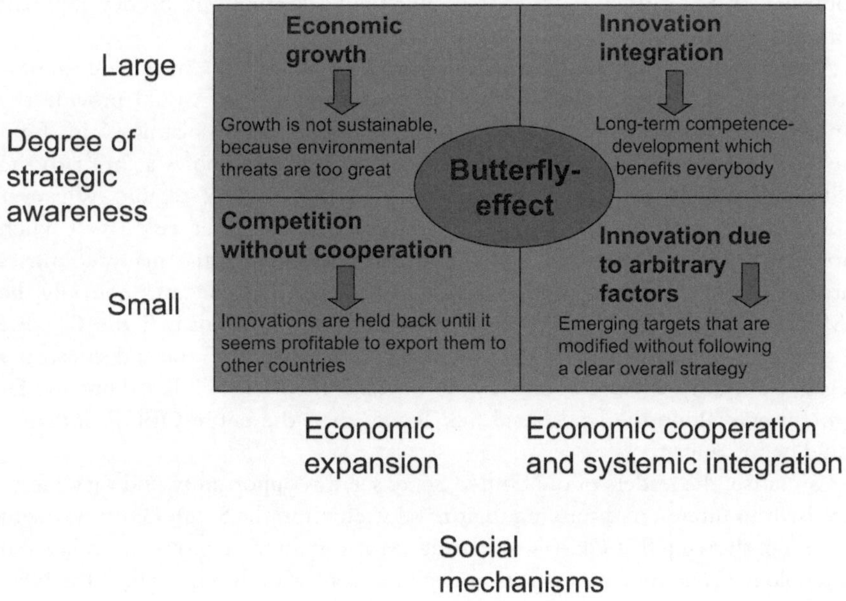

Figure 1.5 Strategic awareness and social mechanisms in relation to the butterfly-effect.

both the land and sea routes. Many of the countries through which the New Silk Road passes do not have high-tech expertise. For these countries, traditional economic expansion will focus on building infrastructure and maintaining it; in addition, these countries will gain economically from the increased trade along the New Silk Road. For other countries along the New Silk Road, e.g. Germany and China, the New Silk Road will function as an innovation generator moving the countries further up the value chain, towards high-tech knowledge production.

The New Silk Road is an economic growth initiative that will take many directions and have different consequences for different countries. However, an interesting point regarding the infrastructure we referred to above is that the United States is not involved in the New Silk Road initiative. This is the most likely cause of the conflict between China and the United States. Of course, the conflict does not stem from the fact that the United States is left out of the Chinese initiative, but due to the fact that some of United States' allies in Europe are included. It is along this line of conflict that we can interpret much of the American aversion to the Chinese technology that is spreading to several countries in Europe, e.g. the US opposition to Huawei and TikTok.

The maritime New Silk Road extends to the ASEAN countries (Association of Southeast Asian Nations) and incorporates them into the overall economic development. The ASEAN community was originally an organization for economic, military and political cooperation, and as a "wall" against communism.[21] In 1990, China, South Korea and Japan became partial members of ASEAN. Later, Australia, New Zealand and India also participated in this community.[22] The maritime New Silk Road therefore has an integrative economic purpose, which aims at taking the economic development of Asia up to a new level. The US military interest in the South China Sea can be understood against the background of this development (Clinton, 2011).

Against this background, it would be a strategic blunder if China were to escalate military tensions in the South China Sea because this would provide the United States and its ideological allies with an argument for isolating China from the ASEAN community as it could be argued that China poses a threat to the ASEAN principle of peaceful development in the ASEAN region. Whatever China may gain from sabre-rattling in this region, they would risk losing much more both economically and diplomatically in relation to the many countries through which the maritime New Silk Road passes. This concerns not only the ASEAN region but along the entire new maritime Silk Road. If the Chinese leadership is not fully aware of the potential conflict that may arise and spread as a negative butterfly-effect, not only along the maritime New Silk Road but also far into Europe, along the land-based Silk Road, then the entire OBOR initiative could be in danger.

Of course, the leaders of the United States see this opportunity, and they therefore have an interest in displaying their naval strength in the South China Sea with the aim of showing that China's economic expansion in the region is in reality also an ideological and military expansion in all the countries through which the New Silk Road passes. Despite the doubtful veracity of such a view, the United States feels it can gain from propagating such a view to the rest of the world.

The United States' growing military build-up in the South and East China Seas can be viewed as a struggle to be the leader in the new emerging technology because the country that is at the forefront of artificial intelligence development will also take on the role of world leader as we enter the Fourth Industrial Revolution. If the United States manages to create a conflict in the South China Sea involving China, their naval presence in the region will have achieved positive strategic results from an American perspective; namely, setting up barriers and building walls along the New Silk Road, isolating China and providing the United States with the opportunity to take the leading global role as we enter the Fourth Industrial Revolution.

Sub-conclusion for strategic awareness

In this section, we have examined the following question: How does the butterfly-effect promote the New Silk Road as an innovation generator?

The short answer is that the New Silk Road has the potential to create economic expansion in China and the countries included in the Silk Road initiative, along both the maritime and the land-based Silk Road. The Silk Road as an innovation generator will be realized by means of the thousands of OBOR projects where small and large innovations will be developed and applied in the countries involved in the projects. The butterfly-effect is reflected in the fact that the economies of many of the countries involved in the projects will be able to create a link between competence development and innovation development. This will then lead to circular connections between innovation and competence, which in their consequences will create many small and some large innovation generators along the New Silk Road.

Co-creation: infrastructure projects along the New Silk Road

In this section, we will examine the following question: How does the co-creation effect promote the New Silk Road as an innovation generator?

Co-creation here relates to the dynamics of the global transformation that large infrastructure and info-structure[23] projects have created in the countries participating in the OBOR projects. The largest single historical initiative we know of, which included thousands of smaller projects, was the US-led Marshall Plan which was launched in Europe after World War II. It is generally viewed that the Marshall Plan was one of the major contributing factors in the recovery of the United States and Europe during the post-war period. Similarly, the OBOR initiative can also be viewed as a type of "Marshall Plan" for Asia, Africa, the Middle East and Europe at the beginning of the Fourth Industrial Revolution.

Narratives for co-creation

Case letter 1: The relative decline of the United States and the progress of other countries due to the co-creation effect

To get an idea of the effects of the New Silk Road, it is advantageous to look at maps of all the countries that the maritime and land-based New Silk Road runs through. In this way, it is not difficult to envision how the initiatives that emerge along this entire route will become important for the development of ideas, innovation, production, trade and consumption.

Further, we can imagine how these initiatives and projects that extend through large parts of Asia, the Middle East, Africa and Europe will affect the geopolitical world order we know today. Whatever one's political point of view, it seems clear that the old world order will be challenged, that is, the old world order as represented by a dominant United States with no other country able to challenge the world's strongest power.

History shows us that empires that are all-powerful and dominate economically, politically, culturally, militarily and diplomatically are eventually, for various reasons, often internal conflicts, reduced to a shadow of what they once were. The United States has obviously not reached this point *yet*, but many writers have indicated that such a development is already underway (Allison, 2018; Beeson & Li, 2016). History also shows us that when one empire falls another will rise in its place. In the 21st century, a new empire is rising. Since the 1980s, China has allowed foreign capital to invest in China. This has enabled the Chinese economy to grow immensely so that it is set to overtake the United States as the world's largest economy in the near future. The New Silk Road may be viewed as an innovation generator, a powerful locomotive pulling a long train of other OBOR countries up the steep gradient of greater economic value creation, especially with regard to value creation linked to high-tech production and consumption.

Losing in a sports competition does not necessarily mean that you perform worse than you did before. It may simply be the case that others have become better than you. It is in this context that one can understand the relative decline of the United States. It is not necessarily the internal conflicts, race issues, the huge economic inequality, the growing debt and the millions of people who cannot afford health insurance that are the reasons for the decline. The decline of the United States can be explained by the fact that many other countries, and especially China, have overtaken the United States with regard to many economic indicators, e.g. the production and distribution of high-tech products related to artificial intelligence and intelligent robots. The economic downturn for the United States may be viewed as a psychological and sociological downturn, i.e. the belief that they are losing in the global competition, despite the fact that the country is not doing significantly worse than before.

Description of co-creation

If we want to discover how the geopolitical world is being transformed, then it is advantageous to look at those regions where economic activities are growing fastest. OBOR is a strategic development initiative involving several countries along the New Silk Road. As mentioned above, the initiative was launched in October 2013 by Xi Jinping (Wah & Menkhoff, 2020: xxiii). In other words, China is the leader of the initiative, while the countries along the New Silk Road are the participants. The success rate of the various countries participating in the initiative is dependent on their degree of systemic involvement. By "systemic involvement", we mean here that the countries that are most likely to succeed are the ones involved in the project from beginning to end. The hypothesis is that the greater the degree of systemic involvement, the greater the probability of success. The importance of involvement was also emphasized by Xi Jinping when he originally announced the Silk Road initiative during an official visit to Kazakhstan in 2013.[24] The fact that the individual countries can contribute and choose to participate, or not participate, in parts of the initiative will be crucial for commitment, motivation and the mutual building of trust between the countries involved. For this to happen, the countries that are part of the various projects along the New Silk Road should have a high degree of cognitive openness. This means that the respective countries should continuously learn from each other and also be open to knowledge and new technology that is developed elsewhere in the world. This will in all probability lead to the countries along the New Silk Road developing what we term here "systemic competence". "Systemic competence" refers to the fact that the entire value chain should be focused on, not just parts of it, that is, the parts where the respective countries reap the most benefits. In order for this gigantic New Silk Road initiative to be successful, it will be crucial that both China, as leader of the initiative, and the countries involved participate in a joint strategic implementation of the initiative. Systemic implementation here means a continuous understanding of the balance between part and whole as well as a balance between the two questions: (1) What serves our interests?; (2) What serves their interests?

The elements above describe the co-creation in this gigantic project, which have as their strategic intention the development of economic corridors along the New Silk Road. While the old Silk Road was largely a trade route with some key points along the route, the New Silk Road concerns a co-creation of production, innovation, distribution and consumption, as well as the development of knowledge centres at key points. Economic growth and prosperity are the strategic intentions. It is not a new Great Wall or an Iron Curtain being built along these economic corridors, but more a bridge that links together people who have more in common than what separates them. This bridge has been called the Eurasian Land Bridge by a leading institute in Berlin, which studies the relations between China and Germany.[25]

Figure 1.6 shows the five elements which are described above. These elements will be examined more thoroughly in Chapter 4. The description here is at a general level only.

Analysis of co-creation

The Eurasian Land Bridge has concrete projects at several places in Europe. One of these projects is the railway that is being built from Piraeus and Thessaloniki in Greece, via Belgrade in Serbia to Budapest in Hungary. This will connect Southern and Eastern Europe to the southern part of the Eurasian land bridge. Both the construction of the railway line and the trade that will go along the completed railway line will increase the positive economic effects. This sub-project is expected to be completed in 2023 (Wah & Menkhoff, 2020: xxiv). If we imagine tens of

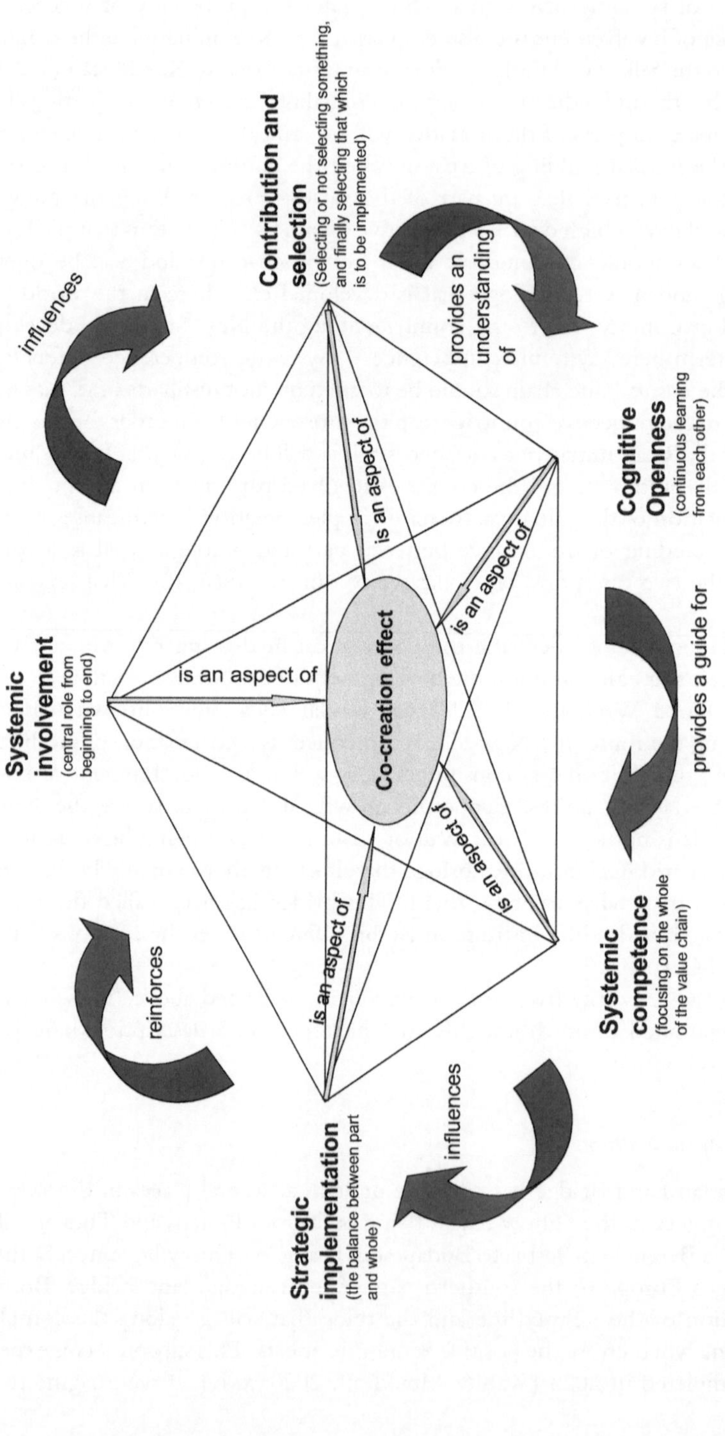

Figure 1.6 The co-creation effect.

thousands of such sub-projects, then we can start to get an idea of the scope of the New Silk Road. From a Chinese perspective, this may be considered as a help to self-help, just as the Marshall Plan was a help to self-help from an American perspective after World War II. There is nothing morally wrong with helping others in order to help oneself. What is more to the point is the fact that the countries and the people will benefit from this railway project; they will benefit in several ways including increased employment and income and improved prosperity through a growth in trade.

Of course, there are already various transport routes today between Greece, Serbia, Hungary and the rest of Europe. Such trade routes have existed since Roman times. However, the point of the new Eurasian Land Bridge in general, and specifically the part that connects Budapest, Belgrade and Piraeus, is that this will be the fastest transport route in the region. Regarding the China–EU cooperation, this sub-project can be the beginning of a new economic cooperation, where China is able to meet the EU's competition standards, as well as quality standards the EU sets for such projects. Both Greece and Hungary are members of the EU. Serbia is not yet a member. Such a project between EU countries and countries that aspire to be EU members can act as a diplomatic multiplicator effect, enabling Serbia to become a member of the EU at an earlier stage.

If the New Silk Road in Europe can promote the integration of the EU and the countries in Europe that aspire to EU membership, then the New Silk Road will have acquired a new function for the European continent. However, it seems reasonable to assume that such an increased integration of the European continent, and at the same time a stronger connection to the Chinese market, would not be in the interest of a relatively weaker United States. If such an assumption is correct, then it is likely that the United States will try to weaken the ties between China and Europe. It is against this background that the strategic partnership that the EU and China have developed over many years can act as a brake on the United States' strategic intention of weakening China's position, while strengthening their own position. This is evident in at least three areas.

Firstly, the United States will exert greater naval presence in the South China Sea. This will also influence the EU countries, many of which are also members of NATO, to take a stand together with the United States in this area of conflict. Once you have taken sides in a conflict, then this can pave the way for constructing an image of "the enemy". It may well be the case that the United States' involvement in the South China Sea does not have a specific military aim but that the intention is rather to break the economic ties that the Eurasian land bridge will create. If the United States manages to raise a barrier against the Eurasian land bridge, then they will open up the possibility of a closer relationship between Europe and the United States. The tensions in the South China Sea can thus be understood and explained from an economic and technological perspective, where the New Silk Road is not only a thorn in the side of the United States but an anchor that can result in China going past the United States both economically and technologically. Therefore, all conflict areas that the United States can build against China will serve its strategic intention. If one reads Hillary Clinton's article "America's Pacific century", published in 2011 in the *Foreign Policy* magazine, from this perspective, then it becomes clear that the United States has long felt intimidated by China's progress in several areas; such as, China's education system where the technological competence at university level has exploded; China's technological expertise regarding artificial intelligence; China's large economic growth rate; China's investment in its defence system; and China's connections to other countries and continents regarding various collaborative projects.

Secondly, there is US concern over human rights abuses in China, such as the reported Chinese abuses against the Hui Muslims in Xinjiang Province. Moreover, the United States is concerned about the political unrest in Hong Kong. The United States has also sought the support of the EU on these issues. However, it seems hypocritical that the United States talks about human rights abuses but does not focus on its own backyard. For instance, the Guantánamo Bay detention centre, which was built by the United States, imprisons people indefinitely, without charge or trial and subjects them to various types of torture with the alleged aim of extracting information.[26] It is also difficult for Europeans to understand the fact that hundreds of thousands of Americans are dying from Covid-19 partly due to the inadequate response by the US government. Moreover, it is a contravention of basic human rights that millions of people in the United States do not receive adequate health care because they cannot afford health insurance, resulting in a higher mortality rate among this sector of the population. Just like the endemic, structural racism in the United States also violates human rights; this violation of human rights has increased in recent years, as shown by the "Black Lives Matter" movement. Viewed in this context, the United States' preoccupation with human rights abuses in China can be considered as no more than a poorly camouflaged intention to disconnect Europe from the Eurasian Land Bridge. This will make it easier for the United States to strengthen ties to Europe and re-establish the transatlantic relationship, which was partly eroded under the Trump administration. However, in this context, the Europeans may ask: Will there be a new "Trump" in 2024?

Thirdly, the United States is intentionally, and with some success, attempting to slow down and hinder China's technological development. This can be explained by the fact that China has come a long way in the competition with the United States regarding the high-tech development that will come to define the Fourth Industrial Revolution. The United States is well aware of the fact that the country or countries that lead this technological development will also be the leaders in the Fourth Industrial Revolution. The preceding three industrial revolutions spanned 50–100 years, and the countries that led these industrial revolutions also took on the mantle of global leadership. The period of US global leadership has lasted about 70 years, since the end of World War II. In order for the United States to continue its global leadership role, it is strategically crucial to put a brake on China's technological development. This seems to be the case if we consider the Huawei issue. The United States has exerted pressure on several European countries to ban Huawei from 5G networks as the company is judged to be a threat to national security because the company may be required to hand over data to the Chinese government if the government demands it.

If the United States, through these three or other social mechanisms, manages to impede China's economic and technological connections to Europe, then this will not affect the New Silk Road to any significant extent, but it could reduce the significance of the New Silk Road initiative for Europe. In its consequences, the US actions could slow down the New Silk Road as an innovation generator for Europe. The United States will in the short term be able to make gains from such a manoeuvre because Europe will become even more strongly connected to the United States. On the other hand, one can assume that the New Silk Road will turn its focus more in a southerly direction and direct the route away from Europe.

Theoretical points related to co-creation

An important point about the maritime New Silk Road is that it has the potential to draw all countries bordering the South China Sea into a multiplier effect for innovation development. In other words, the countries bordering the South China Sea may experience innovation-driven economic growth, which will affect their economic development in the long term. This also applies to the countries in the South Pacific Ocean and Indian Ocean regions. The other countries and regions along the New Silk Road maritime routes may also experience this type of economic growth; this concerns countries in Southeast Asia, Africa and the Middle East. It only takes a glance at a global map to understand that the maritime New Silk Road has the potential to transform the entire geographical belt that is included in the New Silk Road. Against this background, it is highly understandable that the United States is increasing its involvement in these areas. In the short and medium term, economic activities will be affected by the extent of the naval build-up in this corridor (Allison, 2018; Hamilton, 2018).

First, there are the key ports that are being developed along the maritime New Silk Road, which will involve many financial projects related to logistical operations. The countries where these ports are located could end up in a very favourable development position. If the military tension between the United States and China increases, then it is likely that these projects will be put on hold. However, the sooner these projects are launched, the less likely it is that they will be shut down by military tensions between the United States and China (Feng & Liang, 2019). This can be explained, among other things, by the fact that the ports are not only key points along the New Silk Road but also logistical hubs for the respective countries' internal infrastructures, i.e. the goods that are exported and imported will to a large extent use these ports. In other words, these ports have several functions. One function is a logistics function for the country's internal infrastructure. The second function is as a hub for logistics along the New Silk Road. The third function is that these ports will act as economic multipliers for large geographical areas around these ports. The fourth function is that the ports will have the potential to become innovation generators for the countries in which these ports are located.

The maritime New Silk Road connects countries and regions. It has the potential to integrate economies, develop innovations and distribute them to economic centres in the participating countries. However, there are two prerequisites that are crucial for the co-creation effect of the New Silk Road related to its function as an innovation generator. This is the degree of systemic involvement and the degree of cognitive openness. Systemic involvement is linked to the extent the countries

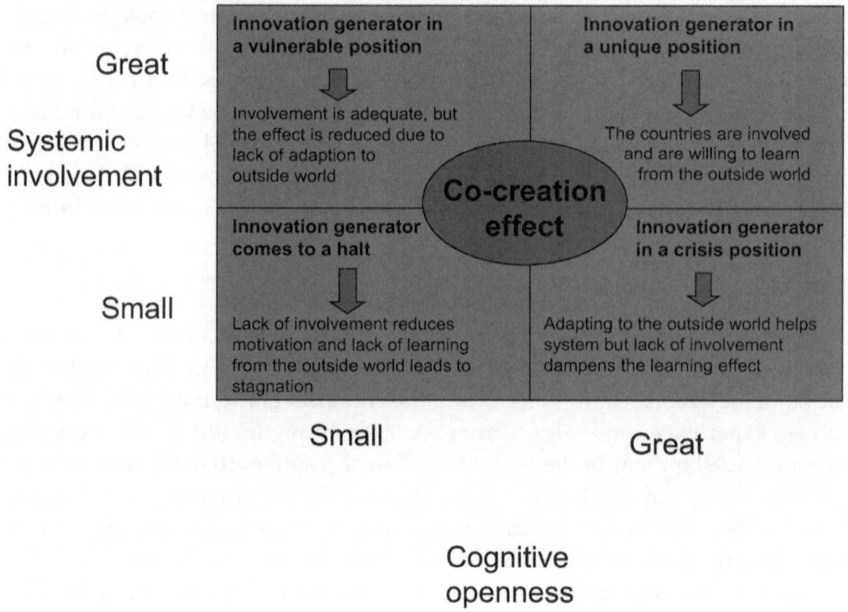

Figure 1.7 Systemic involvement and cognitive openness related to the co-creation effect.

participating in the various projects are involved from beginning to end. Cognitive openness is linked to the extent to which countries are willing to learn from the world around them and their ability to adapt to new developments.

We have developed a typology for the co-creation effect related to systemic involvement and cognitive openness in Figure 1.7.

Proposition: The greater the degree of systemic involvement and the greater the degree of cognitive openness, the greater the probability of developing a unique innovation generator.

Proposition: The greater the degree of systemic involvement and the smaller the degree of cognitive openness, the greater the probability that the innovation generator will be in a vulnerable position.

Proposition: The smaller the degree of systemic involvement and the greater the degree of cognitive openness, the greater the probability that the innovation generator will end up in a crisis position.

Proposition: The smaller the degree of systemic involvement and the smaller the degree of cognitive openness, the greater the probability that the innovation generator will go into a downward spiral and come to a halt.

Practical utility for co-creation

Co-creation along the New Silk Road creates both low-skills jobs and jobs in high-tech technologies in the countries participating in the OBOR initiative. As of 2020, there were 60 countries in Asia, Africa, the Middle East and Europe that had committed to various projects along the New Silk Road (Wah & Menkhoff, 2020: xxv). This indicates that the sum of the projects along the New Silk Road has set in motion a snowball effect that will roll and grow larger as it rolls forward. It is this snowball effect that makes it difficult, if not impossible, for the United States to stop this snowball from growing bigger. One possibility of course is war with China, but in such a war everyone will be a loser.

The financing of the various projects along the New Silk Road has been done by establishing large funds, both Chinese, Asian and financing projects that have been developed between the countries involved and China (Lim & Lim, 2020: 97–125). Many of the Central Asian countries need external funding for the major infrastructure projects that connect the New Silk Road along this route. These countries are Kazakhstan, Kyrgyzstan, Uzbekistan and Turkmenistan (Batzhan et al., 2020: 71–97).

One of the routes on the northern New Silk Road, which runs through Kazakhstan, connects the port cities of China with European cities, e.g. St. Petersburg. Japanese banks and Asian and European development banks are involved in projects related to the northern New Silk Road (Lim & Lim, 2020: 97–125). The transfer of parts of the freight between China and Europe, from ships to electrified trains, will most probably have a positive effect on the environment. Along this route between China and Europe, many key hubs for logistics operations will be developed. These hubs may be developed into central economic centres that serve transport along this route to Europe, and from Europe to China. Moreover, the trade of countries involved will also benefit from this transport route (Batzhan et al., 2020: 71–97).

Another northern route along the maritime New Silk Road is the "Ice Silk Road". This maritime route connects China with Europe via the Bering Strait, Russia, Norway and further southwards in Europe. An important function of this New Silk Road route is to connect to the many gas and oil projects in the Barents region in addition to projects related to tourism, scientific research in the Barents Sea and shipping activities.[27] The "Ice Silk Road" also connects to the Northwest Passage. The Northwest Passage in combination with the "Ice Silk Road" will eventually lead to a much greater focus on the Barents region and Greenland than has been the case before.

President Xi Jinping announced the "New Silk Road" initiative in 2013; this massive Chinese initiative will obviously affect the self-perception of the United States, regarding their geo-economic and geo-political role. For 40 years, from 1980 onwards, the United States has acted as the world police force, while today, it might be said it has become a spectator of a Chinese-driven idea of a new global infrastructure, at sea and on land. If a new Barents route from San Francisco to Rotterdam sees the light of day, aided by Chinese investments in the northern "Ice Silk Road", there is much to suggest that the United States' self-perception will change. One possible scenario is that the United States will become more isolationist and less preoccupied with the rest of the world; we have already witnessed the contours of such a development with regard to the protectionist policies implemented by the Trump administration. It might be said that such a scenario would harmonize American foreign policy with the views of most Americans because foreign policy is not something that the average American citizen is that concerned about (Sandel, 2020).

The northern "Ice Silk Road" in conjunction with the southern maritime route is connecting the regions of the world in completely new ways. China, Asia and Japan are now able to more easily connect to the Barents region. The southern maritime Silk Road connects Japan, China and other countries in Asia to the Middle East, Africa and the Mediterranean via the Suez Canal and the ports in Europe. With these maritime and land-based routes, globalization takes on a completely different meaning than was imagined in the 1980s, and up until 2013 when the New Silk Road initiative was launched. The New Silk Road is not only an institutional innovation but also an innovation generator for the countries affected by the various OBOR projects. With the launching of the New Silk Road, China has taken the step from being an export-driven economy to becoming an innovation-driven economy, where artificial intelligence and all the innovations are generated by the new technology drive development in China, as well as along the New Silk Road.

Sub-conclusion for co-creation

In this section, we have examined the following question: How does the co-creation effect promote the New Silk Road as an innovation generator?

The short answer is that the co-creation effect creates innovations along the New Silk Road, along both the land and sea routes. At the same time, the involvement in the various projects, from beginning to end, will create commitment and motivation in the respective countries. An important element of the New Silk Road as an innovation generator is how the various countries will be able to move up the value chain and focus on high-tech production.

Feedforward: expectations about the future along the New Silk Road

In this section, we will examine the following question: How does the feedforward effect promote the New Silk Road as an innovation generator?

In short, a feedforward effect is the sum of the economic expectations that are created. In our context, it is the expectations concerning the New Silk Road. Feedback relates to information from the past. Feedforward relates to the future through an expectation mechanism. It is the expectations we have for the future that will affect our actions in the present, just as the information we have about the past will affect our actions. This is the assumption related to the feedforward mechanism.[28]

The feedforward effect is related to five elements. First, it is related to how OBOR creates global expectations. Second, it is related to how the New Silk Road initiative project creates shared futures for the various countries included in the projects related to OBOR. Third, the feedforward effect is related to expectations that the projects will create win–win situations for everyone involved. Fourth, the feedforward effect is related to how the New Silk Road initiative creates a new mindset at an overall level. Fifth, the new mindset is related to the fact that the various projects develop a new type of globalization where high-tech projects are included in the OBOR initiatives.

Narratives related to feedforward

Case letter 1: Shared futures take precedence over political intentions

When the United States launched its trade war against China, an interesting triangular trade pattern emerged with regard to bypassing the restrictions on trade between China and the United States. The new trade pattern brought in a third country, Vietnam, which enabled trade to continue between China and the United States. In other words, Vietnam functioned as a midway station between the United States and China.[29] A triangular trade pattern thus quickly developed, with imports to Vietnam from the United States increasing sharply. This increase in imports from Vietnam was contrary to what the Americans believed. The Americans assumed that they had increased their trade with Vietnam.

Although the statistics showed that exports from Vietnam to the United States increased, it was unclear at the time whether some of these goods originally came from China; however, a closer examination of the statistics showed that many of these goods had originated from China. This triangle trade shows that even if when the trading of goods with one specific country is impeded by customs duties, then this can be bypassed by re-directing the goods through a third country – in this case, Vietnam. Figures from the US Commerce Department show that imports from Vietnam to the United States increased by 8.5% in the first half of 2020. However, if we look at the export figures from China to Vietnam in the same period, exports from China to Vietnam increased by 12.3%.[30]

China Daily reports:

> ---, there is reason to believe that Vietnam has been importing materials and components from China, further processing them into finished goods and then shipping them to the US. In other words, the US administration's efforts to decouple with China have had little effect.[31]

One of the purposes of initiating the trade war was to bring American companies back to the United States, i.e. to "reshore" American companies. However, the new trading pattern shows that this has not occurred. *China Daily* writes:

> Instead, they have increased investments in China. In the January–July period (2020) alone, US companies invested in 860 new enterprises in China, because, as *The Wall Street Journal* writes, "US businesses see China as a 'safe haven' for their capital.[32]

Regarding the trade between China and Vietnam, companies have developed new relations which they use to circumvent regulations that do not serve their purposes. In other words, they have a shared future and create new trading patterns in order to circumvent, at an overall level, the various political intentions.

Description related to feedforward

While Deng Xiaoping opened up China to foreign investment in the 1980s,[33] Xi Jinping initiated China's cooperation with various countries along the New Silk Road in 2013, also called OBOR and BRI (Zou, 2018: 6).[34] In 2020, 30 countries were formally associated with the New Silk Road initiative, while many more participated in smaller projects at various levels (Wah & Menkhoff, 2020: xxiii–xxxviii). The New Silk Road is a mega-project that has created global expectations for economic growth and prosperity in many regions (Feng & Liang, 2019). Furthermore, it has integrated many countries in the idea of shared futures linked to development projects for infra- and info-structures in the ASEAN countries (Yue & Fujian, 2019). These projects are presented and perceived as win–win projects by the countries involved (Yuan, 2019). The projects have also developed new mindsets. This becomes evident if we consider that artificial intelligence and intelligent robots are now viewed as something that can also be used to increase productivity in agriculture and fisheries, as well as in many industries that have not previously been considered high-tech (Xing, 2019). The old globalization with a focus on cheap labour and profiting from the differences in labour costs and framework costs seems to be changing with the new globalization that OBOR is driving forward. The new globalization thinking concerns production, distribution and consumption based on an innovation and high-tech driven economic growth.

There are many indications that the feedforward mechanism, as we have conceptualized it here, is transforming China's economy from an export-driven economy to an economy based on domestic demand. Moreover, the new thinking of Xi Jinping in relation to the New Silk Road initiative is based on a cooperation philosophy between the countries involved. China aims to benefit from the cooperation with the New Silk Road countries, especially in relation to the fact that the various New Silk Road projects will be presented as win–win endeavours.

The new way of thinking in international co-operation projects is that no single country should benefit more than any other country; in other words, the entire network of countries should benefit equally. This stands in contrast to the idea behind the Trump administration's "America First" policy.

At all levels of contacts between Chinese leaders and leaders from other countries, BRI/OBOR has had a central strategic role (Zou, 2018: 6). This means that the focus on, and strategic awareness around, the New Silk Road initiative has been given top priority in China.

The Chinese strategic thinking behind the New Silk Road initiative concerns the investment of Chinese capital abroad, increased trade and the increased use of Chinese expertise in projects in other countries (Xing, 2019). In this context, one can understand China's global expectations regarding the New Silk Road – that it should function as an economic corridor that serves China's interests. However, China is aware of the fact that if the countries participating in the OBOR projects do not feel that they have a shared future or that they are participating according to a win–win situation, then it is probable that most of the countries will sooner or later back out, and be easy targets for a US-led economic coalition. Therefore, the new mindset and the new globalization are completely different from the old globalization based on cost differentials and the thinking that the Trump administration clearly expressed, and which has been the premise for all American companies' investments in China, i.e. "America First". The new globalization with a focus on technological and innovation-driven economic growth, where the strategic intention is win–win for all the countries involved in the projects, has a sustainability that the old globalization did not have.

Figure 1.8 shows the five elements described above. These elements will be examined more thoroughly in Chapter 5. In this chapter, they are only described and analysed at a general level.

Analysis related to feedforward

The conflict between the United States and China which we have seen materialize in the South China Sea since 2011 (Clinton, 2011) includes many levels of tension. On a rhetorical level, we constantly hear that the United States and its allies need to protect themselves against Chinese technology companies for national security reasons, e.g. the Huawei case. Of course, such an argument can always be used, because the truth content of the argument can never be verified. However, underlying the argument is the fear that Chinese technological companies will outcompete the US technological companies. This situation is reminiscent of how Japan was treated in the 1980s, when they invested in the United States. While the launching of Sputnik in 1957 gave American politicians a wake-up call regarding the technological advances made in the Soviet Union, Japanese investment and competition with American cars and motorcycles gave American politicians a wakeup call in the 1980s, regarding the emerging industrial power of Japan. In particular, the sale of Honda motorcycles in the United States is often highlighted, because Honda was competing with the American icon Harley Davidson. Similarly today, Chinese technology companies, such as Huawei and TikTok, are considered hostile investments, which are excluded in the United States and by many of their allies for national security reasons.

Against this background, the New Silk Road provides an economic corridor towards the ASEAN countries, the Middle East, Africa and Europe. It will be crucial for the initiative's success that the countries participating in the various OBOR projects believe that they have a shared future and can participate in win–win situations. In this way, China can circumvent the American sabre-rattling in the South China Sea and the East China Sea, as well as the United States' attempts to isolate the Chinese technology giants in the United States and Europe.

There are two social mechanisms that can disrupt the United States' attempt to exclude Chinese technology companies. First, it will be important to ensure that co-operation takes precedence over competition, and that co-operation projects involving various countries should be based on shared futures and win–win strategies. The second social mechanism is to develop a new globalization based on a common idea of a high-tech innovation economy, where projects are driven by a new mindset that team efforts are better than individual efforts.

The New Silk Road, and its feedforward effect, is a new strategic positioning for shared futures for all the countries that are part of OBOR. One example of this

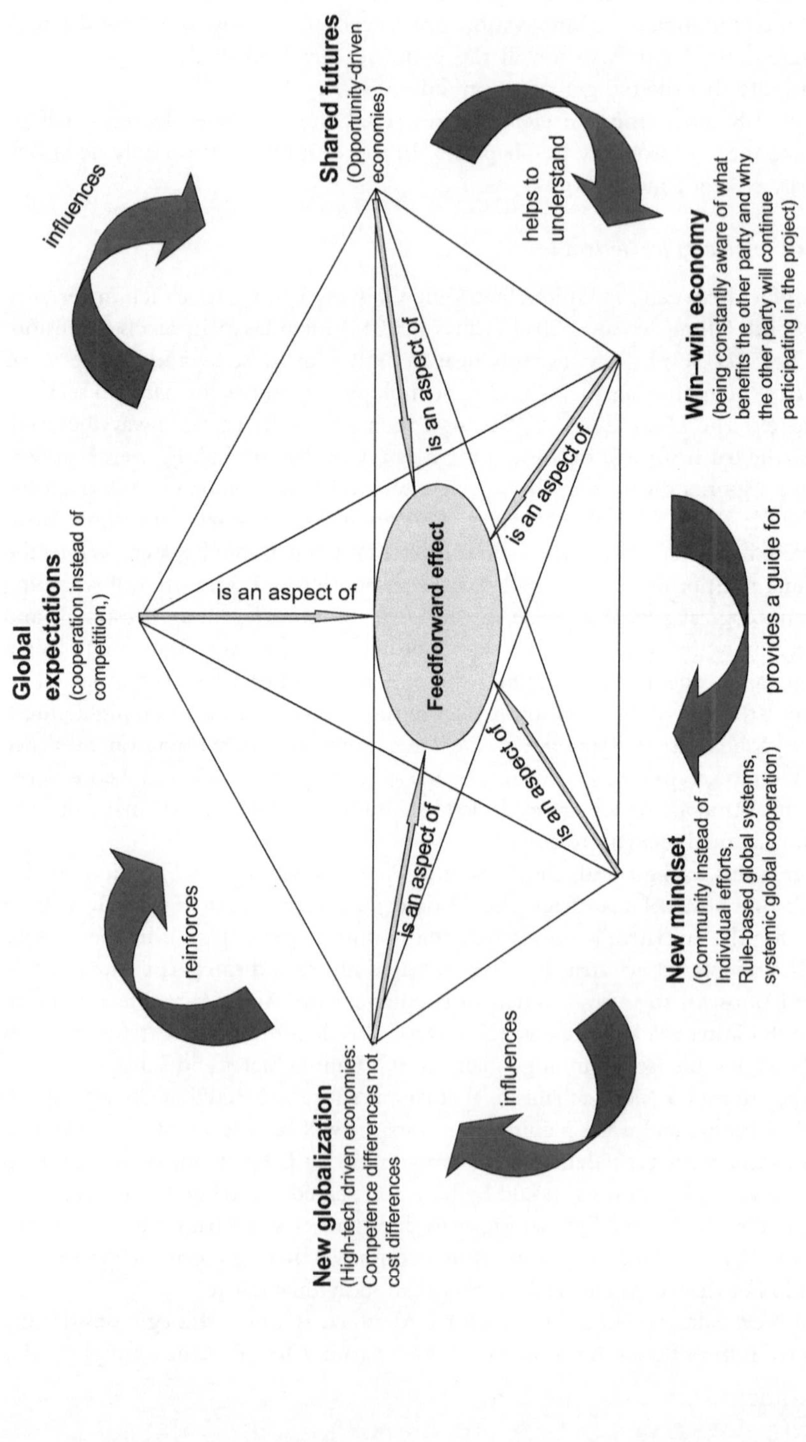

Figure 1.8 The feedforward effect.

is the world's largest free trade agreement, the Regional Comprehensive Economic Partnership (RCEP), which China has helped to establish (signed in November 2020). The signatory countries are the ten ASEAN[35] countries, as well as other countries.[36] The signatory countries of the free trade agreement have a total population of 2.3 billion, and stand for 29% of the world's economic activities, according to the Peterson Institute for International Economics.[37] The United States is not one of the signatories in this free trade agreement, and is viewed as a direct competitor. Under the Obama administration the Trans-Pacific Partnership (TPP) trade agreement was proposed, which was signed by the United States; however, the United States withdrew from the agreement during the Trump administration, so the agreement never entered into force.[38] However, China has been working to establish the RCEP trade agreement since 2012, when the agreement was first proposed, and when Xi Jinping became president of China.[39]

Within and outside the New Silk Road, China is working to create a new global world order, which includes free trade, and with a new mindset characterized by the ideas inherent in the concepts of "shared futures" and "win–win" projects (Angang, 2014: 1–10). This is not to suggest that China has a higher business morality than countries such as the United States, but because China has learnt from experience that trade where one party over time earns disproportionately more than the other(s), will sooner or later run into problems. In other words, this is part of China's history, since Deng Xiaoping first opened up China's market to foreign investment in 1978, and beyond into the 1980s.[40] When China opened up its market to foreign capital, and up until the New Silk Road (2013), knowledge and technology flowed into the country, while since 2013, China has begun to export its own technology to large parts of the world.

Theoretical points related to feedforward

The New Silk Road is an innovation generator that creates the conditions for the "Chinese Dream", which in short is about raising all the Chinese people to a middle class income level (Brown, 2018). However, the New Silk Road is more than this; the New Silk Road, and its feedforward mechanism is also part of a national security strategy (Zou, 2018: 11). This security strategy can generally be understood as an attempt to emerge from a one-sided economic and military confrontation with a somewhat wing-clipped American eagle. By investing in the New Silk Road and other multinational collaborations, e.g. as mentioned above the RCEP, Chinese national security is able to shift from a one-sided focus on China's borders and the PLA's[41] role, to a global engagement in which many nations are integrated into the many OBOR projects. In this way, national security is no longer just a matter of China's security, but also the economic, political and diplomatic security of all the countries involved in the projects along the New Silk Road, along both the land and sea routes. In this way, the New Silk Road sends a clear message from all countries involved in the OBOR projects: We are all working together for a shared future, and we are all dependent on the success of the projects. The message carries on: An economic attack on one of the countries that is part of OBOR will constitute an attack on all the countries.

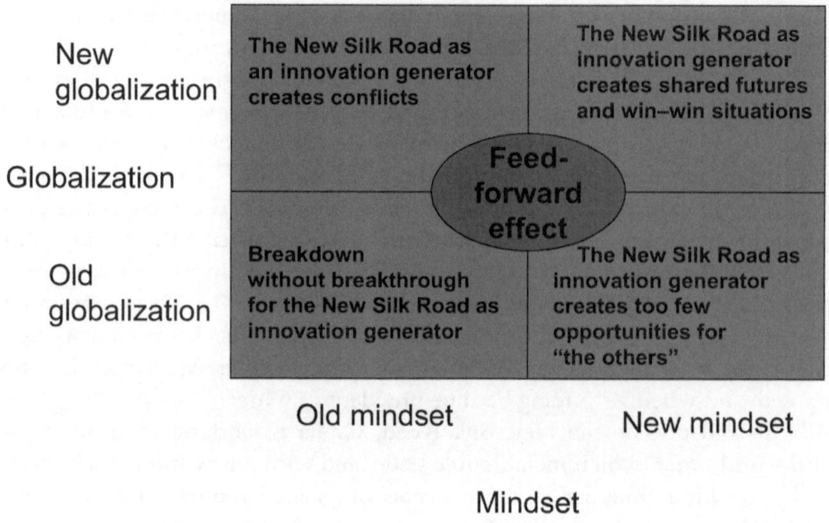

Figure 1.9 Globalization and mindset in relation to the feedforward effect.

The transition from the old globalization to the new globalization is the most significant aspect of the feedforward effect. The old globalization was mainly driven by profitability based on wage differentials. The new globalization is an innovation-driven economic green growth based on high technology, artificial intelligence and intelligent robots. It is the competence differentials, not wage differentials, that is the central social mechanism in the new globalization. Furthermore, the feedforward effect is based on a transition from an old mindset to a new mindset. The old mindset was driven by competition and win–lose thinking. The new mindset is driven by a collaborative philosophy and win–win thinking.

The new globalization and the new mindset are of strategic importance to the Chinese leaders, because it will transform China's role from one where the country was open to foreign investment, into a role where an opening has been created in the outside world for Chinese technology and expertise. Chinese leaders have developed a new strategic awareness in relation to the process where China first imported technological knowledge from the 1980s up until 2013, when China began to export its own technology[42] (Batzhan et al., 2020; Bougon, 2017).

Figure 1.9 shows a typology of the feedforward effect related to old and new globalization, as well as old and new mindsets.

Proposition: The more the new globalization and the new mindset are in focus, the greater the probability is that the New Silk Road will function as an innovation generator.

Proposition: The more the new globalization and the old mindset are in focus, the greater the probability is that the New Silk Road will create conflicts as an innovation generator.

Proposition: The more the old globalization and the new mindset are in focus, the greater the probability is that the New Silk Road as an innovation generator creates too few opportunities for "the others".

Proposition: The more the old globalization and the old mindset are in focus, the greater the probability is that the New Silk Road as an innovation generator will collapse.

Practical utility for feedforward

The most important practical usefulness of the feedforward mechanism is the expectation created regarding economic cooperation, and employment for people in the countries that participate in the New Silk Road (Zou, 2018: 13). It is the interconnection that takes place at different levels between the countries participating in the OBOR projects, which can be viewed as the overall practical utility value. This interconnection is economic, social, political, technological and cultural. It is this interconnection that ensures stability in the regions in which the OBOR projects are implemented. The more projects connect the countries together, the less likely it is that military conflicts will arise. The RCEP free trade agreement signed in November 2020 will further increase the importance of the New Silk Road, because economic activity will receive a boost due to the agreement.[43] In this way, the feedforward effect will combine with the locomotive-effect.

An important aspect of the New Silk Road is that it is an open and inclusive initiative, and not closed like the RCEP free trade agreement. The Chinese leaders have expressed that the New Silk Road aims to include all the countries interested in participating (Wang, 2016). In other words, economic cooperation and inclusion, not exclusion, is an important principle in the projects along the New Silk Road (Wang, 2017b).

From a Chinese perspective, the New Silk Road is divided into three phases. The first phase concerns international and national mobilization. This phase lasted from 2013 to 2016. The second phase concerns strategic planning (from 2016 to 2021). The third phase concerns strategic implementation; this phase will be implemented from 2021 up until 2049 (Wang, 2015, 2017c). The end-date of the last phase is not accidental; 2049 marks 100 years since the Chinese Revolution of 1949.

From this long-term perspective up until 2049, China is interested in establishing and maintaining relations with the countries along the New Silk Road. In this context, collaborative thinking with regards to global expectations and shared futures in relation to the feedforward mechanism play a crucial role, at the same time as the projects are perceived as win–win projects by all the participating countries. A key element of OBOR is the importance of ensuring that the interests of all the countries involved in the initiative are maintained, and not that some countries benefit more than others. In other words, if the countries involved in the OBOR project were to adopt the type of unilateral thinking associated with the "America First" policy, this would in all probability lead to the derailment of the New Silk Road, and a downturn of the OBOR initiative as it moves towards 2049.

The overall strategic architecture of the New Silk Road is shown in Figure 1.10.

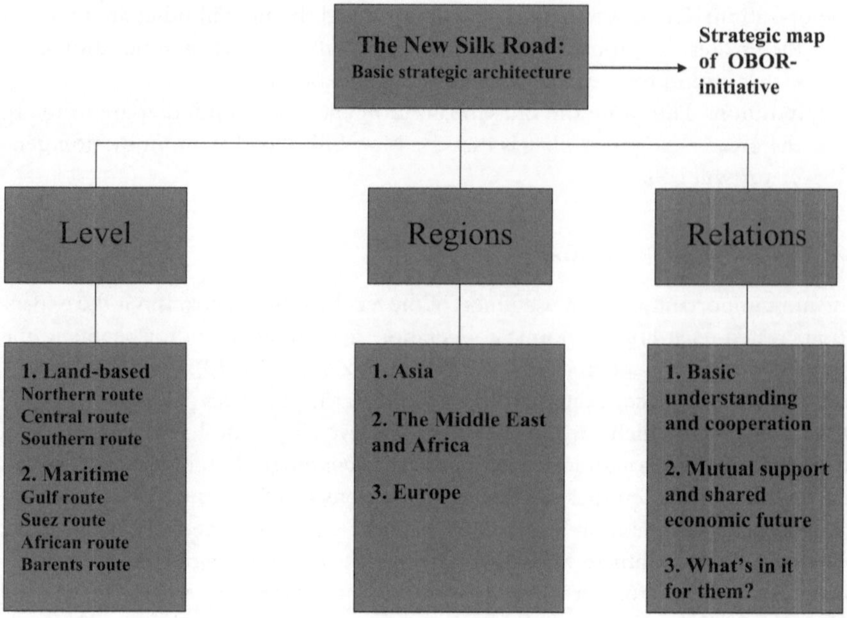

Figure 1.10 The New Silk Road: The basic strategic architecture.

Sub-conclusion for feedforward

We have examined the following question: How does the feedforward effect promote the New Silk Road as an innovation generator?

The short answer is that the feedforward effect promotes the New Silk Road as an innovation generator through cooperation where the future opportunities for the countries involved are based on a mutually helpful basic relationship, and where the projects are continuously assessed in relation to win–win possibilities. The measurement indicators are linked to what all the project participants have gained from the projects. This is where the new mindset in the feedforward mechanism is crucial, i.e. multilateral initiatives and not unilateral initiatives that give priority to one project participant before another, that is of the type of unilateralism associated with the "America First" policy.

Main conclusion for the New Silk Road as an innovation generator

In this chapter, we have addressed the following research problem: What social mechanisms are promoting the New Silk Road as an innovation generator?

The short answer is that there are five social mechanisms that promote the New Silk Road as an innovation generator. These are: the locomotive-effect, the butterfly-effect, the co-creation effect, the feedforward effect and the competence-network effect. These social mechanisms can be viewed in relation to the transition of China from an export-driven economy (1980–2012) to an innovation-driven economy, which dates from 2012, when Xi Jinping became president of China. According to Xi-Jinping,[44] there are five drivers that will promote innovation-driven growth. These drivers are:

1 Technological innovation
2 Greater connectivity internally in China and between the countries along the New Silk Road
3 An open economy
4 Greater emphasis on the digital economy
5 Reciprocity and the implementation of win–win projects along the New Silk Road.

Critics of the New Silk Road mainly come from the United States, Europe, Australia, Japan and India, in other words, those countries and regions that are not involved in the OBOR projects, or only involved to a small extent. Some critics claim that China's projects have a global intention. It may very well be that China has geo-political and geo-economic intentions, but why should this be a criticism of the projects along the New Silk Road. The United States has had global intentions for 100 years or more, if one takes a look back at American history. The same may be said of Europe. It is not having global intentions that is essentially wrong, but what these intentions entail. The United States' intention behind criticizing and finding arguments against the New Silk Road can be viewed in conjunction with the American trade war against China. The main argument seems to be that China's economic expansion threatens American interests in the regions affected by the New Silk Road.

One social mechanism that has not been mentioned, but which is crucial when answering the research problem above, is the importance of making sure corruption does not flourish because this will hinder and eventually bring to a halt the development of an innovation-driven economy, like all other economic growth. The major campaign against corruption in China, headed by Xi Jinping, cracked down on both corrupt high-level officials and local civil servants. Corruption, or more specifically graft, concerns an official's or a politician's unscrupulous use of his or her position for personal gain. If corruption flourishes, people's trust in the political system will be eroded, and consequently their social commitment and motivation will also be reduced. This is one of the reasons why the fight against corruption is a priority area for Xi Jinping, also for the projects along the New Silk Road.

Figure 1.11 shows a model based on the description above.

The economic inequality, which we can observe resulting from the introduction of many technological innovations and the companies that grow up around these innovations, is creating a new aristocracy. This aristocracy is growing in power, which they use to strengthen the economic inequality.

Technological innovations create breakthroughs for some companies, while others are destroyed. They result in economic crises for some companies, while other companies experience economic growth. The innovations tend to gather around specific geographical locations; it has been empirically shown that they emerge in relation to five social mechanisms. These five social mechanisms are as follows:

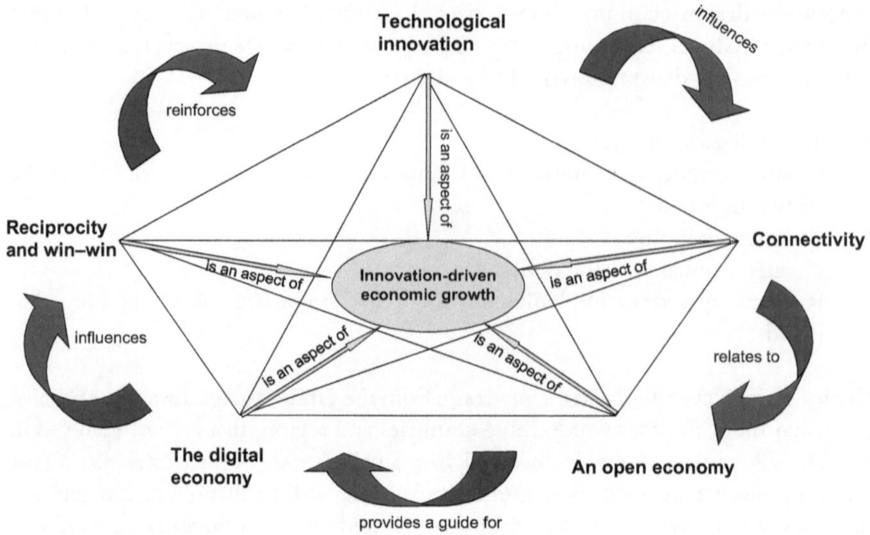

Figure 1.11 Innovation-driven growth.

1 First, as a general rule, innovations emerge where the relative productivity is declining.
2 Second, innovations emerge where the relative quality of various products and services is declining.
3 Third, innovations emerge in those areas where the relative competence is declining.
4 Fourth, innovations emerge in those areas where the relative costs are rising.
5 Fifth, innovations tend to emerge in those areas where knowledge can be quickly transformed into technology.

Sometimes one or a few of these social mechanisms together will trigger innovations. Other times, it may be all five of the social mechanisms in combination that trigger an innovation.

Figure 1.12 shows a model where innovations may emerge.

As a general rule, the large technology companies seize the opportunities that the new innovations generate, for instance, companies such as Amazon, Apple, Google, Facebook, Instagram, Tesla, Huawei, Tencent, etc. The combined wealth of the first four companies in the list above may be compared to the wealth of a large European country. Almost half of the major technology companies are located in China. The innovations that are driven by the various social mechanisms, and the companies that grow out of these innovations, are located around geographical areas, e.g. in the United States and China.

The difference between the incomes of the top leaders and the salary of the average worker in these technology companies is formidable. Capital is centralized, as well as the location of the companies, while wealth is clustered and under the control of the very rich.

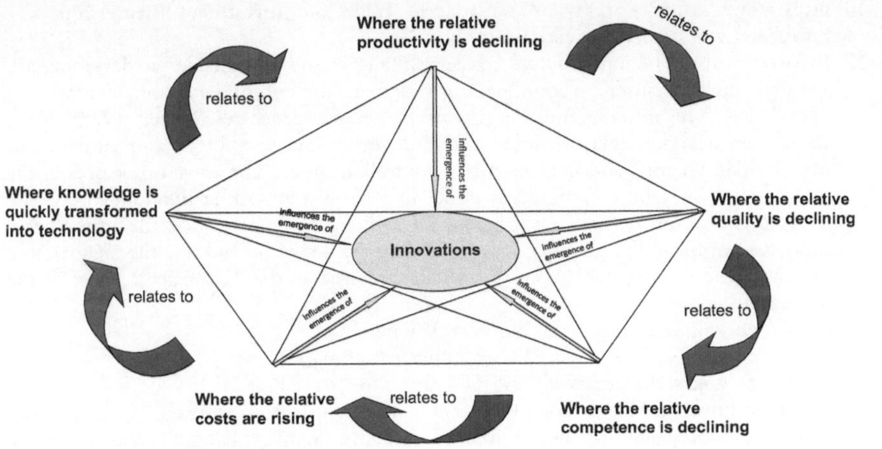

Figure 1.12 Why and where innovations emerge.

At the beginning of the Fourth Industrial Revolution, we are witnessing a high-tech development, with a focus on artificial intelligence and intelligent robots. This high-tech production promotes and is promoted by innovation processes. The synergy of high-tech production and the innovation processes leads to economic and social crises because the old mode of production and associated skills become superfluous. This results in unemployment among those working in industries based on the old mode of production, at least in the short-term perspective. The sum of high-tech production, innovation processes and economic crises leads in its consequences to a very strong economic and social inequality. In turn, these processes promote a feudal capitalist development.

Notes

1 OBOR stands for One Belt One Road, also known as BRI, Belt and Road Initiatives, or, in everyday speech, the New Silk Road.
2 Allison (2018); Beeson & Li (2016); French (2015); Hamilton (2018); Macaes (2020); Mahbubani (2020); Mantzopoulos & Shen (2011); Mearsheimer (2010); Vangeli (2017, 2018, 2019); Wang (2017a, 2017b, 2017c, 2020).
3 *People's Daily*, 29 March, 2015:2.
4 http://www.srilankaguardian.org/2020/10/secretary-pompeos-travel-to-india-sri.html.
5 https://en.wikipedia.org/wiki/Law_of_Jante.
6 https://news.cgtn.com/news/2020-09-28/19th-CPC-Central-Committee-to-hold-5th-plenary-session-Oct-26-to-29-U9HMnelwwE/index.html.
7 https://news.cgtn.com/news/2020-08-24/Xi-Jinping-China-must-strive-for-breakthroughs-in-key-technologies-TdN8iZqBWw/index.html.
8 https://news.cgtn.com/news/2020-06-03/A-look-at-Western-approach-to-national-security-laws-R1tFcKkg5a/index.html.
9 CEE stands for relations between China and Central and Eastern Europe. These countries are: Albania, Bosnia and Herzegovina, Bulgaria, Croatia, the Czech Republic, Estonia, Hungary, Macedonia, Montenegro, Latvia, Lithuania, Romania; Poland, Serbia, Slovakia and Slovenia (Pavlicevic, 2019: 273).

10 https://en.wikipedia.org/wiki/Transatlantic_Trade_and_Investment_Partnership.
11 https://en.wikipedia.org/wiki/Butterfly_effect.
12 **Infostructure**. The infostructure concerns the processes that enable the development, transfer, analysis, storage, coordination and management of data, information and knowledge. The infostructure consists of 11 generic processes (Miller, 1978): input transducer, decoder, encoder, internal transducer, output transducer, associator, memory, decider, channel and net, boundary controller, timer. The eleven processes in the infostructure may be considered as nodes in a social network at different levels, e.g. team, organization, society, and region, all in the global space. Together, the eleven processes comprise the totality of the infostructure. It may be said that the *info*structure has the same importance in the knowledge society as the *infra*structure had in the industrial society.
13 https://en.wikipedia.org/wiki/Norbert_Wiener.
14 https://en.wikipedia.org/wiki/List_of_universities_in_China.
15 https://en.wikipedia.org/wiki/List_of_universities_in_China.
The nine universities are Fudan University, Shanghai, Harbin Institute of Technology, Harbin, Heilongjiang province, Nanjing University, Nanjing, Jiangsu province, Peking University, Beijing, Shanghai Jiao Tong University, Shanghai, Tsinghua University, Beijing, University of Science and Technology of China, Hefei, Anhui province, Xi'an Jiaotong University, Xi'an, Shaanxi province, and Zhejiang University, Hangzhou, Zhejiang province.
16 *China Daily*, 11 April 2020 (https://global.chinadaily.com.cn/a/202011/04/WS5fa1e59ea31024ad0ba82e20.html).
17 https://simple.wikipedia.org/wiki/Renaissance.
18 In Europe, Johannes Gutenberg is credited with inventing the printing press in 1439. However, book printing had existed in China since the 5th century, albeit on a different technical platform than the one invented by Gutenberg (https://en.wikipedia.org/wiki/Johannes_Gutenberg).
19 https://en.wikipedia.org/wiki/Zheng_He.
20 The following is a selection of researchers that support the pragmatic perspective: Bougon (2017); Boutrup (2019); Brown (2018, 2019); Economy (2018); Johannessen (2021); Magnus (2018); Ross & Bekkevold (2016); Wasif Khan (2019); Yang (2015); Zhang (2015).
21 https://en.wikipedia.org/wiki/ASEAN.
22 https://en.wikipedia.org/wiki/ASEAN.
23 Info-structure here stands for information structure. This concerns all the information and communication processes in organizations, institutions and societies.
24 https://en.wikipedia.org/wiki/Belt_and_Road_Initiative.
25 https://en.wikipedia.org/wiki/Mercator_Institute_for_China_Studies.
26 https://en.wikipedia.org/wiki/Guantánamo.
27 https://moderndiplomacy.eu/2018/03/18/ice-silk-road-from-dream-to-reality/. Date of reading 29.11.2020.
28 https://en.wikipedia.org/wiki/Feedforward.
29 The information in this case letter was sourced from Global China Daily 8.11.2020 (https://global.chinadaily.com.cn/a/202011/07/WS5fa60463a31024ad0ba83b41.html).
30 Ibid.
31 Ibid.
32 Ibid.
33 https://en.wikipedia.org/wiki/Deng_Xiaoping.
34 OBOR stands for "One Belt One Road", while BRI stands for "Belt and Road Initiative".
35 ASEAN: The Association of Southeast Asian Nations.
36 Vietnam, Thailand, the Philippines, Laos, Cambodia, Myanmar, Singapore, Indonesia and Brunei – as well as Australia, China, Japan, New Zealand and South Korea.

37 https://www.piie.com/system/files/documents/wp20-9.pdf.
38 https://en.wikipedia.org/wiki/Trans-Pacific_Partnership.
39 https://edition.cnn.com/2020/11/16/economy/rcep-trade-agreement-intl-hnk/index.html.
40 https://en.wikipedia.org/wiki/Deng_Xiaoping.
41 People's Liberation Army.
42 Xi Jinping focuses on this in his speech; see the following link: https://www.chinadaily.com.cn/a/202011/09/WS5fa89e50a31024ad0ba83e75.html.
43 Regional Comprehensive Economic Partnership (RCEP) (https://en.wikipedia.org/wiki/Regional_Comprehensive_Economic_Partnership).
44 Global China Daily, 21.11.2020 (https://global.chinadaily.com.cn/a/202011/21/WS5fb8ae4ea31024ad0ba95991.html).

References

Allison, G. (2018). *Destined for war: Can America and China escape Thucydides trap?* Scribe, London.

Angang, H. (2014). Silk Road economic belt: Strategic considerations, positioning and implementation routes. *Journal of Xinjiang Normal University*, 2: 1–10.

Batzhan, A., Alpysbayeva, S. & Kapsalyamova, Z. (2020). The Belt and Road initiative: Case of Kazakhstan. In Wah, C.Y., Menkhoff, T. & Low, L. (Eds.), *China's Belt and Road initiative: Understanding the dynamics of a global transformation*, World Scientific, London. pp. 71–97.

Beeson, M. & Li, F. (2016). China's place in regional and global governance: A new world comes into view. *Global Policy*, 7, 4: 491–499.

Billington, D.P. (2020). *From insight to innovation*, MIT Press, Boston, MA.

Bougon, F. (2017). *Xi Jinping*, Hurst & Company, London.

Boutrup, C. (2019). *The great tech revolution, how China is shaping our future*, Saxo Business, Copenhagen.

Brown, K. (2018). *China's dream*, Polity, London.

Brown, K. (2019). *The world according to Xi*, I.B. Tauris, London.

Clinton, H. (2011). America's Pacific century. *Foreign Policy*, 189, 11 Oct.

Economy, E.C. (2018). *The third revolution, Xi Jinping and the new Chinese state*, Oxford University Press, Oxford.

Feng, D.H. & Liang, H.M. (2019). *Belt and Road initiative: Chinese version of Marshall Plan*, World Scientific, London.

Frank, T. (2020). *People without power*, Scribe, London.

French, H.W. (2015). *China's second continent*, Random House, London.

Gleick, J. (1997). *Chaos: Making a new science*, Vintage, New York.

Hamilton, C. (2018). *Silent invasion: China's influence in Australia*, Hardie Grant Books, New York.

Hudson, C.F. (1961). *Europe & China: A survey of their relations from the earliest times to 1800*, Beacon, Boston, MA.

Jianglin, Z. (2020). *21st century maritime Silk Road initiative, aims and objectives, implementation strategies and policy recommendations*, World Scientific, London.

Johannessen, J.-A. (2021). *The innovation economy in China*, Routledge, London.

Kissinger, H. (2015). *World order*, Penguin, New York.

Lim, J. & Lim, D. (2020). Financing the OBOR initiative. In Wah, C.Y., Menkhoff, T. & Low, L. (Eds.), *China's Belt and Road initiative: Understanding the dynamics of a global transformation*, World Scientific, London. pp. 97–125.

Linehan, P.M. (2018). *The culture of leadership in contemporary China*, Lexington Books, London.

Linggui, W. (2020). Foreword. In Jianglin, Z (Ed.), *21st century maritime Silk Road initiative, aims and objectives, implementation strategies and policy recommendations*, World Scientific, London. pp. v–xiii.

Macaes, B. (2020). *Belt and Road: A Chinese world order*, C. Hurst, London.

Magnus, G. (2018). *Red flags, why Xi's China is in jeopardy*, Yale University Press, New Haven, CT.

Mahbubani, K. (2020). Has China won? *Public Affairs*, 3, 4: 381–396.

Mantzopoulos, V. & Shen, R. (2011). *The political economy of China's systemic transformation*, Palgrave, London.

Mearsheimer, J. (2010). The gathering storm: China's challenge to US power in Asia. *Chinese Journal of International Politics*, 3, 4: 381–396.

Miller, J.G. (1978). *Living systems*, McGraw-Hill, New York.

Pavlicevic, D. (2019). A power shift underway in Europe? China's relationship with central and eastern Europe under the Belt and Road initiative. In Xing, L. (Ed.), *Mapping China's One Belt One Road initiative*, Palgrave, London. pp. 249–278.

Robert, J.-N. (2005). *From Rome to China: Silk Road of the Roman empire period*, Guangxi Normal University, Guangxi.

Ross, R. & Bekkevold, J.I. (2016). *China in the era of Xi Jinping*, Georgetown University Press, Washington, DC.

Sandel, M.J. (2020). *The tyranny of merit: What's become of the common good?* Allen Lane, New York.

Vangeli, A. (2017). China's engagement with the sixteen countries of central, east and southeast Europe under the Belt and Road initiative, *China & World Economy*, 25, 5: 101–124.

Vangeli, A. (2018). Normative foundation of the Belt and Road Initiative. In Wenhua, S., Nuotio, K. & Zhang, K. (Eds.), *Normative readings of the Belt and Road initiative*, Springer, London. pp. 59–83.

Vangeli, A. (2019). A framework for the study of One Belt One Road initiative as a medium of principle diffusion. In Xing, L. (Ed.), *Mapping China's One Belt One Road initiative*, Palgrave Macmillan, London. pp. 57–89.

Wah, C.Y. & Menkhoff, T. (2020). Introduction: Understanding the transformational power of China's Belt and Road initiative. In Wah, C.Y., Menkhoff, T., & Low, L. (Eds.), *China's Belt and Road initiative: Understanding the dynamics of a global transformation*, World Scientific, London. pp. xxiii–xxxviii.

Wang, D. (2020). *Reigning the future*, New Degree Press, New York.

Wang, Y. (2015). *One Belt One Road: Opportunities and challenges*, People's Press, Beijing.

Wang, Y. (2016). *The Belt and Road initiative: What will China offer the world in its rise*, New World Press, Beijing.

Wang, Y. (2017a). *Belt and Road initiative: China's responsibilities in its rise*, People's Press, Beijing.

Wang, Y. (2017b). *China connects the world: What behind the Belt and Road initiative*, China Intercontinental Press, Beijing.

Wang, Y. (2017c). *The world is connected: The logic of Belt and Road initiative*, The Commercial Press, Beijing.

Wasif Khan, S. (2019). *Haunted by chaos, China's grand strategy from Mao Zedong to Xi Jinping*, Harvard University Press, Cambridge, Mass.

Wright, G.H.v. (1996). *At forstå sin samtid*, Munksgaard, København.

Xing, L. (2019). Understanding the multiple facets of China's "One Belt One Road" initiative. In Xing, L. (Ed.), *Mapping China's One Belt One Road initiative*, Palgrave Macmillan, London. pp. 29–56.

Yang, J. (2015). China's new diplomacy under the Xi Jinping administration. *China Quarterly of International Strategic Studies*, 1, 1: 1–17.

Yuan, F. (2019). The One Belt One Road initiative and China's multi-layered multilateralism. In Xing, L. (Ed.), *Mapping China's One Belt One Road initiative*, Palgrave, London. pp. 91–116.

Yue, Y. & Fujian, L. (2019). *The Belt and Road initiative: ASEAN countries' perspectives*, World Scientific, London.

Zhang, J. (2015). China's new foreign policy under Xi Jinping: Towards peaceful rise 2.0? *Global Change, Peace & Security*, 27, 1: 5–19.

Zou, L. (2018). *The political economy of China's Belt and Road initiative*, World Scientific, London.

2 Hi-tech competence

The driving force for the new globalization

Key points in this chapter

- A locomotive-effect is a social mechanism that initiates and then reinforces a trend.
- Unlike the old globalization, which was about cost differentials, the new globalization is about competence differentials.
- In this context, the locomotive-effect initiates and reinforces the development of competence along the New Silk Road.
- Multilateralism, i.e. global cooperation and global coordination, is the fundamental concept underlying the New Silk Road.
- The innovation economy will be characterized by economic growth based on innovations.
- The "Dual Circulation Development Paradigm": This new Chinese economic paradigm (2020) can be explained in a single sentence: China needs to rely on its own resources and not allow itself to become dependent on hi-tech components from the United States and other Western countries. In addition, this new paradigm focuses on increasing domestic demand.
- Paradoxically, the American trade war against China led to China developing a strategy for becoming self-sufficient in the hi-tech products that it had previously imported from the United States. Viewed in this light, Trump's actions contributed a positive locomotive-effect for technological innovation in China.
- The Greater Bay Area (GBA) can be understood as a huge regional cluster, where the focus is on innovation development.
- It can be anticipated that the new globalization, which is linked to competence differentials rather than cost differentials, will be the decisive factor for China in the innovation economy.
- The New Silk Road is a strategic pillar for preventing China from being forced back behind a new "Iron Curtain" erected by American interests.
- Note that there is a qualitative difference between the "American Dream" and the "Chinese Dream". The American Dream is based on the idea that anyone can achieve their goals, as long as they work hard enough. The Chinese Dream is based on the idea that everyone should be able to enjoy a middle-class income as long as they work together to reach that goal.

DOI: 10.4324/9781003316978-2

- The trend in China has been an opening up to foreign investment in accordance with Deng Xiaoping's strategic thinking from the 1980s onwards, and an increase in Chinese exports of hi-tech products and expertise, in accordance with Xi Jinping's strategic plan, from 2013 onwards.
- The New Silk Road can be understood as a general abstract concept for the new Chinese economic policy. The BRI (Belt and Road Initiative) can be understood as an initiative that results in agreements for possible projects. OBOR (One Belt One Road) can be understood as a realization of the BRI agreements in specific projects that are implemented in the various countries and regions along the New Silk Road. This division of these three concepts makes them distinct, but at the same time interlinked.

Introduction

A locomotive-effect is the social mechanism that initiates and then reinforces a trend. The mechanism is metaphorically like a locomotive, which puts wagons into motion and then drags them up the side of the valley. Further, we can imagine this locomotive pulling a cargo of new ideas along the corridor created by the New Silk Road. These ideas have within them the potential to reduce American dominance; the American ideas and assumptions that the United States will be the leading power in this new world. Unlike the old globalization, which was about cost differentials, the new globalization is about competence differentials. New economic activity will no longer be generated by the lowest relative costs but by relatively higher hi-tech competence. In this context, the locomotive-effect initiates and reinforces the development of competence along the New Silk Road.

The new globalization is leading to strategic autonomy for the countries along the New Silk Road in contrast to the former American dominance. It is in this context that the Chinese leaders emphasize the importance of multilateralism, i.e. global cooperation and global coordination.

From the US perspective, independent of which administration is in power, relative strategic autonomy is viewed as an attack on its economic, political and military dominance. In other words, the United States and its allies view such a development as something which can lead to an unstable balance of power, which is perceived as chaos.

It is put forward as a thesis by the United States and its allies that a modernized and high-tech China will primarily act to promote Chinese interests and is thus a threat to Western interests (Jacques, 2012: 585, 637). One may ask: What's new about this? Since the early 16th century, European nations have conquered and exploited large areas of the world, not least China, which was invaded in the 19th century. Similarly, since its creation in 1776, the United States has launched numerous wars of foreign aggression and played a dominant world role since 1945, involving foreign wars as well as considerable investments in other countries. In other words, both the Europeans and the Americans have followed their own unilateral interests and have often instigated wars to promote these interests, making considerable investments in other countries. Why should it be imagined that

China has a different and more "moral" strategy. Trump's unilateral policy "America First" is nothing new. Such unilateral policies and actions are at least as old as the first Portuguese and Spanish conquistadors that swept through the Americas from the 15th century onwards (Hobsbawn, 1989, 1995).

Since, 2012, Xi Jinping and the other Chinese leaders have made it clear that the creation of new technological innovations is crucial to drive China into a position where they can be a leading nation at the start of the Fourth Industrial Revolution.[1] From around 2020, this technological innovation development was aligned with the "Dual Circulation Development Paradigm". In short, this strategy can be explained in one sentence: China needs to rely on its own resources and not become dependent on high-tech components from the United States and the West. In addition, the new paradigm stresses the importance of increasing domestic demand. This new strategy may be understood in relation to the trade war launched by the Trump administration. In the medium-term perspective, the consequence for China of this trade war is that the Chinese economic locomotive is now running along two main tracks. One track runs along the New Silk Road, along the land and sea routes. The second track is much more powerful. It is a multifaceted track that is spreading throughout the Chinese domestic economy.

The opening to the West and the New Silk Road are important elements in the Dual Circulation Development Paradigm.[2] This paradigm was established in May 2020. Zhang Qi, who is director-general of the Research Department of Foreign Economic Relations at the Development Research Center (DRC) of the State Council, defines "dual circulation" as follows: " 'dual circulation' allows the domestic and overseas markets to reinforce each other, with the domestic market as the mainstay".[3]

Zhang also points out that China needs to develop free trade zones (FTZ) and free trade ports with a high degree of autonomy. In June 2020, China developed an overall plan for these FTZ so that by September 2020 there were 21 such zones, and more are under development. The purpose of these zones is to develop creativity and innovation. The zones will then function as the starting point for the government's measures to develop high-tech infra- and info-structure projects, both in China and along the New Silk Road. In addition, Zhang says that such projects will also function as a locomotive-effect for the free trade agreement, RCEP.[4]

The basis for bringing about this paradigm shift is that China needs to expand creativity and innovation, which will be a necessary prerequisite to develop an innovation-driven economy. The Chinese education system is also a necessary prerequisite for the development of the future Chinese innovation economy. The sufficient prerequisite, however, are the centres in China for creativity and innovation linked to Chinese universities. These centres will deliver the practical innovations to entrepreneurs around China.

The position that China adopts with its new Dual Circulation Development Paradigm will most probably be opposed by the United States and its allies because the implementation of the paradigm will result in China becoming strategically independent of US technology; moreover, China will be able to develop its own technology and economy regardless of what happens in the United States. Such a de-coupling from the United States will paradoxically result in the United States and its allies becoming more interested in the developments taking place along the New Silk Road. The reasoning is simple. If China exerts a relatively stronger economic and technological grip on the countries along the New Silk Road, this will result in a relative decline of US dominance. In such a situation, the United States may fall into Thucydides' Trap (2009). Thucydides' Trap is a metaphor used to describe the effect of an emerging great power (China) on an existing great power (the United States). According to Thucydides' Trap, the great power will tend to attempt to hinder the development of the emerging power, often using military force (Allison, 2018).

This book, as well as this chapter, will focus on the following problem: the battle for new technology, artificial intelligence and intelligent robots, and how China can come to lead the innovation economy.[5]

In this chapter, we will examine the following research problem: How does the locomotive-effect promote the New Silk Road as an innovation generator?

The research questions we investigate in order to answer this research problem are:

RQ1: How will technological innovations influence the New Silk Road as an innovation generator?
RQ2: How will the "Dual Circulation Development Paradigm" influence the New Silk Road as an innovation generator?

The objective of the chapter is to provide inputs to, and perspectives on, the emergent Chinese innovation economy as we head towards the Fourth Industrial Revolution.

The knowledge basis of this chapter is systemic thinking.

The introduction is figuratively shown in Figure 2.1. Figure 2.1 also shows how this chapter is organized.

Technological innovations

In this section, we will examine the following question: How will technological innovations influence the New Silk Road as an innovation generator?

The classic globalization was driven by cost differentials. The new globalization is driven by competence differentials. An additional element in the new globalization is that it is the areas where competence has the potential to become new technology that innovations will be created. It was the American companies that mainly profited from the old globalization. As the new globalization emerges, it is the United States (under the Trump administration) at the political level, not the corporate level, which is trying to prevent this new globalization. The reasoning is simple. The United States does not want to fall behind in the new globalization, where competence becomes a competitive parameter. Therefore, the United States has imposed trade restrictions on China regarding high-tech equipment, among others, chips for intelligent robots and artificial intelligence (Jianglin, 2020).

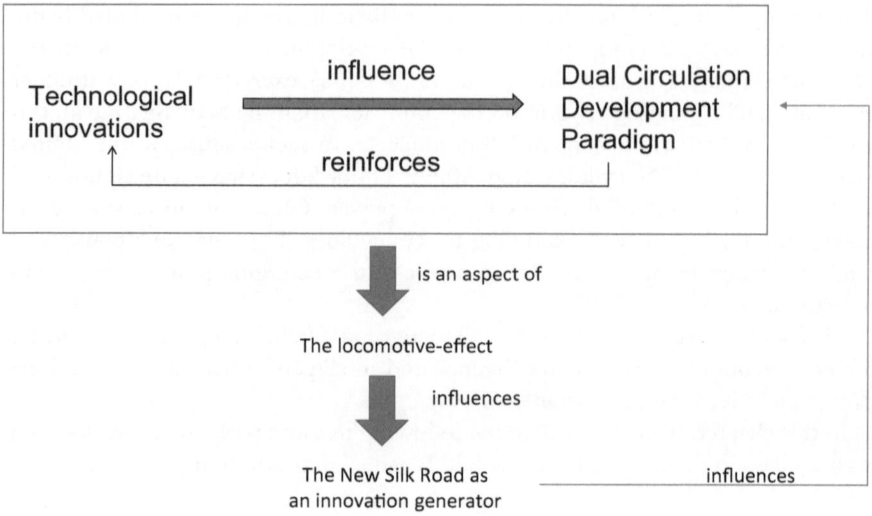

Figure 2.1 The locomotive effect.

Narratives for technological innovations

Case letter 1: Paradoxically, the United States loses out by preventing exports to China

The United States has imposed restrictions on the export of chips, semiconductors and other high-tech equipment to China.[6] This has resulted in the Chinese companies having to develop their own technology to meet the demand for these products from Chinese companies.[7] The American companies are now experiencing that competition has been reduced because they have been excluded by their own political leaders from a growing market. In the short and medium term, this will limit the innovation development in these American companies because they do not have that little extra incentive to innovate to compete. By imposing restrictions on the sale of technological equipment to China, no matter how good the reasoning is, the Americans are shooting themselves in the foot by such a manoeuvre because they will become less competitive when innovation development is hindered.

Guandong in the 1990s was an example of the old globalization. It was here that Deng Xiaoping first opened up the free economic zones. This attracted American investment, and American investors were able to reap higher profits than from investments in the US domestic market. Guandong and several other free economic zones, in the 1990s and at the beginning of the 21st century, mass produced cheap industrial and consumer goods that were exported to the United States and Europe.

Twenty to thirty years after Guandong first became a free economic zone, it is less profitable to operate companies based on wage differentials between the West and the East. Of course, it is cheaper to produce consumer goods in Guandong than in an American city such as Chicago, but the differences are relatively small, and therefore the interest from American companies to invest has also diminished. In other words, the wage costs in Guandong and other similar economic zones have increased so that the relative differences in wage costs between East and West have narrowed. Another point is that the expertise and technology used in Guandong and similar economic zones as an input factor in production and distribution has increased sharply. Jacques (2012: 174) writes that this development has led to, among other things, 1000 shoe factories closing down in Guandong in 2007. From 2007 to 2020 China has been banned from parts of the world trade in high-tech products. This has resulted in the establishment of the new Dual Circulation Development Paradigm in China.[8] In short, this paradigm focuses on China developing its own high-tech products for its high-tech industry; there is also a focus on increasing domestic demand as well as demand stemming from the economic corridor created via the New Silk Road. Moreover, China will be able to increase its trade through the new free trade agreement, RCEP, which came into force in September 2020.[9] The United States has withdrawn from the TTP free trade agreement, thus paving the way for China to enter the RCEP agreement. In other words, the United States has continually shot itself in the foot in terms of economic integration in Southeast Asia. This may explain why the United States is starting to increase its presence in the South China Sea.

Case letter 2: The engine of the new globalization

China's innovation-driven economy is the result of the gigantic investment in education at all levels over the past 40 years. In 2017, there were 2,914 universities and colleges in China, with 20 million students enrolled.[10] It is this education industry, which constitutes the input into the innovation economy in China (Linehan, 2018: 128–143). The technological cooperation within China, as well as between China and the countries along the New Silk Road, will contribute to an innovation-driven globalization. However, it is also possible that this globalization will be limited if the United States and its allies hinder cooperation with China. This limited globalization may emerge as a dynamic regional innovation-driven economy throughout the ASEAN area, the countries included in the RCEP free trade area and also the countries that are part of the New Silk Road. Such a development will in all probability not benefit Europe because it will de-couple them from the dynamic economic developments in South-East Asia. On the other hand, it is possible that regional alliances based on a decentralized power structure will benefit many countries that do not belong to the US-led alliance.

Description of technological innovations

There is much to suggest that China will be at the forefront of the future development of high-tech expertise (Fannin, 2019). However, two necessary preconditions and one sufficient precondition must be present for this to happen. The first of the two preconditions is that China needs to develop strategic autonomy by developing regional innovation clusters (Feng & Liang, 2019). The second necessary precondition is that China needs to develop strategic competence in artificial intelligence (Drache et al., 2019). The sufficient condition is that China needs to develop artificial intelligence that can be used in practical applications that can increase value creation in China and also for its most important alliance partners along the New Silk Road (Boutrup, 2019; Brown, 2018).

It would be erroneous to view China today as a country that still needs to imitate Western technology (Fannin, 2019). Around 2020, the Chinese innovation economy shifted from imitation to innovation (Johannessen, 2021). Paradoxically, the United States' trade war with China resulted in China being able to develop a strategy to become self-sufficient in the high-tech products it had previously imported from the United States. Viewed from this perspective, the trade war benefitted China with regard to the development of technological innovations in China. It might be said that Trump's trade war against China functioned as a locomotive-effect that self-started the development of technological innovations in China that resulted in high-tech products being produced by Chinese industry. It's not just that China has learned from its competitors. The competitors, in this case the United States under President Trump, have pursued a strategy toward China that has resulted in China becoming technologically self-sufficient. In this way, Trump's strategy has led to the United States losing in the technological competition, while China has minimized competition related to the development of technological innovations.

From 2000 to 2020, Shenzhen, known as the "Silicon Valley of China", has established itself as a regional innovation cluster, according to China expert Rebecca Fannin (2019). If this is related to the recent American strategy towards China, then it is not difficult to understand how and why China is developing strategic autonomy from the United States. In addition to the many regional innovation clusters that have emerged in China since 2000, major private and state-owned high-tech Chinese companies, such as Baidu, Alibaba, Tencent, Huawei, etc., can today compete with the largest companies in the United States and Europe. It is through this "two-sided systemic strategy" that China makes gains with its technological innovations. The two-sided systemic strategy referred to here is China's strategic autonomy and its regional innovation clusters that are systemically connected to the major technology giants mentioned above. In addition, there are also a number of slightly smaller technology companies such as Xiaomi, Toutiao, ByteDance and Meituan Dianping which are also very important for China, as well as China's alliance partners (Fannin, 2019).

China's development of technological strategic autonomy and regional innovation clusters, as well as strategic expertise focusing on the development of artificial intelligence and intelligent robots are also very much in evidence in the Greater Bay Area (Berlie & Hung, 2020: 77–100), which is also important for developing the New Silk Road. The Greater Bay Area can be viewed as a giant regional innovation cluster.

Hong Kong is an important city in the Greater Bay Area because it has a strong financial infrastructure, which is not only necessary for developing technological innovations but also important with regard to the development of various projects along the New Silk Road. The new giant bridge, the HZM Bridge that connects

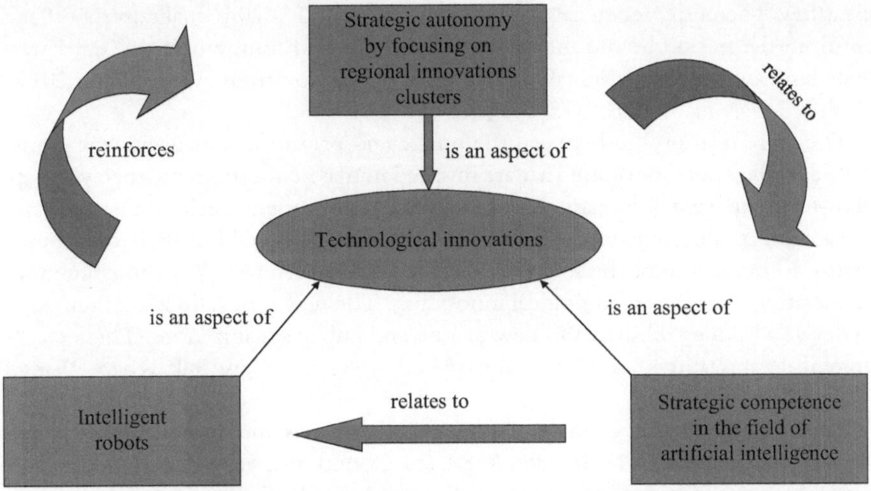

Figure 2.2 Policy prerequisites for the development of technological innovations.

Hong Kong with Zhuhai and Macau may be viewed as a symbol of the power that the New Silk Road has for connecting economies that previously operated as "islands" with only loose connections to other economies (Berlie & Hung, 2020: 77).

Considerable foreign investment in China has been an indicator of China's economic and financial globalization. However, this indicator is expected to change sharply as China's technological strategic autonomy is strengthened, and there is more focus on domestic demand (i.e., the new Dual Circulation Development Paradigm). The competence differentials rather than labour costs differentials in China will function as a decisive indicator for China in relation to the new Chinese globalization in the innovation economy.

Figure 2.2 summarizes the above and shows aspects of the prerequisites for the development of China's technological innovations.

Analysis of technological innovations

The technological revolution in China is driven by a close cooperation between the public and private sectors (Fang & Fu, 2020). The ten largest privately owned companies in China are Mide Group, Byte Dance, JD Group, Huawei, Pinduoduo, Ant Group, Ping An Insurance, Meituan, Alibaba and Tencent.[11] These companies create many technological innovations in consumer goods. These goods are sold in China to the countries along the New Silk Road and to the rest of the world. Private entrepreneurship in China is highly developed as these private companies show.

High-tech entrepreneurship based on technological innovations is the future that Chinese leadership has envisioned as a growth engine for China going forward (Wang, 2020). It is the new spirit of entrepreneurship that has enabled private sector actors from the 1980s onwards to develop new enterprises in China. Before the 1980s, the Chinese leadership envisioned completely different strategic measures. The entrepreneurial system in China around 2020 is qualitatively different from the period before the 1980s and ensures both innovation and entrepreneurship based on institutional and technological innovations (Wasif Khan, 2019; Weih & MacMillan, 1991: 375–379).

The close relationship between the public and private sectors is evident if one considers the enormous sums that are invested in mass-educating students with top high-tech expertise (Linehan, 2018). The graduate students seek employment in private and public organizations, and some are able to establish their own businesses. In other words, the scientific focus of the government has contributed to accelerating Chinese technological innovation. The new innovations are then used to develop both established and new private and public organizations. These technological innovations are also being applied along the New Silk Road (Wang, 2017a, 2017b, 2017c).

The strategy of the Chinese Communist Party has unquestionably changed since the period before 1980. After 1980, the Communist Party uses the opportunities that exist, e.g. market, profit, motivation for individuals to get rich, etc., to achieve the goal of the "Chinese Dream", namely a middle-class income for everyone in China (Bougon, 2017; Brown, 2018). The strategy of the Communist Party has changed qualitatively between 1980 and 2020. Moreover, Xi Jinping has added a new strategic intention, namely to focus on the development of high-tech innovation, high-tech entrepreneurship, RCEP, the Dual Circulation Development Paradigm and the New Silk Road (Brown, 2019; Yue & Fujian, 2019). By means of Xi Jinping's strategy, the technological innovations developed in China function as an innovation generator for the countries along the New Silk Road. The New Silk Road may also be viewed as a strategic pillar that will prevent China from being pushed behind a new "Iron Curtain" established by American interests.

By focusing on a combination of private and public organizations, Chinese leaders have a greater variety in their strategic tools to achieve their goal, which is expressed as the Chinese Dream (Brown, 2018). The governing authorities are able to develop a policy for the private organizations so that they are continuously involved in steering the Chinese economy towards the Chinese Dream. However, note that there is a qualitative difference between the "American Dream" and the "Chinese Dream". The 'American Dream' is that all Americans have the opportunity to become rich, just as long as they work hard enough. The Chinese Dream is that everyone can be raised to a middle-class income, as long as they work together to achieve the goal (Brown, 2018).

Xi Jinping has greatly changed the Chinese strategy from 2012, just as Deng Xiaoping greatly changed the Chinese strategy after 1980. Xi Jinping is developing China into a modern innovation state by developing technological innovations with a focus on artificial intelligence. In order to become independent of US investments, which Deng Xiaoping encouraged, Xi Jinping has established a clear strategy of becoming self-sufficient in the critical components needed for the technological innovations which are developed in order to promote the production of artificial intelligence-based products.

It would be a mistake to view this change in strategy as representing a greater degree of closure of Chinese society. It is only a necessary strategic change to facilitate the export of innovative knowledge-based products. In other words, the strategic development has changed between the 1980s and 2020. Deng Xiaoping's strategy was to encourage foreign investment in China. Xi Jinping's strategy is to facilitate the export of Chinese high-tech products and expertise. This should be viewed in connection with the New Silk Road, which is an economic corridor that functions as a highway for the Chinese export of high-tech innovative products to all the countries along both the land and sea routes.

Theoretical points for technological innovations

The strategic competence in China is linked to two axes. First is the education system that provides millions of students every year with high-tech skills and competencies (Linehan, 2018: 128–143). Second, there is the strong emphasis on private entrepreneurship (Economy, 2018; Huang, 2017). At the same time as China is developing its own type of strategic competence, they are also developing a strategic autonomy based on regional innovation clusters. The strategic autonomy related to the economic system is a consequence of the realization that China's dependence on high-tech equipment, especially from the United States, makes them vulnerable to the policies and actions of changing administrations in Washington. The need for this strategic autonomy became especially evident during the Trump administration, which launched a trade war against China in 2018. China's exports to the United States in 2020 amounted to approximately 20% of all Chinese exports, so obviously a US embargo on China regarding certain products, and the raising of tariffs on other goods, is damaging to the Chinese economy, but not something that cannot be repaired. It is precisely in this context that the New Silk Road can act as a buffer. The biggest threat to China's economy related to the US embargo and raising of tariffs is the time-lag that occurs between an embargo and the raising of tariffs being fully implemented and the time it takes China to compensate for the loss by focusing on other countries in the region and along the New Silk Road.

Initially, China tried to circumvent the embargo by moving production to other countries, e.g. Vietnam and South Africa. From a longer term perspective, however, China needs to focus on producing certain goods, especially high-tech components for its own domestic industry. China's way out of the US trade embargo can be said to be based on a five-pronged strategy:

1. The Dual Circulation Development Paradigm
2. Domestic technological innovation[12]
3. The New Silk Road
4. "Made in China 2025"[13]
5. RCEP[14]

1, 2, 4 and 5 also constitute the strategic prerequisites for the New Silk Road as an innovation generator.

Figure 2.3 shows a typology of how technological innovations can be an innovation generator, as a function of strategic autonomy and regional innovation clusters on the one hand, and strategic competence and artificial intelligence on the other.

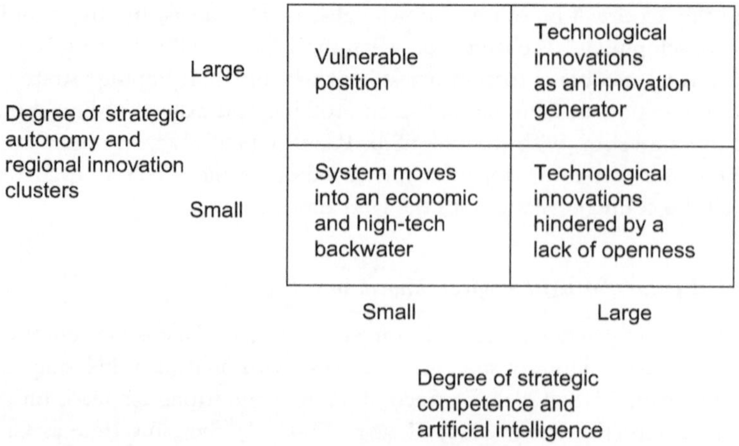

Figure 2.3 Typology for technological innovation as an innovation generator.

Proposition: The greater the degree of strategic autonomy and regional innovation clusters China develops, as well as the greater the degree of strategic competence and artificial intelligence that is developed, the greater the likelihood of developing technological innovations that can act as an innovation generator along the New Silk Road.

Proposition: The greater the degree of strategic autonomy and regional innovation clusters that China develops, and the smaller degree of strategic competence and artificial intelligence that is developed, the greater the likelihood that the development of technological innovations that can act as an innovation generator along the New Silk Road will end up in a vulnerable position hindering intentions.

Proposition: The smaller the degree of strategic autonomy and regional innovation clusters that China develops, as well as the greater the degree of strategic competence and artificial intelligence that is developed, the greater the probability will be that the development of technological innovations that can act as an innovation generator along the New Silk Road will be hindered.

Proposition: The smaller the degree of strategic autonomy and regional innovation clusters that China develops, as well as the smaller degree of strategic competence and artificial intelligence that is developed, the greater the likelihood that the development of technological innovations that can act as an innovation generator along the New Silk Road will end up in an economic and high-tech backwater.

Practical utility for technological innovations

In the Fourth Industrial Revolution, technological progress will be inseparable from scientific progress. Of course, China has realized this. This is evident if we consider the following statement made by Wang Zhigang, the Chinese Minister of Science and Technology:

> Research has almost doubled since 2015, reaching 133.6 billion yuan last year. China has also doubled the value of its technology market since 2015. China now has 169 national-level high-tech development zones and over 225,000 high-tech companies, up from 79,000 in 2015. (…). The number of full-time R&D personnel in the nation grew from 3.76 million in 2015 to 4.8 million last year.[15]

It also emerges from the above statement that the Chinese regional innovation centres named by Wang, as "national-level high-tech development zones", are important for the development of technological innovations in China.

Science and technology are global languages that know no national borders. Consequently, it is possible to compare the different countries in relation to their technological and innovative progress. The Global Innovation Index provides detailed information about the innovation performance of various countries. Wang Zhigang also points out that "China's ranking on the Global Innovation Index (…) jumped from 29th in 2015 to 14th in 2020."[16] We can therefore assume that the advances China has made regarding technological innovations shown here will have a direct impact on the projects along the New Silk Road.

The rapid progress China is making in developing technological innovations indicates that the Chinese leadership views such technological progress as an important mechanism for becoming a leader in the Fourth Industrial Revolution.

By developing win–win projects, focusing on cooperation and co-creation along the New Silk Road, as well as applying and developing the new technology in these projects, the probability is high that the New Silk Road will function as an innovation generator for all the countries participating in OBOR projects.

Figure 2.4 summarizes the practical benefits of the technological innovations for the countries along the New Silk Road.

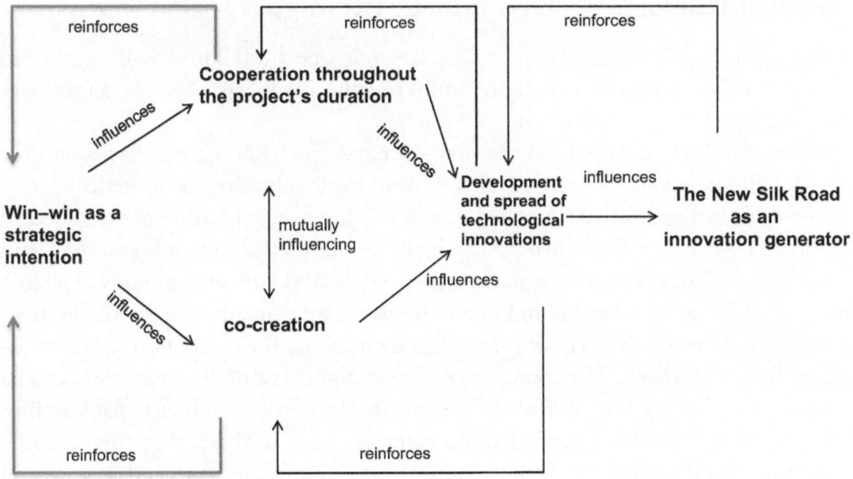

Figure 2.4 The New Silk Road as an innovation generator: Some practical prerequisites.

Sub-conclusion for technological innovations

In this section, we have examined the following research question: How will technological innovations influence the New Silk Road as an innovation generator?

The short answer is that there are three policy prerequisites, four strategic prerequisites and four practical prerequisites that must exist in order for the technological innovations to promote the New Silk Road as an innovation generator.

Policy prerequisites:

1 Strategic autonomy
2 Strategic competence
3 Intelligent robots

Strategic prerequisites:

1 The Dual Circulation Development Paradigm
2 The development of technological innovations domestically
3 "Made in China 2025"
4 RCEP

Practical prerequisites;

1 Win–win projects
2 Collaboration throughout the life of the project
3 Co-creation for efficiency and innovation
4 The development and dissemination of technological innovations

The Dual Circulation Development Paradigm

In this section, we will examine the following question: How will the "Dual Circulation Development Paradigm" influence the New Silk Road as an innovation generator?

Briefly, the basic idea behind the new development paradigm is that economic growth will be driven forward by an economic and technological locomotive that will be mainly based on domestic demand. The new paradigm was launched in China's five-year plan 2021–2025, which also included the launching of "Made in China 2025". These two concepts are internally linked and have roughly the same rationale. The main idea behind them is that China needs to rely on its own resources and not be dependent on foreign technology for its economic and technological development. Therefore, the new paradigm is not only a paradigm linked to economic factors but also to education, regional development, partnerships along the New Silk Road, as well as cooperation and co-creation in the new free trade zone (RCEP). RCEP is the world's largest free trade zone and includes all ten ASEAN countries as well as five other countries.[17]

Narratives for the Dual Circulation Development Paradigm

Case letter 1: RCEP as part of the Dual Circulation Development Paradigm

The RCEP free trade agreement includes the ten ASEAN countries and five of the largest trading partners of the ASEAN countries. This free trade zone constitutes the world's largest free trade bloc with a combined population of 2.27 billion people, a total GDP of more than $26 trillion and a total trade value of $10.4 trillion.[18]

For China, RCEP will provide the opportunity for the country to develop its Dual Circulation Development Paradigm by participating in trade and technological co-creation with the other RCEP countries. This will strengthen the Chinese economy, but it will also strengthen the development of the economies of the 14 other RCEP countries. The RCEP agreement will be able to function as an economic mechanism that can kick-start the new economic paradigm in China. The new free trade area will represent a challenge for both the EU and the United States because any form of strategic independence will relatively weaken these areas. In particular, the agreement is a threat to the United States because the country wasted its chance to lead in another free trade agreement (TPP[19]), which the Trump administration withdrew from. Thus, this opened a door for China, which was not initially involved in the free trade discussions. In this way, it was the United States, which, by withdrawing from the TPP, worsened its economic position in the area of free trade throughout South-East Asia.

Case letter 2: The implementation of the RCEP agreement

In general, goods, services and people will be able to flow across the borders of the RCEP countries, once the agreement has reached a certain level of implementation. In the short term, this will promote technological cooperation projects throughout this large free trade area. It is not difficult to foresee how this free trade area will contribute to integrating the economy in a region that covers approximately 30% of the world's total GDP.[20] An important point of the RCEP agreement in the context of the new economic paradigm is that China's domestic demand and the demand that will result from the RCEP agreement will reinforce each other, and act as an economic high-speed locomotive for the Chinese economy, and for the economy of the whole RCEP free trade zone.

Case letter 3: The RCEP as an economic upward spiral

The RCEP area can act as an upward economic spiral, making China less dependent on trade with the United States. By means of the RCEP agreement, which may be viewed as a "gift" from Donald Trump because he withdrew the United States from an ongoing free trade agreement, China was not part of (TPP); China can become strategically independent of the United States and strengthens the development of the concept "Made in China 2025". The RCEP agreement will greatly contribute to regional economic integration in South-East Asia. The agreement also represents a threat to those countries that are attempting to establish a greater degree of protectionism and unilateral policies in the world economy.

Case letter 4: OBOR and the Dual Circulation Development Paradigm: a practical case

OBOR, RCEP and "Made in China 2025" are concepts that in practice promote the new economic paradigm in China. Specifically, China plans to build new railways both in China and between China and several of the countries along the New Silk Road. It is possible that some countries that are part of the RCEP will also be included in these plans. China has previously developed rail systems in Nigeria, Angola, and from Djibouti to several cities in Ethiopia.

CRRC Tangshan CO. Ltd. is a high-speed train-making company located in Hebei Province in China. This company has developed high-speed trains with a maximum speed of 400 km/h. The train system can operate in different temperature zones between −25 °C and 50 °C.[21] The point of highlighting this here is to show that China's investment in infrastructure projects will bind regions and countries together so that trade will be more easily facilitated, and thus positively affect the many businesses and companies along the New Silk Road. Several other countries that China has connections to at different levels, such as Turkey, Indonesia and Malaysia, have also started planning to use railway development as an essential part of the economic integration in regions and between countries. Using high-speed trains, such integration could literally have a locomotive-effect on the economy of the countries that are developing such high-speed railways.

Description of the Dual Circulation Development Paradigm

Since the New Silk Road initiative was proposed by Xi Jinping in 2013, progress has been made in planning, the implementation of specific projects, and a large-scale coordination of policies between the countries participating in the New Silk Road. The projects are linked to different sectors and have been integrated into the various countries' development policies, which has integrated the countries and created a regional development the likes of which has rarely been seen before. Partnerships at different levels are linked and implemented through various physical projects (Zou, 2018: 235). Coordination, connectivity, regional development and partnership are also aspects of the concept Dual Circulation Development Paradigm.[22]

This new paradigm was adopted by the Central Committee of the Communist Party of China (26–29 October 2020). Briefly, the paradigm concerns a change in China's economic development, from being mainly oriented towards exports to now having a greater focus on economic growth by increasing domestic demand and trading with selected key countries. Some of the key countries are those involved in the New Silk Road initiative from 2013 onwards, as well as the 14 other countries that are part of the new free trade area (RCEP).

The connections between the New Silk Road, the RCEP countries, the strategic plan, "Made in China 2025"[23] and a greater focus on policy integration between the BRICS countries (Brazil, Russia, India, China and South Africa), will, although it was not necessarily the intention, transform the Dual Circulation Development Paradigm into a high-speed economic locomotive for the economies of all the countries involved (Macaes, 2020). We can now make out the contours of the economic tectonic plates that are forcing new economic mountain ranges into existence. It will be important for Western countries to avoid exclusion from this economic growth and to avoid becoming unable to cross the passes through these emerging ranges of economic mountains.

With these changes, the old globalization has now been consigned to history (Mahbubani, 2014). The new globalization is based on competence, technological innovations and China as an economic locomotive. The Dual Circulation Development Paradigm may prove to have greater consequences for the global economy than many have anticipated because the strategy was launched at a time when the United States was no longer able to shoulder the burden of global leadership (Mahbubani, 2018). Among other things, internal problems and conflicts have contributed to the United States being unable to continue the leadership role it has had since 1945 (Mahbubani, 2009, 2010, 2020).

China's new economic paradigm will lead to China becoming self-sufficient in new technology and thus less dependent on the United States' technology. The new economic paradigm linked to the RCEP and "Made in China 2025" will lead to China becoming the leading economic force in the new globalization. This can be partly explained by the Chinese higher education revolution which has enabled China to create the necessary competence (Linehan, 2018). In this new globalization, the United States may very well end up in the backwaters of global economic development.

"Made in China 2025" was launched by the Chinese Prime Minister Li Keqiang in 2015.[24] The main aim of the plan is to downscale China's labour-intensive industries, which rely heavily on the availability of cheap labour, and instead of focusing increasingly on industries developing hi-tech products. It is here that the links to the new economic paradigm that was launched in October 2020, and to the RCEP, which was signed by 15 countries in South-East Asia that same autumn, will have the effect of metaphorically shifting the economic driver from a steam-driven engine to a high-speed locomotive.

Figure 2.5 shows the new economic paradigm and the role it will have for the New Silk Road as an innovation generator.

Analysis of the Dual Circulation Development Paradigm

Many critics expect that China will surpass the United States as the world's largest economy around 2035 (Mahbubani, 2018, 2020). The United States is trying to convince its allies that China poses a future threat. However, it is not only the Republicans under the Trump administration who stood for this viewpoint. As early as 2011, the former Secretary of State, Hillary Clinton, wrote the article "America's Pacific century" that was published in the *Foreign Policy* magazine, which emphasized the Obama administration's foreign policy perspective, which was not that different from the Trump administration's views regarding concerns about China's global progress (2016–2020) (Mahbubani, 2018, 2020).

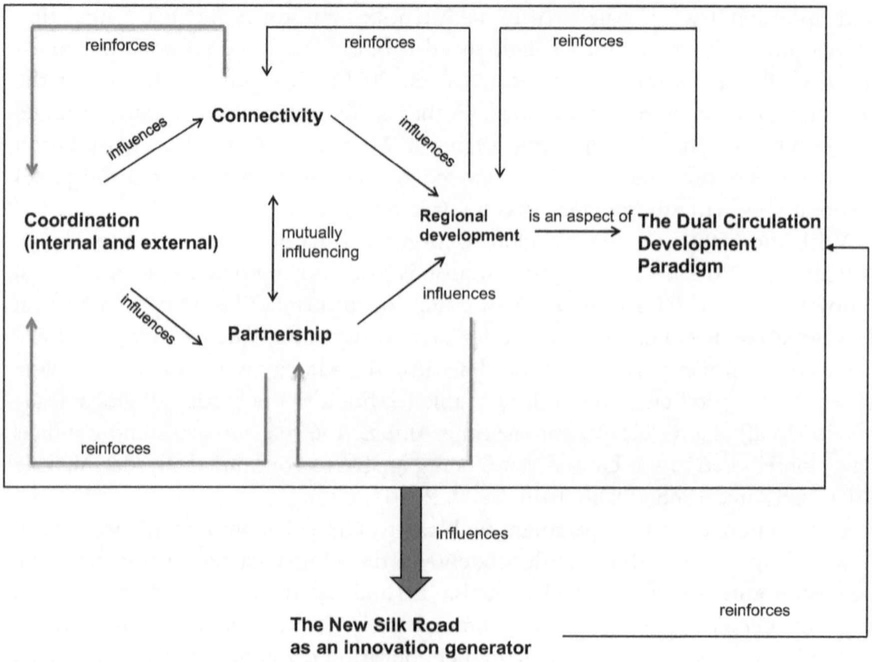

Figure 2.5 The dual circulation development paradigm.

The United States has advanced two main arguments regarding the Chinese "threat" (Clinton, 2011; Magnus, 2018; Mahbubani, 2020).

1 China is using its dominant economic position to take control of other countries.
2 China is spreading its political ideology to the countries it dominates economically.

Based on these two main arguments, the United States believes that China should have developed in a way that corresponds to the political and economic ideology of the United States and Western countries, that is, a liberal Western capitalism. In the past, this has provided an important argument for making investments in China; that is, it was believed that as soon as the Chinese economy became "free", the political system would follow suit and also become "free", that is, imitate Western liberal capitalism (Mantzopoulos & Shen, 2011; Mearsheimer, 2010). However, the Chinese political system has not changed significantly since China opened up to foreign investment in the 1980s (Beeson & Li, 2016; Ross & Bekkevold, 2016). The Chinese political system is centralist and pragmatic and uses the market as an instrument to achieve overall economic and technological goals (Zou, 2018). However, the "market" is not a capitalist invention. It existed long before merchant capitalism was developed in the Netherlands in the early 17th century (Johannessen, 2018).

Since Deng Xiaoping opened up China to foreign investment in 1978, China has lifted 800 million people out of extreme poverty (Mahbubani, 2020). To put this into perspective, there are at present 29 million in the United States who do not have enough to eat every day.[25]

The New Silk Road will most probably have a great impact as an innovation generator, together with the RCEP. In the period, from the 1980s up until today, the Chinese middle class has grown to approximately 200 million people (Mahbubani, 2020). During the same period, the American middle class has been sharply reduced and "de-classed" (Kotkin, 2020; Reves, 2018). Today, China has the world's largest middle class. This development also corresponds to the vision of the "Chinese Dream" (Brown, 2018). The economic development along the New Silk Road also corresponds with the dreams of many countries participating in the OBOR projects (Drache et al., 2019). The point being made here is that the New Silk Road is part of the new Dual Circulation Development Paradigm and will generate both economic and technological advances as the economic locomotive picks up speed (Jianglin, 2020; Lim & Lim, 2020).

At the same time as China's economic growth is benefitting the majority of the Chinese population, we are witnessing more and more crises emerging to the surface in American society. The 2020 US presidential election seemed to indicate that American democracy is in crisis, with the incumbent president initially refusing to accept the election result and the attack by right-wing groups on the Capitol in Washington, DC. The crisis in the economy is manifested in many ways; as mentioned above, 29 million do not have enough to eat every day, according to the world food program. Incomes have stagnated during the last 30 years, while a few have become extremely rich (Bartels, 2008). In addition, race relations in the United States have deteriorated in recent years (Frank, 2020). Against this background, one may ask: Why should the United States be the economic and political model that Europe and the rest of the world should look up to and be dominated by?

The United States is governed by the wealthy. China is governed by the leaders of the Communist Party. China's strategy from 1949 to the present has changed several times. Deng Xiaoping's opening of China to foreign capital perhaps contributed most to China's economic development and the increase in the standard of living for the majority. Xi Jinping's strategy after becoming leader in 2012, with the launching of the New Silk Road, "Made in China 2025", the Dual Circulation Development Paradigm and a focus on technological innovations and green industrial investment may change the Chinese economy even more than the changes that were brought about by Deng Xiaoping's opening of China to foreign investment. Deng Xiaoping adopted a policy to stimulate industrial development by attracting foreign investment, and the policies of Xiaoping aimed at preparing China to take on a leading global role in the Fourth Industrial Revolution. Against this background, it is understandable that the United States fears China, just as Sparta feared the rise of Athens. In this context, we might refer to the phenomenon termed the Thucydides' Trap, named after the historian of the same name (Thucydides, 2009). The Thucydides' Trap is a political metaphor used to describe the effect of a rising great power on the dominant great power. According to

Thucydides' hypothesis, the great power that is falling from its dominant position will tend to hinder the development of the emerging power, often by using military force (Allison, 2018).

Theoretical points for the Dual Circulation Development Paradigm

It is not difficult to understand that the New Silk Road will function as an economic engine that will fulfil the aims of the Dual Circulation Development Paradigm with regard to foreign demand (Vangeli, 2017, 2018, 2019). Coordination and connectivity internally in the countries along the New Silk Road, as well as between the countries, will function as the necessary conditions to ensure that China's domestic and overseas markets (along the New Silk Road) will reinforce each other. However, coordination and connectivity will not be sufficient for the Dual Circulation Development Paradigm to function as an innovation generator for the countries included in the OBOR projects. A high degree of partnership and regional development will also be needed to meet the sufficient condition.

Policy coordination is the starting point for achieving the aims of the Dual Circulation Development Paradigm (Zou, 2018: 236). According to Zou (2018: 236), Chinese diplomacy focused on the countries participating or planning to participate in the projects along the New Silk Road between September 2013 and the beginning of 2015. The Chinese diplomacy, conferences, regional meetings and other information and communication arenas were used to develop the understanding that the New Silk Road projects aim to be win–win projects, where economic partnerships will be emphasized. This involved Asian countries, African countries, Arab states and some countries in Europe. Coordination, connectivity, partnership and regional development were central themes in these communication arenas. In order to foster the interest of the Arab states, there were three areas that were important: energy, infrastructure and mutual investment. One would think that the Arab states were primarily interested in fossil fuels; however, the Arab–Chinese partnership regarding energy was to develop new forms of energy linked to nuclear energy, solar energy and other forms of renewable energy (Zou, 2018: 236–237).

Regarding the Sino–Pakistani Silk Road, infrastructure projects are crucial because they will strengthen Pakistan's economic development. This concerns partnerships based on win–win projects that will function as economic drivers along the New Silk Road (Zou, 2018: 238–239).

We have developed a typology for the Dual Circulation Development Paradigm as an innovation generator in Figure 2.6.

Proposition: The larger the degree of coordination (internal/external) and connectivity, as well as the larger the degree of partnership and regional development that takes place along the New Silk Road, the greater will be the probability of developing a Dual Circulation Development Paradigm as an innovation generator along the New Silk Road.

Proposition: The larger the degree of coordination (internal/external) and connectivity, as well as the smaller the degree of partnership and regional development that takes place along the New Silk Road, the greater will be the likelihood of developing a Dual Circulation Development Paradigm as an innovation generator along the New Silk Road that will end up in a vulnerable position.

Proposition: The smaller the degree of coordination (internal/external) and connectivity, as well as the larger the degree of partnership and regional development that takes place along the New Silk Road, the greater the likelihood that the development of the Dual Circulation Development Paradigm as an innovation generator along the New Silk Road will lack an overall strategy.

Proposition: The smaller the degree of coordination (internal/external) and connectivity, as well as the smaller the degree of partnership and regional development that takes place along the New Silk Road, the greater the likelihood that the countries operating under these conditions will be closed in and stuck in an economic backwater.

Practical utility for the Dual Circulation Development Paradigm

The New Silk Road may be understood as a general abstract concept for the new economic policy in China. The BRI (Belt and Road Initiative) may be understood as an initiative that involves agreements on various projects. The OBOR (One Belt One Road) may be understood as a concretization of the BRI agreements in relation to the specific projects that are implemented in the various countries and regions along the New Silk Road. Such a categorization of these three concepts makes them distinct, but at the same time connected to each other. This also creates an abstraction hierarchy, where all three concepts can be applied. With such an understanding, the New Silk Road was established by Xi Jinping in 2013. The BRI agreements were entered into at different times and with various countries. The specific OBOR projects have been carried out in the various countries from 2013 onwards.

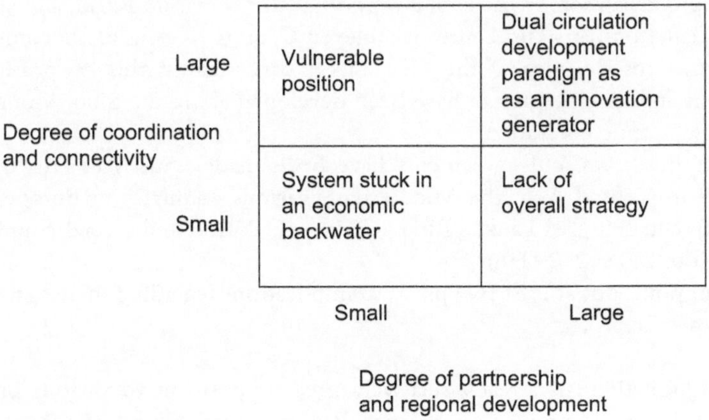

Figure 2.6 A typology for Dual Circulation Development Paradigm as an innovation generator.

For example, an agreement between China and Pakistan was established on 20 April 2015, when Xi Jinping visited Islamabad. This agreement was aimed at securing the construction of future infrastructure projects along the China–Pakistan Economic Corridor (CPEC).[26] Infrastructure projects along the CPEC have been under construction throughout Pakistan since 2013 (but the formal agreement was signed in 2015). These infrastructure projects include the building of motorways and railways, as well as the development of ports in Gwadar and Karachi, which will enable these seaports to link up with northern Pakistan. CPEC's importance to Pakistan has been compared to the Marshall Plan launched by the United States in post-war Europe, which helped Europe get back on its feet after the destruction of the Second World War. Pakistani estimates have calculated that the CPEC will create 2.3 million jobs between 2015 and 2030. The projects alone will lead to increased economic growth of approximately 2.5%.[27]

CPEC has led to policy coordination and a large degree of connectivity in the region, as well as a strong economic partnership and regional development (Zou, 2018: 238). Regarding the Dual Circulation Development Paradigm, it is precisely these conditions (which we have pointed out above), which will enable the paradigm to function as an innovation generator along the New Silk Road.

Pakistan has entered into similar agreements with other countries concerning various projects, e.g. agreements with Kazakhstan (which is where Xi Jinping, in 2013, launched the idea of the New Silk Road).

In addition to roads and railways, there are many sub-projects involving cooperation between China and Kazakhstan that include deeper integration, coordination and connectivity in the industrial sector. This includes projects in the steel, cement, chemical and textile industries and metal development, among others (Zou, 2018: 239).

Apart from Kazakhstan, there are other countries that have signed similar agreements that have resulted in the implementation of specific projects. This applies to projects in Indonesia, Armenia, Belarus and Kyrgyzstan, to name a few countries. Following Russia's somewhat cool reception of the New Silk Road, and after the Western sanctions on Russia after it annexed Crimea, Russia has become more positive towards the idea of the New Silk Road. Against this background, an agreement and specific project have been developed along the Sino–Mongolian–Russian economic corridor.[28]

Similar initiatives and agreements have been made with Vietnam, the EU, countries in Central Asia, the Middle East, various countries in Europe, Saudi Arabia, Egypt, Iran, Sri Lanka, Turkey, Hungary, Poland and several countries in Africa (Zou, 2018: 242–276).

We can point out at least two practical implications regarding these agreements and the specific projects.

1 Although there is already relatively great opposition to various projects, e.g. from the United States, the projects are so well anchored and advanced that it will be impossible to stop them, even if the United States desires to do so.

2 The projects will lead to economic gains for the countries involved. As a whole, the projects will strengthen the new Dual Circulation Development Paradigm with regard to foreign trade and foreign relations.

Sub-conclusion for the Dual Circulation Development Paradigm

In this section, we have examined the following question: How will the Dual Circulation Development Paradigm influence the New Silk Road as an innovation generator?

The short answer is that the Dual Circulation Development Paradigm acts as an innovation generator along the New Silk Road when there is a large degree of coordination and connectivity at the same time as there is a large degree of partnership and regional development in the areas in which the OBOR projects are implemented.

Main conclusion for hi-tech competence

In this chapter, we have addressed the following research problem: How does the locomotive-effect influence the New Silk Road as an innovation generator?

The answer to the research problem is that the locomotive-effect is based on two central drivers. These are technological innovations and the Dual Circulation Development Paradigm.

Technological innovations are in turn driven by three social mechanisms.

The first social mechanism is strategic autonomy. This is promoted by focusing on regional innovation clusters.

The second social mechanism is strategic competence in artificial intelligence. This is promoted by a strong educational system that provides university-level education for millions of students in technological studies.

The third social mechanism is the development of intelligent robots. These are being developed in collaborative efforts between university environments and entrepreneurs in China and along the New Silk Road.

The large degree of strategic autonomy and regional innovation clusters together with a large degree of strategic competence and expertise in artificial intelligence facilitate the development of technological innovations and thus function as an innovation generator along the New Silk Road.

The necessary political approach needed to drive forward technological innovations is based on four social mechanisms. These are win–win as a strategic intention, co-creation, collaboration throughout a project's lifetime and development and dissemination of technological innovations along the whole of the New Silk Road.

The Dual Circulation Development Paradigm is driven by four social mechanisms that together constitute the New Silk Road as an innovation generator. These four social mechanisms are coordination, partnership, connectivity and regional development. When there is a large degree of coordination and connectivity, and a large degree of partnership and regional development, then the Dual Circulation Development Paradigm is able to function as an innovation generator along the New Silk Road.

Figure 2.7 illustrates the answer to the research problem in this chapter.

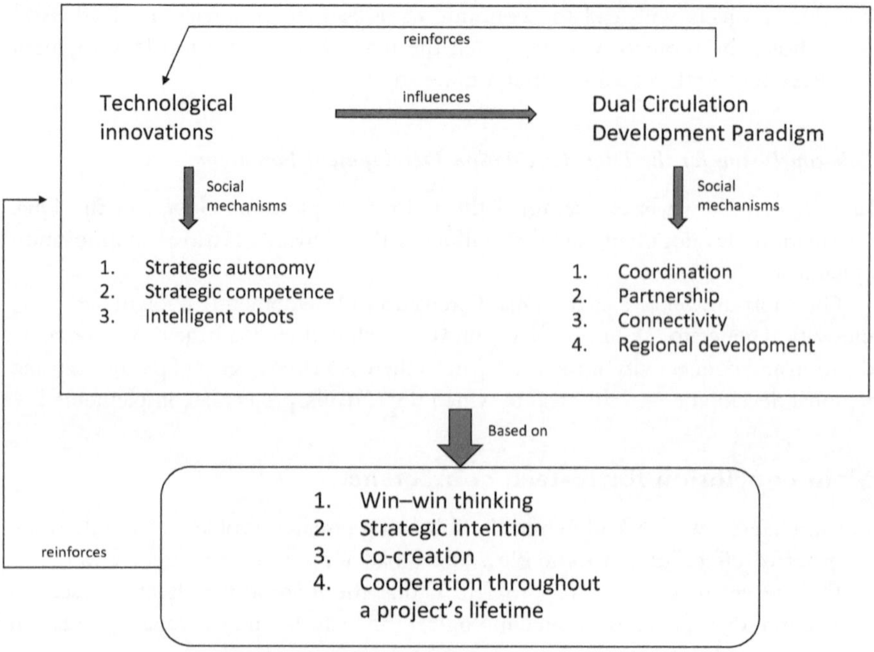

Figure 2.7 How does the locomotive-effect influence the New Silk Road as an innovation generator?

Notes

1 Zou (2018); Zhang (2015); Yang (2015); Yuan (2019); Xing (2019).
2 https://www.chinadaily.com.cn/a/202011/27/WS5fc0bb93a31024ad0ba9806b.html
3 Ibid.
4 RCEP: Regional Comprehensive Economic Partnership (https://en.wikipedia.org/wiki/Regional_Comprehensive_Economic_Partnership).
5 We define the innovation economy here as an economic process in which economic growth is based on innovation.
6 https://en.wikipedia.org/wiki/China–United_States_trade_war.
7 Refer to the "Dual Circulation Development Paradigm" discussed above.
8 https://news.cgtn.com/news/2020-11-19/China-s-future-Dual-circulation-tech-innovation-and-market-reform-VxzT1hQwVy/index.html (Date of reading: 22 Nov. 2020).
9 https://en.wikipedia.org/wiki/Regional_Comprehensive_Economic_Partnership (Date of reading: 18 Dec. 2020).
10 https://en.wikipedia.org/wiki/List_of_universities_in_China.
11 http://www.chinadaily.com.cn/a/202012/07/WS5fcd5dc0a31024ad0ba9a022_1.html.
12 "In 2019, China's research and development spending reached 2.21 trillion yuan ($332 billion), up from 1.42 trillion yuan in 2015. R&D spending on basic research has almost doubled since 2015, reaching 133.6 billion yuan last year.
China has also doubled the value of its technology market since 2015. China now has 169 national-level high-tech development zones and over 225,000 high-tech companies, up from 79,000 in 2015. ---. The number of full-time R&D personnel in the nation grew from 3.76 million in 2015 to 4.8 million last year (http://english.www.gov.cn/statecouncil/ministries/202010/22/content_WS5f90d7a6c6d0f7257693e3b7.html).

13 "Made in China 2025" is perceived as a threat by the United States because this strategy will result in China becoming self-sufficient in high technology by 2025 (Economy, 2018). "Made in China 2025" focuses on the following industries: IT, robotics, aerospace technology, the marine industry, biomedicine, new materials and energy. To achieve this, China is already investing approximately 2.3% of its gross domestic product on R & D.
14 Although tariffs outside the RCEP may rise by 15%, the economy within the RCEP could still expand, according to reports from the RCEP (https://en.wikipedia.org/wiki/Regional_Comprehensive_Economic_Partnership).
15 http://english.www.gov.cn/statecouncil/ministries/202010/22/content_WS5f90d7a6c6d0f7257693e3b7.html.
16 Ibid.
17 https://www.chinadaily.com.cn/a/202012/11/WS5fd2b403a31024ad0ba9b224.html.
18 Ibid.
19 https://en.wikipedia.org/wiki/Trans-Pacific_Partnership.
20 https://www.chinadaily.com.cn/a/202012/08/WS5fcede9ea31024ad0ba9a818.html.
21 https://www.chinadaily.com.cn/a/202012/11/WS5fd2c757a31024ad0ba9b2f5.html.
22 One of the channels provided by China Global Television (https://news.cgtn.com/news/2020-10-25/Guide-to-China-s-dual-circulation-economy-US8jtau4h2/index.html).
23 https://en.wikipedia.org/wiki/Made_in_China_2025.
24 https://en.wikipedia.org/wiki/Made_in_China_2025.
25 https://www.information.dk/debat/2010/01/usas-stoerste-problem-sult.
https://en.wikipedia.org/wiki/World_Food_Programme.
26 https://en.wikipedia.org/wiki/China–Pakistan_Economic_Corridor.
27 https://en.wikipedia.org/wiki/China–Pakistan_Economic_Corridor.
28 https://www.thebricspost.com/china-russia-mongolia-to-create-economic-corridor/.

References

Allison, G. (2018). *Destined for war: Can America and China escape Thucydides trap?* Scribe, London.

Bartels, L. (2008). *Unequal democracy*, Princeton University Press, Princeton, NJ.

Beeson, M. & Li, F. (2016). China's place in regional and global governance: A new world comes into view. *Global Policy*, 7, 4: 491–499.

Berlie, J.A. & Hung, S. (2020). The Greater Bay Area and the role of Hong Kong and Macau SARs in the Belt and Road initiative. In Berlie, J.A. (Ed.), *China's globalization and the Belt and Road initiative*, Palgrave, London. pp. 77–100.

Bougon, F. (2017). *Xi Jinping*, Hurst & Company, London.

Boutrup, C. (2019). *The great tech revolution, how China is shaping our future*, Saxo Business, Copenhagen.

Brown, K. (2018). *China's dream*, Polity, London.

Brown, K. (2019). *The world according to Xi*, I.B. Tauris, London.

Clinton, H. (2011). America's Pacific century. *Foreign Policy*, 189, 11 Oct.

Drache, D., Kingsmith, A.T. & Qi, D. (2019). *One road many dreams: China's bold plan to remake the global economy*, Bloomsbury, New York.

Economy, E.C. (2018). *The third revolution, Xi Jinping and the new Chinese state*, Oxford University Press, Oxford.

Fang, N. & Fu, Y. (2020). *China's Political system*, Springer, London.

Fannin, R.A. (2019). *Tech titans of china*, Nicholas Brealey Publishing, London.

Feng, D.H. & Liang, H.M. (2019). *Belt and Road initiative: Chinese version of Marshall Plan*, World Scientific, London.

Frank, T. (2020). *People without power*, Scribe, London.

Hobsbawn, E. (1989). *The age of empire 1875-1914*, Abacus, New York.

Hobsbawn, E. (1995). *Age of extremes, the short twentieth century 1914–1991*, Abacus, New York.

Huang, Y. (2017). *Cracking the China conundrum: Why conventional economic wisdom is wrong?* Oxford University Press, Oxford.

Jacques, M. (2012). *When China rules the world*, Penguin, London.

Jianglin, Z. (2020). *21st century maritime Silk Road Initiative, aims and objectives, implementation strategies and policy recommendations*, World Scientific, London.

Johannessen, J.-A. (2018). *Innovation leads to economic crises*, Palgrave, London.

Johannessen, J.-A. (2021). *The innovation economy in China*, Routledge, London.

Kotkin, J. (2020). *The coming of neo-feudalism: A warning to the global middle class*, Encounter Books, New York.

Lim, J. & Lim, D. (2020). Financing the OBOR initiative. In Wah, C.Y., Menkhoff, T. & Low, L. (Eds.), *China's Belt and Road initiative: Understanding the dynamics of a global transformation*, World Scientific, London. pp. 97–125.

Linehan, P.M. (2018). *The culture of leadership in contemporary China*, Lexington Books, London.

Macaes, B. (2020). *Belt and Road: A Chinese world order*, C. Hurst, London.

Magnus, G. (2018). *Red flags, Why Xi's China is in jeopardy*, Yale University Press, New Haven, CT.

Mahbubani, K. (2009). *The new Asian hemisphere: The irresistible shift of global power to the east*, Public Affairs, London.

Mahbubani, K. (2010). *Can Asians think?* Marshall Cavendish, Singapore.

Mahbubani, K. (2014). *Great convergence: ASIA, the West, and the logic of one world*, Public Affairs, New York.

Mahbubani, K. (2018). *Has the west lost*, Allen Lane, New York.

Mahbubani, K. (2020). *Has China won?* Public Affairs, London

Mantzopoulos, V. & Shen, R. (2011). *The political economy of China's systemic transformation*, Palgrave, London.

Mearsheimer, J. (2010). The gathering storm: China's challenge to US power in Asia. *Chinese Journal of International Politics*, 3, 4: 381–396.

Reves, R.V. (2018). *Dream Hordes: How the American upper middle class is leaving everyone else in the dust. Why that is a problem and what to do about it*, Brooking Institution Press, Washington, DC.

Ross, R. & Bekkevold, J.I. (2016). *China in the era of Xi Jinping*, Georgetown University Press, Washington, DC.

Thucydides. (2009). *The Peloponnesian war*, Oxford University Press, Oxford.

Vangeli, A. (2017). China's engagement with the sixteen countries of central, east and southeast Europe under the Belt and Road Initiative. *China & World Economy*, 25, 5: 101–124.

Vangeli, A. (2018). Normative foundation of the Belt and Road Initiative. In Wenhua, S., Nuotio, K. & Zhang, K. (Eds.), *Normative readings of the Belt and Road initiative*, Springer, London. pp. 59–83.

Vangeli, A. (2019). A framework for the study of One Belt One Road initiative as a medium of principle diffusion. In Xing, L. (Ed.), *Mapping China's One Belt One Road initiative*, Palgrave Macmillan, London. pp. 57–89.

Wang, D. (2020). *Reigning the future*, New Degree Press, New York.

Wang, Y. (2017a). *Belt and Road initiative: China's responsibilities in its rise*, People's Press, Beijing.

Wang, Y. (2017b). *China connects the world: What behind the Belt and Road initiative*, China Intercontinental Press, Beijing.

Wang, Y. (2017c). *The world is connected: The logic of Belt and Road initiative*, The Commercial Press, Beijing.

Wasif Khan, S. (2019). *Haunted by chaos, China's grand strategy from Mao Zedong to Xi Jinping*, Harvard University Press, Cambridge, MA.

Weih, W. & MacMillan, I.C. (1991). A review of entrepreneurial development in the People's Republic of China. *Journal of Business Venturing*, 6, 6: 375–379.

Xing, L. (2019). Understanding the multiple facets of China's "One Belt One Road" initiative. In Xing, L. (Ed.), *Mapping China's One Belt One Road initiative*, Palgrave Macmillan, London. pp. 29–56.

Yang, J. (2015). China's new diplomacy under the Xi Jinping administration. *China Quarterly of International Strategic Studies*, 1, 1: 1–17.

Yuan, F. (2019). The One Belt One Road initiative and China's multi-layered multilateralism. In Xing, L. (Ed.), *Mapping China's One Belt One Road initiative*, Palgrave, London. pp. 91–116.

Yue, Y. & Fujian, L. (2019). *The Belt and Road initiative: ASEAN countries' perspectives*, World Scientific, London.

Zhang, J. (2015). China's new foreign policy under Xi Jinping: Towards peaceful rise 2.0? *Global Change, Peace & Security*, 27, 1: 5–19.

Zou, L. (2018). *The political economy of China's Belt and Road initiative*, World Scientific, London.

3 Strategic awareness

Understanding and explaining some aspects of the Chinese innovation economy

Key points in this chapter

General

- This chapter aims to provide an understanding of, and explain, the consequences of the Chinese innovation economy.
- This chapter attempts to explain the importance of understanding the significance of stable and efficient institutions at a time when everything else is changing and when the very basis for stability is precisely change and innovation.
- The innovation economy is defined in this book, and this chapter as economic growth is based on innovations in general and technological innovations in particular.
- When discussing the steps upwards in the value chain, we will mainly refer to the shift towards high-tech production based on artificial intelligence.
- We define the butterfly-effect in relation to four social mechanisms. These are as follows:

  Strategic awareness
  Economic expansion and systemic integration
  The Chinese Dream
  The steps upwards in the value chain.

- When the four mechanisms operate as one system, this creates innovation at different levels, also at a high-tech level.
- While the old and classic globalization was based on cost differentials in general and wage differentials in particular, the new globalization is based on competence differentials in general and high-tech competence in particular.
- The struggle to acquire high-tech competence will determine which country will take the lead in the innovation economy and, thus, which country will lead as we move towards the Fourth Industrial Revolution.

DOI: 10.4324/9781003316978-3

Strategic awareness

- The new China represents the new globalization, where it is the differences in relative competence levels between countries, which will be the decisive competitive factor.
- The new globalization is reflected in the development of technological innovations, high-tech production and global competition based on competence, especially within the field of technological innovations.
- Independent of what the future of Chinese technology companies in the West will look like, the New Silk Road will provide a back door out of the stranglehold that the United States and the West have attempted to exert on the development of Chinese technology. It is through the New Silk Road that China's strategic awareness will become evident, and their economy and technology will grow and develop.

Economic expansion and systemic integration

- The new globalization is characterized by high-tech expertise.
- High-tech production in China will reduce its strategic dependence on high-tech products from the United States and other countries.
- Systemic integration will depend on a strong Chinese high-tech university system, interconnected at all levels so as to strengthen the development of technological innovations.
- One aim of the New Silk Road is to increase economic growth in China so that more and more Chinese people can share in economic growth (the Chinese Dream).
- Innovation in general and technological innovations in particular will be able to transform the economy so that it is not affected by constraints on economic growth.
- To overcome the constraints on growth, China is adopting a two-sided strategy. One element in this strategy is a new economic paradigm, the Dual Circulation Development Paradigm. The second element is the concept "Made in China 2025". In addition, China is investing in the development of economic, political and diplomatic relations along the land-based and maritime New Silk Road.
- If Europe chooses to stay out of projects along the New Silk Road, there is much that suggests that this will harm the economic dynamism of many European countries.
- Economic expansion and systemic integration will be ensured by innovation-driven economic growth, based on global cooperation through international rule-based institutions, which will thus influence the development of the New Silk Road as an innovation generator.

The Chinese Dream

- In short, the Chinese Dream is to raise the Chinese to a "middle class" income level by investing in collective solutions.

- Innovation in general and technological innovation in particular are the engine of the innovation economy, as well as the driving force behind the new globalization.
- Before the opening up of China to foreign capital in 1978, there was a greater degree of economic equality in China. However, some cynical voices might say this was a meaningless equality, as there was little to share.
- The trade agreement between China and the EU is intended, from China's viewpoint, to be a driving force for the fulfilment of the Chinese Dream. This agreement covers four areas. The first is common market access. The second is common competition rules. The third is an interest in finding solutions to any disagreements that may arise. The fourth area, which will be crucial for the environment and sustainability, is a common understanding that economic development must be based on the UN's sustainability goals.
- The fulfilment of the Chinese Dream is based on the following key concepts: technological innovations, high-tech education, entrepreneurship, the Dual Circulation Development Paradigm, "Made in China 2025", the free trade agreements (RCEP, EU–China), the New Silk Road, co-creation, shared futures, global cooperation, and multilateralism.
- In 1978, the Gini coefficient, which is a measure of wealth inequality within a nation, was only 0.12 in China, while in 2012 it was 0.46.[1] In other words, there has been an increase of economic inequality in China between 1978 and 2012, which is attributed to urbanization and economic growth.
- The Chinese Dream can be realized through economic growth and institutional innovations. These social mechanisms drive the economic dynamism along the New Silk Road, but they also promote economic inequality, which can turn out to be the Achilles' heel of the Chinese Dream.

The steps upwards in the value chain

- The innovation economy presupposes that production, distribution and consumption are pushed up the value chain.
- Tight political control is only a necessary condition for economic transformation and economic growth. The sufficient condition is a flexible economic philosophy. This flexibility was evident when China opened up to foreign investment in 1978, and also in 2012 with the development of a new economic philosophy.
- The necessary and sufficient social mechanisms have resulted in the development of ten of China's leading innovative regions. These regions are as follows: Guandong, Beijing, Jiangsu, Shanghai, Zhejiang, Shandong, Hubei, Shaanxi, Chongqing and Shenzhen.
- Balanced development, coordination and systemic connections are key concepts with regards to pushing the economy up the value chain.
- Using political control internally, a win–win strategy externally, and a joint coordination of the projects along the New Silk Road, so that systemic connections become a reality at all levels, the steps upwards in the value chain will enable the New Silk Road to function as an innovation generator.

- By balancing traditional infrastructure projects with high-tech projects, there will be a demand for different types of competencies, at different levels, for the different projects, traditional as well as high-tech.

Introduction

The butterfly-effect is the idea that a small change in one place can lead to major changes in other places. The explanation is that systems, both in physical and social environments, are complexly connected with feedback mechanisms that mutually influence each other. The main research problem in this chapter is: How does the butterfly-effect influence the New Silk Road as an innovation generator? In Chapter 1, the butterfly-effect was divided into five elements: strategic awareness, economic expansion and systemic integration, the Chinese Dream and the steps upwards in the value chain.

In order to address the research problem, we have formulated four research questions:

RQ1: How does strategic awareness influence the New Silk Road as an innovation generator?
RQ2: How does economic expansion and systemic integration influence the New Silk Road as an innovation generator?
RQ3: How does the "Chinese Dream" influence the New Silk Road as an innovation generator?
RQ4: How do the steps upwards in the value chain influence the New Silk Road as an innovation generator?

This chapter aims to provide inputs to, and perspectives on, the emergent Chinese innovation economy as we head towards the Fourth Industrial Revolution. The knowledge base we use is systemic thinking. The methods we use are economic historical method, scenario thinking, and conceptual generalization (Adriaenssen & Johannessen, 2016). The point of using these various methods is to offer different perspectives on the problem and the research problem under investigation.

The chapter aims to provide an understanding and explanation of the consequences of the Chinese innovation economy, especially in relation to developments in China's domestic economy and the economies along the New Silk Road. The chapter will also attempt to provide an understanding and explanation of the importance of stable and efficient institutions at a time when everything is changing, and where the very basis for stability is precisely change and innovation (Johannessen, 2018, 2020, 2021). It is precisely the lack of stability of the American institutions that Carney (2020) believes can explain "the mess" the United States finds itself in.

The strength and stability of Chinese institutions is important, because China is a multicultural country, rather than a homogeneous one (Fang & Fu, 2020). China consists of many "realities", says Kristoffersen (2020: 12). Therefore, it is important that its institutions are strong and dynamic at the same time. Butterfly-effects tend to change social systems in ways we cannot predict (Anderson, 2014). Therefore, strong, stable and dynamic institutions are crucial.

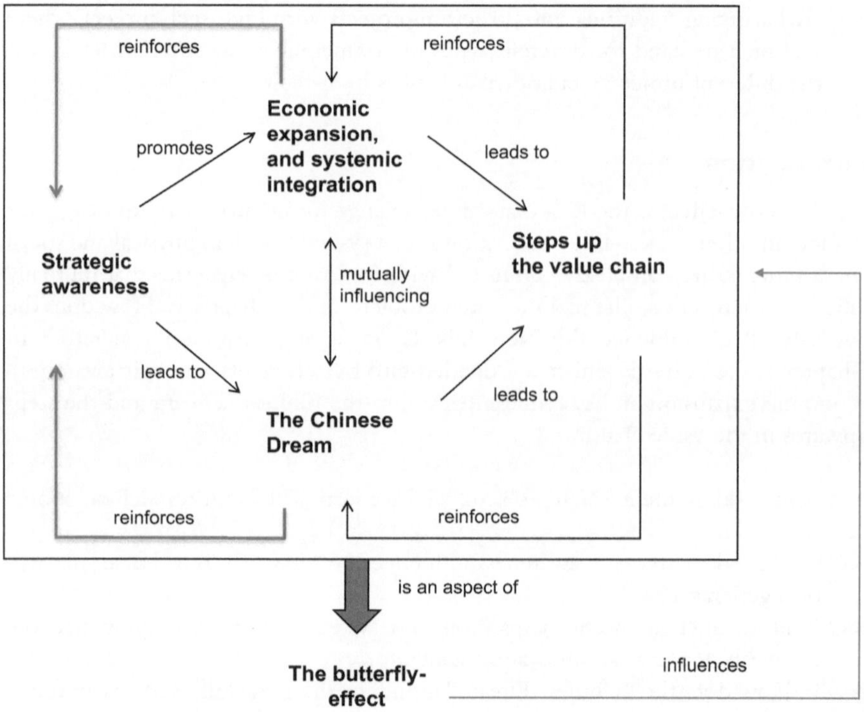

Figure 3.1 The butterfly-effect.

We have illustrated the research problem and research questions in Figure 3.1. Figure 3.1 also shows how the chapter is organized.

Strategic awareness and the New Silk Road

In this section, we will examine the following question: How does strategic awareness influence the New Silk Road as an innovation generator?

The New Silk Road related to the land routes was announced by Xi Jinping, when he visited Kazakhstan in 2013. The maritime New Silk Road was announced by Xi Jinping, the same year, on a visit to Indonesia (Jianglin, 2020a: 3). Both of these meetings and the presentation of the different New Silk Road routes indicate a very strong strategic awareness related to China's economic expansion. In other words, China launched the New Silk Road more or less in its entirety as early as 2013.

Firstly, it is important to note that this occurred only one year after Xi Jinping became president and leader of the Chinese Communist Party.

Secondly, this initiative indicates that China's economy was entering a new phase. The new phase was shown by the fact that China started to transform its economy and economic philosophy from being an economy based on producing cheap consumer goods to becoming an economy producing high-tech products based on technological innovations.

Thirdly, China's increased focus on developing the New Silk Road along both the land and sea routes may be understood against the background of the growing tensions between the USA and China, among others, in the South China Sea, but also in the East China Sea and especially in relation to Taiwan (Clinton, 2011).

Narratives for strategic awareness

Case letter 1: The world's largest free trade agreement

On 15 November 2020, 15 countries signed the RCEP agreement, which is the world's largest free trade agreement.[2] The signatory countries were Vietnam, Thailand, the Philippines, Laos, Cambodia, Myanmar, Singapore, Indonesia and Brunei – as well as Australia, China, Japan, New Zealand and South Korea.[3] This agreement came about after the Trump administration withdrew the United States from the Trans-Pacific Partnership (TTP), another agreement that was under development in the region.[4] China's signing of the RCEP agreement shows a clear strategic awareness on the part of China's Communist leadership in general and Xi Jinping in particular.[5] The member countries of the RCEP agreement have a total population of 2.2 billion, and stand for about 30% of the world's economic activities.[6] If one is to talk about a butterfly-effect and strategic awareness, then it is precisely the RCEP agreement that is important. In addition to the RCEP agreement, China is developing the maritime New Silk Road – also in many of those areas that are part of the RCEP agreement (Jianglin, 2020a: 3–30).

The RCEP agreement will undoubtedly have a huge impact on China. According to the Peterson Institute for International Economics, China's gross domestic product could increase by $85 billion.[7] The United States did **not** participate in the signing of the RCEP. The agreement is seen as a direct threat to US dominance in the region. It was during the Obama administration that the TTP was proposed to counterbalance China's growing dominance in the region. However, when the Trump administration withdrew the United States from the TTP agreement, they provided the strategically aware China with an opportunity, which China seized as an initiator of the RCEP agreement. The agreement will be ratified by the member states in 2022, so it remains to be seen how the new U.S. administration will react to this new situation. China's actions in relation to the RCEP agreement show that a new strategically aware China is emerging, with Xi Jinping at the helm (Wasif Khan, 2019).

Description for strategic awareness

With the signing of the RCEP free trade agreement and the launching and development of the New Silk Road, we can observe a new China emerging; a new china which has left behind the old globalization based on cost differentials in general, and wage differentials in particular, between the West and China. The new China represents the new globalization, where it is the differences in relative competence levels between countries, which will be the decisive competitive factor. The new globalization is characterized by technological innovations, high-tech production and global competition based on competence, especially within the field of technological innovations. It is against this background that one can understand why several Chinese companies have faced opposition in the West, especially Huawei. Sweden, the UK, Australia, France, the United States and several other countries have excluded Huawei from participating in the development of the new 5G network.[8] This has been explained by the fact that Huawei could be forced to hand over data to the Chinese government if the government required it, because of Chinese national security laws. Yet, such laws also exist in most Western countries, including the United States. Independent of what the future of Chinese technology companies in the West will look like, the New Silk Road will provide a back door out of the stranglehold that the United States and the West have attempted to exert on the development of Chinese technology. It is in relation to the New Silk Road that China's strategic awareness will become evident, and that their economy and technology will grow and develop.

Along the entire Silk Road, both the maritime (MSR) and the land-based (LSR), structural changes are taking place, where new infrastructure projects are being launched at an ever increasing rate (Jianglin, 2020a: 4). Relations with the countries in the region are changing, both regarding the RCEP agreement, and the specific projects that are continuously being developed along the New Silk Road. Both the RCEP and the New Silk Road are expressions of a high degree of strategic awareness on the part of the Chinese government. One indication of this strategic awareness is the speed with which China helped finalize the RCEP trade agreement after the Trump administration withdrew the United States from the TTP agreement.

Analysis of strategic awareness

The economic and technological architecture of China has completely changed with the implementation of the New Silk Road. Firstly, this concerns a transition from quantity to quality, i.e. from producing cheap "shoes" for Western markets, to producing high-tech products for domestic and foreign markets. Although restrictions have been imposed on Chinese products by some countries, countries in the world market, including the RCEP countries and the New Silk Road countries, are such strong trading and project partners (collaborating on win–win projects), that it will be useless to attempt to hinder Chinese economic progress in the region; that is, along the New Silk Road, which has routes through large parts of Africa, in European countries, Russia, and a maritime route through the Arctic. Secondly, the strategic awareness related to the economy is linked to focusing on domestic demand, and not only on export-driven economic growth. The closed aspect of China's economic and political system is now changing to a greater degree of openness, especially in relation to the signing of the RCEP agreement and the implementation of the New Silk Road.

"Made in China 2025" is also an indication that both China's economic architecture, but also globalization, has changed. The new aspect of globalization in relation to the Chinese economy is the transition from focusing on cost differentials to focusing on competence differentials, and especially technological competence.

In sum, China has moved away from being dependent on the exports of cheap products to the West, and is now moving towards becoming more strategically independent.

We have illustrated China's new economic architecture in Figure 3.2.

Theoretical points related to strategic awareness

As China manages to become independent of Western technology, by developing its own technology, the strategic dependence on the West will be reduced. This is the main focus of the strategic plan "Made in China 2025".[9] Although there is a great deal of government interest and involvement in the development of technological innovations in China, it is primarily the privately-owned companies that are dependent on Western technology.[10] China's solution to this dilemma can be found along four axes:

Axis 1: First, there is development towards a high-tech innovation economy in conjunction with a well-developed higher education system, especially related to high-tech innovation (Linehan, 2018).

Axis 2: Second, there is development towards a high-tech innovation economy in relation to a greater degree of integration of technological transfers between the private and public sectors, e.g. innovation projects linked to private enterprises, where the technical universities are strategic partners (Mahbubani, 2010, 2014, 2018, 2020).

Axis 3: Third, there will be an increased focus on developing the domestic market and markets along the New Silk Road (Vangeli, 2017, 2018, 2019).

Axis 4: Fourth, the development of local, regional and international innovation centres will enable China to become more strategically independent and less dependent on Western technology. The international innovation centres can be located along the New Silk Road in order to achieve systemic integration (Wang, 2015, 2016, 2017a, 2017b, 2017c).

From	To
Quantity	Quality
Export-driven growth	Innovation-driven growth
Dependent on the West	Strategic independence
Closed economy	Balanced economy

Figure 3.2 Aspects of the new economic architecture in China.

Making innovation development the strategic priority of companies may be said to represent the core of the new globalization. Regarding China, this is crucial for developing products high up on the value creation ladder, because from approx. 1980 to 2012, China has had its main focus on competing on costs, not on quality and innovation. However, initiatives such as "Made in China 2025" and the new "Dual Development Economic Paradigm" are expected to radically change the course of the entire Chinese economy. Of course, it takes time to change an economy as large as the Chinese one. China's economy will be transformed from a focus on low cost advantages, to a focus on quality and innovation benefits, where competence constitutes the fundamental competitive factor.

Practical utility for strategic awareness

The theoretical points mentioned above, as well as the analysis, point to six integrated factors that promote the practical utility of strategic awareness for developing the New Silk Road as an innovation generator.

The six integrated factors are:

1 Education
2 Technology transfers
3 Technologically self-sufficient
4 Increased degree of free trade (e.g. RCEP and the China-EU trade agreement)
5 Domestic demand balanced against exports (the Dual Circulation Development Paradigm)
6 Systemically integrated innovation system: local, regional and global.

These factors can easily be developed into practical policy recommendations, and implemented at various levels, both in China, along the maritime New Silk Road (MSR) and the Land-Based Silk Road (LSR). In order for these factors to function as an integrated holistic system, two pre-conditions are necessary, if not sufficient. The two necessary pre-conditions are increased inter-connectivity and regional cooperation (Jianglin, 2020a: 5). An assumed consequence of the six integrated factors, and the two necessary preconditions, is that a new globalization is developed. The new globalization will be based on competence differentials, not cost differentials, which characterized the old globalization. The driving force of the new globalization is innovation in general, and technological innovations and artificial intelligence in particular.

Figure 3.3 illustrates the six integrated factors in a holistic model, showing how the factors are systemically integrated.

Sub-conclusion related to strategic awareness

We have examined the following question: How does strategic awareness influence the New Silk Road as an innovation generator?

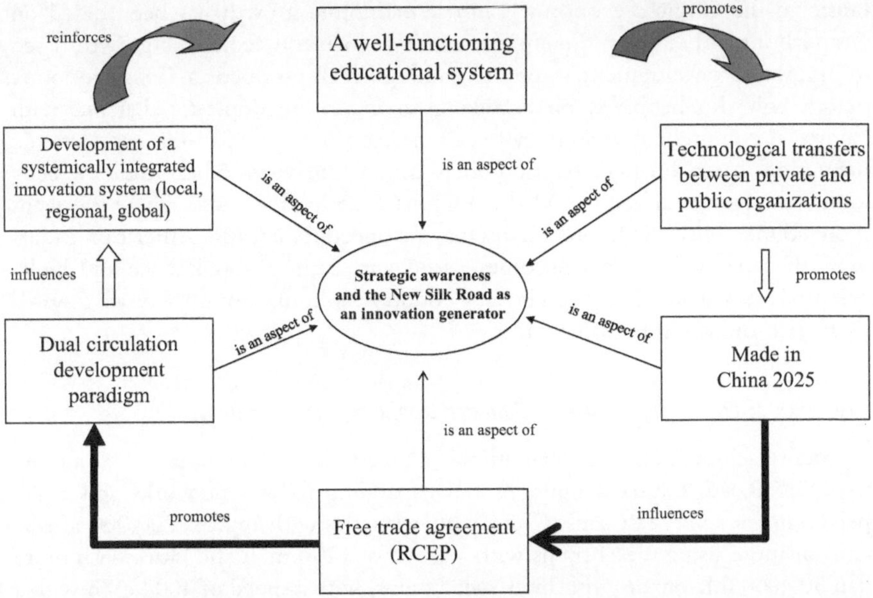

Figure 3.3 Strategic awareness and the New Silk Road as an innovation generator.

The very short answer is that this is done by keeping a focus on the new globalization and facilitating conditions at all levels and in all collaborative structures for the development of technological innovations.

Economic expansion and systemic integration

In this section, we will examine the following question: How does economic expansion and systemic integration influence the New Silk Road as an innovation generator?

Economic expansion and systemic integration are distinct but interconnected and related concepts. Economic growth up to a certain level is possible without systemic integration. Above a certain threshold level, there needs to be systemic integration for further economic growth. National economic growth is often measured in terms of gross domestic product. Systemic integration, on the other hand, is a more diffuse concept, but is linked to the following variables at local, regional and global level: cooperation, co-creation, win–win intention, joint development and dissemination of technological innovations, partnership, connectivity and joint coordination (Zou, 2020). Systemic integration is a strategic intention behind the New Silk Road initiative (Jianglin, 2020a, 2020b).

Narratives for economic expansion and systemic integration

Case letter 1: Dual Circulation Development Paradigm linked to "Made in China 2025"

Possibly the best example of systemic integration can be found in the strategic plan: the Dual Circulation Development Paradigm. This strategic plan aims to transform the Chinese economy. Chinese economic growth has been based on cheap labour and exports; the current aim is to focus on economic growth based on innovation development, expertise and high-tech production. This economic growth will also be based on balancing an increasing domestic demand with exports. A comprehensive strategy for Chinese economic expansion and systemic integration, based on high-tech products comes into view, when this new economic paradigm is linked to "Made in China 2025". This is also where the seeds of the conflict with the United States may be traced to, because American leaders know that the country that becomes a leader in artificial intelligence and high-tech products will also become a leading country economically as we move towards the Fourth Industrial Revolution.[11]

Case letter 2: High-tech competence characterizes the new globalization

In order to achieve systemic integration at a practical level in China, and along the New Silk Road, China is building and expanding railway networks and high-speed trains at a very fast pace. China connects cities with approx. 200,000 inhabitants or more using diesel trains with a speed of 120 km/h and cities with more than 500,000 inhabitants with high-speed trains, with a speed of 400 km/h with a target of 600 km/h.[12] With such infrastructure projects, the foundation for systemic integration will be established on the physical level. An important side effect of these infrastructure projects will be the increase in economic growth due to investments and activities focused on developing the railway networks at the research and development centres, and for increased employment for unskilled, semi-skilled and highly skilled workers (Wang, 2017a, 2017b, 2017c).

This economic expansion will also increase domestic demand and strengthen economic growth (Yuan, 2019). At the same time, an emphasis on high-tech production in China will reduce the strategic dependence on high-tech products from the USA (Zou, 2018). Such a transformation will depend on a strong Chinese high-tech university system that is also interconnected to strengthen the development of technological innovations (Linehan, 2018; Macaes, 2020). This will, as we will discuss in more detail in a later chapter, drive Chinese production up the value chain. In practice, this means less focus on using cheap labour as a competitive advantage and more focus on upgrading skills (Mahbubani, 2018).

Description of economic expansion and systemic integration

Economic growth may be measured in gross national product per capita. The gross national product per capita is the value of a country's output divided by its population; i.e., it says something about the average income of a country's inhabitants (Picket, 2017; Piketty, 2014, 2016). Economic growth in China was high from the 1980s until the financial crisis in 2008 (Ross & Bekkevold, 2016). After the financial crisis, economic growth slowed, but remained at a relatively high level, between 6 and 8%.[13] However, the average income in China is much lower than in the United States and Europe. While the average income in Europe lies between 40,000–60,000 dollars, varying from country to country, the average income in

China is 6,000 dollars, i.e., approx. one-tenth of what Americans and Europeans earn (Jianglin, 2020a: 61). One of the aims of investing in the land-based and maritime New Silk Road is to reduce this gap in incomes between China and the developed world. In other words, it is hoped that the development of the New Silk Road will increase economic growth in China so that more and more Chinese people can share in the economic growth (Vangeli, 2017, 2018, 2019).

When Chinese economists and policy makers look to the West, there is one feature that stands out. When a Western national economy reaches a certain level, it seems as if a special phenomenon occurs. This phenomenon can be described as the limitation on economic growth, which seems to be restricted to around 1–2%, while both unemployment and debt increases, and countries get stuck in an economic quagmire, where they are unable to transform the economy, so that it is able to become dynamic again (Wah & Menkhoff, 2020). China aims to circumvent this problem by its implementation of the Dual Circulation Development Paradigm. In addition, China is focusing on increasing economic expansion and systemic integration with the countries along the land-based and maritime New Silk Road (Wang 2015, 2020; Zou, 2018).

It seems that innovations in general and technological innovations in particular are the key factors that can transform an economy that is locked in a circle of low economic growth. It is this transformation that China is attempting by the measures the country is taking regarding the New Silk Road, the new economic paradigm, and the strategic plan "Made in China 2025".

Analysis of economic expansion and systemic integration

In order to avoid economic stagnation that characterizes the western economies and the Japanese economy, especially after the financial crisis of 2008, the Chinese leaders are attempting to transform the Chinese economy (Vangeli, 2017, 2018). The overriding action to avoid economic stagnation was the launching of the land-based and maritime New Silk Road (Pavlicevic, 2019).

As previously shown, China has implemented various strategic plans to avoid strategic dependence on the United States, and technological dependence on American companies. One of these strategic plans is "Made in China 2025". The purpose of this strategic plan is to enable China to be self-sufficient in technology, so they are not strategically dependent on the United States. The second economic strategy is the implementation of the "Dual Circulation Development Paradigm", which aims to increase domestic demand, which will benefit the Chinese people, while at the same time reducing its strategic dependence on the United States.

Specifically, China and the United States are leading a transition to a new type of globalization, a globalization based on innovation and high-tech expertise. In this new type of globalization, it is no longer cost differences in general, and wage differences in particular, that are the driving force in globalization, but differences in expertise and competencies. To achieve this transformation, China is developing several innovation clusters internally in China, along the New Silk Road and in other countries that are showing interest (Mahbubani, 2018, 2020). In order for

China to cope with this transformation, they have also initiated a large-scale urbanization with mass education at university level (Linehan, 2018). This will enable China to gain more high-tech expertise that will be an input factor in the innovation-driven economic expansion and systemic integration.

Figure 3.4 shows how economic expansion and systemic integration will enable the New Silk Road to function as an innovation generator.

Theoretical points related to economic expansion and systemic integration

If we view the New Silk Road as a new type of "Marshall Plan" for the areas through which the New Silk Road passes, how will this affect China and the countries along the New Silk Road? The original Marshall Plan after World War II involved investments of approx. $100 billion, while the New Silk Road has investment plans for more than $1,000 billion (Yunker, 2014: 47). There is an ongoing debate in Europe regarding whether China's investments in the New Silk Road will result in Europe becoming more dependent on China than without the New Silk Road? If international investment and increased trade make countries more dependent on each other, then it is of course the case that investments along the New Silk Road, which also includes countries in the EU, will make China and these countries more dependent on each other. However, this has always been the case; that is, that international investment and increased trade make countries more dependent on each other – at least since the First Industrial Revolution from around 1750 onwards. The more trade and the more investments that take place between countries, the greater the likelihood of interdependence. However, it is not so much dependence that is harmful, but that one country dominates and uses its strength to prioritize its own interests, often to the detriment of other countries.

The point in this context is that interdependence, without one country using its power to dominate others, may well be the social mechanism that prevents tensions and war, not the opposite. Although many, including Holslag (2019), argue that the New Silk Road will make Europe more dependent on China; this may be true, but it does not have to be bad news for Europe. On the contrary, investments along the New Silk Road may increase the revenues of European companies participating in the projects. Holslag's objections are that China's leaders have committed themselves to strengthening the Communist Party's position in China. However, this is nothing new, but has been the aim of many Chinese leaders, among others, Xi Jinping; moreover, this has constituted the fundamental idea of the Chinese Communist Party since its founding in 1921.[14] Why should this be a threat to Europe that China wants to maintain a political system, which has, at least since 1980, managed to lift hundreds of millions of Chinese out of extreme poverty?

Practical utility for economic expansion and systemic integration

Being dependent on another party is not necessarily something that needs to be negative. However, negative relationships can develop when one party dominates the other. To avoid such dominant structures, and the development of negative

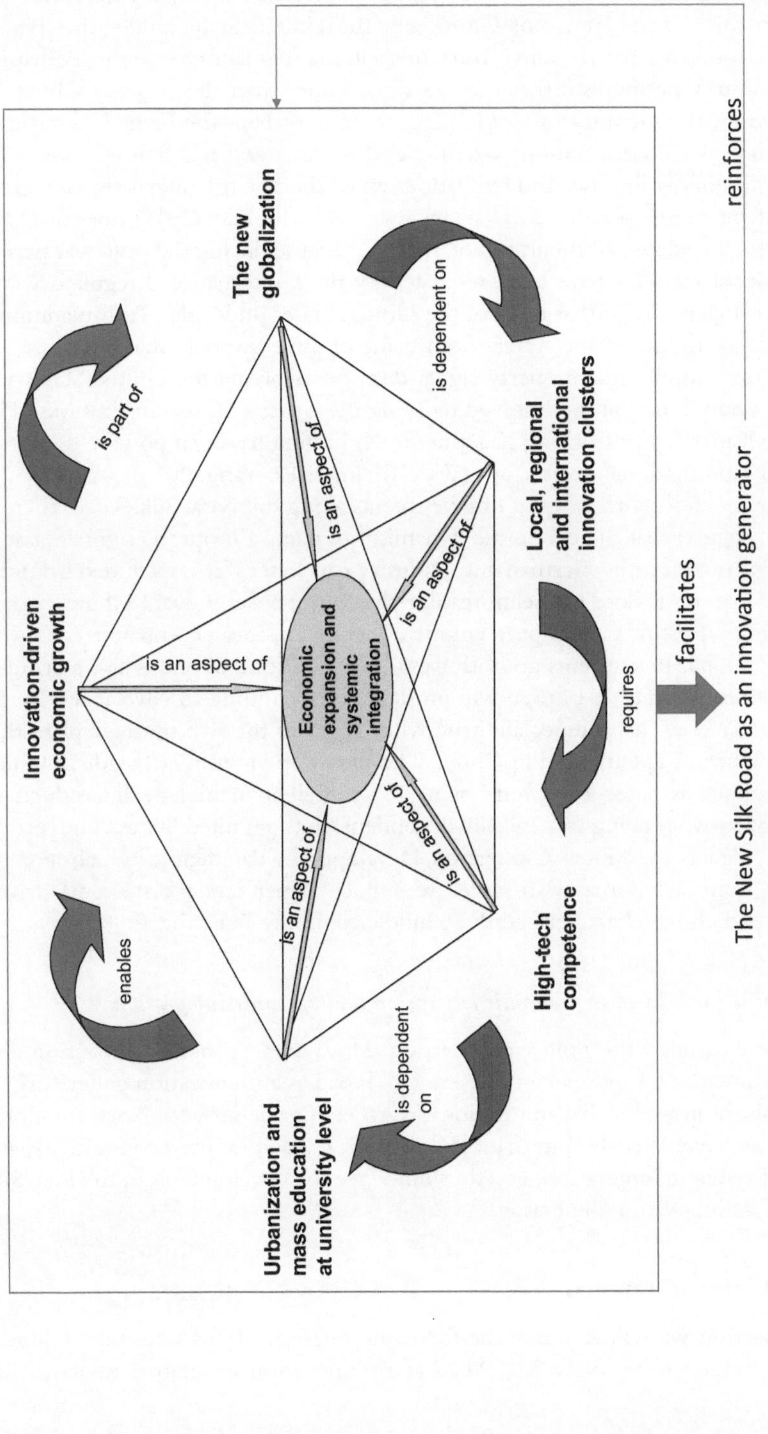

Figure 3.4 Economic expansion and systemic integration as an innovation generator.

relationships, global cooperation institutions have been established, such as the WHO (World Trade Organization), the IMF (International Monetary Fund), and many other global institutions which aim to secure international rule-based systems. In this context, it is not China, but the United States under the Trump administration that has retreated from international regulatory systems. Perhaps it is the rise of Communism that the US fears, rather than the country China. In other words, the memory of Cold War Europe is perhaps the biggest obstacle to developing global cooperation systems based on laws and regulations. Countries that do not follow the laws and regulations established by the international regulatory systems can be penalized in various ways. Why Holslag (2019) does not have faith in such systems is difficult to understand, because during the post-war period international relations have been regulated by these international regulatory systems (Kissinger, 2015); that is, until the United States under the Trump administration chose to ignore and retreat from many of these international systems.

Moreover, intellectual property rights' disputes involving the United States and the EU, and China, can be resolved by using these international institutions. The Chinese leadership from Deng Xiaoping to Xi Jinping has been positive to participating in international institutions (Wasif Khan, 2019; Yang, 2015).

If Europe chooses to stay out of investments along the New Silk Road, there is much to suggest that the economic dynamism of many European countries could suffer. For instance, the German auto industry can suffer if it is excluded from the Chinese market. It does not seem feasible that Europe can prevent Chinese companies from investing in European countries, while European companies can invest freely in China. Investments go both ways, and a critique of one is also a critique of the other. Therefore, Europe will profit from continuing to have access to the Chinese market. This is especially true with regard to the two strategic plans that have now been implemented in China. The first strategic plan is "Made in China 2025", which is based on China being self-sufficient in high-tech products in order not to avoid being strategically dependent on the United States. The second strategic plan is the "Dual Circulation Development Paradigm", which aims to increase domestic demand in order to reduce dependency on export-driven growth (which has characterized the Chinese economy since the 1980s).

Sub-conclusion related to economic expansion and systemic integration

We have examined the following question: How does economic expansion and systemic integration influence the New Silk Road as an innovation generator?

The short answer is that innovation-driven economic growth, based on global cooperation regulated by international institutions, will ensure economic expansion and systemic integration, and thus influence the development of the new Silk Road as an innovation generator.

"The Chinese Dream"

In this section we will examine the following question: How does the "Chinese Dream" influence the New Silk Road as an innovation generator? In short, the

Chinese Dream is to raise everyone in China up to a middle-class income (Brown, 2018). This dream, or idea, was transformed from rhetoric to practical action with the launching of the New Silk Road in 2013. Project agreements have been entered into with many countries along both the land and sea routes (Yue & Fujian, 2019). These collaborative production, trade and research projects aim to not only lift the Chinese people to a higher standard of living, but also the people of the countries participating in the projects (Wang, 2017c). This concerns countries in Africa, Asia, the Middle East and Europe (Xing, 2019).

Narratives for "the Chinese Dream"

Case letter 1: The "Chinese Dream" and the countries in Europe

Negotiations between China and the EU on a mutual investment agreement have been ongoing since 2013.[15] In the autumn of 2020, at the 35th round of negotiations, it was determined by both sides that great progress had been made and that the agreement was just within reach. On Wednesday 30 December, the agreement between the EU and China was signed, with strong support from German Chancellor Angela Merkel.[16] Ironically, it might be said that it was the policies and actions of Donald Trump throughout his presidency that contributed to the agreement between the EU and China finally being ratified.

Case letter 2: Technological innovations and economic growth

China's annual growth rate in 2020 was forecast to be 1.9%, while the other major economies are forecast to have a negative rate of growth, according to the IMF (International Monetary Fund).[17] Chinese economists believe that the growth is the result of the new Chinese "Dual Circulation Development Paradigm". The paradigm aims to increase domestic demand, while balancing this with trading and exports, especially with countries along the New Silk Road.

In order to increase domestic demand, and thus push the Chinese Dream one step forward, large investments have been made in 5G networks in China. In addition to the implementation of 5G, Chinese researchers have begun developing 6G. In 2020 alone, 330,000 new 5G base stations were set up in China. In addition, 144 million new 5G smartphones were sold by 199 different suppliers. It is estimated that China will have 450 million 5G connections by 2025.[18]

Case letter 3: The new technology and the New Silk Road

In addition to 5G, China is focusing on increasing domestic demand by investing in and expanding "smart" cities, as well as implementing major infrastructure projects. Many of these infrastructure projects are also linked to the countries along the New Silk Road. In this way, the New Silk Road will be impacted by the Chinese Dream and establish itself as an innovation generator. Innovation in general and technological innovations in particular constitute the engine of the innovation economy, as well as the driving force of the new globalization. If countries choose not to participate in the projects launched along the New Silk Road, this may be compared to refusing to participate in the First Industrial Revolution. Countries that stay on the side-lines in the development of new technology in general and artificial intelligence in particular risk ending up in the backwaters of the global economy and technological development.

Description of "the Chinese Dream"

The year 2020 was a turning point for the Chinese Dream. The free trade agreement RCEP was signed. An agreement between the EU and China was also finalized on 30 December 2020.[19] The EU–China agreement had been under negotiation since 2013. The agreement marks a transition from China as a producer of cheap consumer products to a country involved in high-tech cooperation and high-tech innovation development. From this perspective, the agreement can be understood as a transition from the old globalization to the new globalization. The old globalization was based on cost differences. The new globalization is based on differences in competence. In this context, China's education system, with millions of students enrolled at university, gives China a competitive advantage (Linehan, 2018).

The agreement between China and the EU marks the end of an era, in which China under Deng Xiaoping opened up the Chinese economy to foreign investment, and the start of a new era, in which China under Xi Jinping has started to invest abroad, such as in the EU countries amongst others. In this way, the agreement with the EU can be understood as an important pillar of the new Dual Circulation Development Paradigm, which aims to balance increased domestic demand, with foreign trade and investment.

The agreement also addresses cooperation on high-tech development, both within the green transformation of the economy and in many branches of industry that are important for European companies. In this context, it is worth noting that the French President Emmanuel Macron and the German Chancellor Angela Merkel were both heavily involved in pushing the agreement over the finish line. The agreement has a clear intention of greater market access for European companies in China, and vice versa. Understood in this way, the agreement can have a multiplier effect for both the Chinese and EU's economic development. This economic development can be understood as a transformation of the economy towards a green economic growth based on the UN's sustainability goals established in 2021. Thus, the EU–China agreement could be an important social mechanism for economic growth in Europe as we move towards the Fourth Industrial Revolution. The agreement also states that the countries undertake to follow rules and laws established by global regulatory institutions, such as the World Trade Organization.

Analysis of "the Chinese Dream"

The EU–China agreement covers four areas. The first is common market access. The second is common competition rules. The third is the committed willingness of the parties to find solutions to disagreements should they arise. The fourth area, which will be crucial for the environment and sustainability, is a common understanding that economic development should be based on the UN's sustainability goals.

In addition to these four areas, the agreement also focuses on four key areas of cooperation between China and the EU, such as: cooperation in relation to future pandemics; cooperation on the development of the green economy; cooperation on development strategies, so that they are in line with the overall intention of the agreement. In this context, the importance of problems may arise related to intellectual property rights. It is possibly in this area that the future challenges lie for both the EU and China. Finally, collaboration ensuring multilateral[20] development in the areas of geo-economics[21] and geo-politics[22] will also be important.

The EU–China agreement is important to China for many reasons. The Chinese Dream of raising the Chinese to a middle class income level will be able to progress one step forward with the signing of the agreement, because the agreement focuses on the Chinese economy, which to a great extent is anchored in European high-tech production. Another unwritten aspect of the agreement, which we may term a "hidden" strategic intention, is the relationship with the United States. The Chinese leader Xi Jinping, the German Chancellor Angela Merkel and the French President Emmanuel Macron all wish to establish economic policies that are strategically independent. Therefore, it can be assumed that it was important for the above three leaders and for the European Commission's President Ursula von der Leyen to conclude the agreement quickly before a new president took over in the White House (2021).[23]

Theoretical points related to "the Chinese Dream"

In his book *Keywords* (1976), Raymond Williams developed a method which may be applied to clarify the underlying strategy of the "Chinese Dream". Williams shows in his book how the meaning of concepts develop and materialize through a historical process, taking on lives of their own so to speak. He does this by conducting an etymological[24] and cultural study, examining the origins of key concepts, and how they develop and often change radically in relation to their original meaning. This method is not unlike the genealogical methods of Foucault and Nietzsche involving tracking the lineages of key concepts and changes in meaning in relation to historical, social and cultural contexts (Osborn, 2020).

In our context, we can apply the method to examine the key concepts most commonly used by leaders, or more specifically used by the current leader of China, Xi Jinping. We will abstract these key concepts into a conceptual model, or a framework, in order to gain an understanding of the relationships between the concepts used. In particular, we will focus on the key concepts used by Xi Jinping in his speeches.[25] Amongst others, he uses the following key concepts: Technological innovations, high-tech education, entrepreneurship, "Dual Circulation Development Paradigm", "Made in China 2025", free trade agreements (RCEP, EU–China), the New Silk Road, co-creation, shared futures, global cooperation, and multilateralism.

We have abstracted these concepts and illustrated them in the model in Figure 3.5.

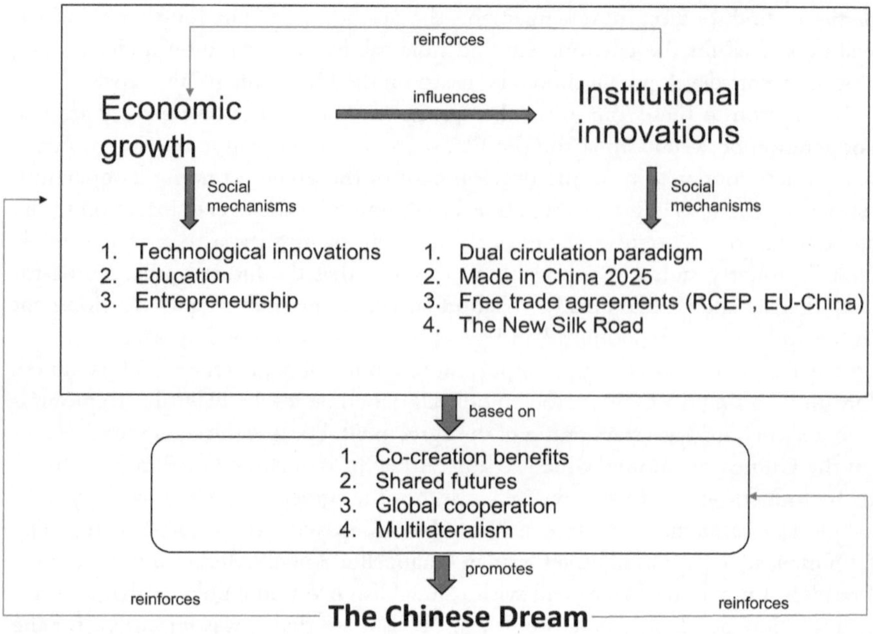

Figure 3.5 The necessary prerequisites to realize the "Chinese Dream" and to enable the New Silk Road to become an innovation generator.

Practical utility related to "the Chinese Dream"

To realize the Chinese Dream, as expressed by Xi Jinping, certain preconditions have to be fulfilled, which the Chinese leaders agree on. One important pre-condition may be linked to Chinese history. The "century of humiliation" is a term used in China today to describe the one hundred years of national humiliation stretching from the mid-nineteenth century to the mid-20th century, when China was repeatedly invaded by imperialist and aggressive foreign powers. In this context, one can mention the Opium Wars (1839–1842 and 1856–1860) and the Second Sino-Japanese War (1937 to 1945),[26] amongst others. In other words, with these humiliating events of the past still in the collective historical memory of the Chinese people, the Chinese leaders believe that it is vital to ensure that China is never again overrun by foreign military forces. Consequently, an important prerequisite for realising the Chinese Dream is to build a strong economy and a strong military system (Brown, 2018: 132). It is important to understand this historical context, in order to understand the thoughts and actions of the Chinese leaders today (Johannessen, 2021).

Parts of China have already reached a relatively high income level. However, it is in urban areas that we find the Chinese Dream if not fully realized, then not far from it, but to a lesser extent in the rural areas. In other words, the increase in prosperity has occurred at the same time as a strong forced urbanization of China. In 1978, before Deng Xiaoping opened the country to foreign investment, only 17.9% of the population lived in urban areas. By 2020, this had rapidly increased to 60.6%.[27] Urbanization has gone hand in hand with economic growth in China, and thus also the increase in prosperity for the majority. It might be said that the Chinese Dream is linked to an extensive urbanization. On the other hand, urbanization, economic growth and the use of market forces to bring about this growth have also led to a sharp increase in economic inequality between people in China. In 2010, the OECD estimated that there were ten megacities in China. A megacity is a city of more than ten million people.[28] In these megacities we also find many of China's dollar billionaires,[29] but also many of China's poor.

Before the opening up of China to foreign capital in 1978, there was a high degree of economic equality in China. However, some cynical voices might say this was a meaningless equality, as there was little to share (Brown, 2018: 132–133). Although the Chinese economy grew from 1978 to 2020, so did economic inequality. In 1978, the Gini coefficient, which is a measure of wealth inequality within a nation, was only 0.12 in China, while in 2012 it was 0.46.[30] In other words, there has been an increase of economic inequality in China between 1978 and 2012, which is attributed to urbanization and economic growth. We emphasize this here, because it constitutes one of the largest challenges that the Communist Party faces in the future (Jacques, 2012; Wasif Khan, 2019).

Sub-conclusion for "the Chinese Dream"

We have examined the following question: How does the Chinese Dream influence the New Silk Road as an innovation generator?

The short answer is that the Chinese Dream can be realized through economic growth and institutional innovations. These social mechanisms drive the economic dynamism along the New Silk Road, but they also promote economic inequality, which can turn out to be the Achilles' Heel of the Chinese Dream.

The steps upwards in the value chain

In this section we will examine the following question: How do the steps upwards in the value chain influence the New Silk Road as an innovation generator?

The steps upwards in the value chain are linked directly to investments in technology and infrastructure, together with a continual focus on education in high technology fields. An example of value creation shifting upwards in the value chain can be found in the fisheries sector. One can catch a fish and sell it. Or a fish can be caught, filleted and then sold as a fillet directly to the customer. Or through the application of sophisticated biotechnology, a fish that undergoes yet more processing can become a source of fat and protein for health supplements. In this way, one can move upwards along the value chain in the fisheries industry. All sectors can move upwards along the value chain. Hi-tech value creation is dependent, however, on hi-tech competence at all levels and in all aspects of a product's potential for development.

Narratives for the steps upwards in the value chain

Case letter 1: Innovation and value creation

If a country aims to invest in high-tech value creation, then one pre-condition is to establish an education system that offers education at a high technological level. When China opened up to foreign investment in 1978, the economic philosophy was based on export-driven growth.

However, China changed its economic philosophy in 2012, when Xi Jinping took over as leader of China. Xi Jinping's economic philosophy was based on innovation along several parameters, and value creation aimed at pushing China up the value chain (Drache et al., 2019). Figure 3.5 above shows how the institutional innovations created the necessary preconditions for economic growth higher up the value chain (Fang & Fu, 2020).

This is not the first time China has tried to move up the value chain. Mao Zedong attempted to move the country forward economically and socially by launching the Great Leap Forward (1958–1962).[31] However, the Great Leap Forward was a disaster for both China and the Chinese workers. The Great Leap Forward only ended up stumbling backwards, leading to economic decline, pushing the country many years back. In 1959, Chinese steel production had reached an acceptable level, as part of the Great Leap Forward state plan, but much of the steel that was produced was largely useless, as it was low quality pig iron. It was against this background that Deng Xiaoping allowed the Chinese market to play a crucial role in bringing the Chinese economy to a qualitatively better level than had been achieved by one-sided state planning (Huang, 2017). In other words, the Chinese leadership in attempting to learn from its mistakes of the past adopted a more pragmatic approach to planning. This is also evident under the current leadership of Xi Jinping who has adopted a new Chinese economic philosophy, based on the new Dual Circulation Development Paradigm and the New Silk Road initiative (2013). In order to achieve the aims of the initiative, it will be crucial that the countries along the New Silk Road can contribute to creating an economic multiplier effect, which can push all the countries up the value chain, increasing employment, incomes and security (Lim & Lim, 2020).

Current Chinese economic policies aim at combining central state planning and local initiatives, with the goal of increasing value creation in order to achieve the Chinese Dream. The centralized planning policies of Mao Zedong's Great Leap Forward, and the Soviet central planning, led to a lack of flexibility, increasing complexity, bureaucracy, and a waste of resources. Attempting to learn from the mistakes of the past regarding centralized planning, current planning policies are based on a balance between central management and local initiatives with the aim of moving up the value chain (Linggui, 2020).

Description of the steps upwards in the value chain

The innovation economy presupposes that production, distribution and consumption are pushed up the value chain. Therefore, the innovation economy is increasingly focused on what drives innovations in general and technological innovations in particular. There is much to suggest that the key drivers are coordination and connectivity (Angang, 2014; Batzhan et al., 2020). In addition, technological development is linked to the development of automation. In other words, future technological innovations may increase unemployment (Billington, 2020). To avoid such possible future problems regarding unemployment, China has linked innovation development to a focus on green industrial development, i.e., a transition to industrial development that is not based on fossil fuels, but on renewable energy sources (Berlie & Hung, 2020). Such a development will be labour intensive, requiring low-skilled, semi-skilled and skilled labour that can be employed in infrastructure projects, such as the construction and application of wind turbines, the development of hydropower, and road construction in the areas where the wind turbines are located, etc. (Billington, 2020). If the focus is only on the development of technological innovations, a situation may arise where the demand for labour will be mainly directed towards people with high-tech competence. However, in a balanced development, where the focus is on the simultaneous development of high-tech projects and more traditional projects, there will be a need for a balanced development where all categories of labour will be in demand. It is this balanced demand for all types of competencies and categories of labour that will strengthen the New Silk Road as an innovation generator.

A central coordination of high-tech projects driven by technological innovations presupposes connections at all levels, i.e. systemic connections to balance the development and application of both high-tech competencies and traditional competencies. If such coordination is not achieved, an imbalance in the demand for labour may quickly evolve, resulting in unemployment for certain sections of the population and creating social tensions. We have witnessed such social tensions in the United States, caused by unemployment and social exclusion of some sections of the population (Frank, 2020, Reves, 2018). An imbalance in the demand for labour may also result in reduced demand for high-tech competencies, or the traditional competencies associated with infrastructure projects. It seems reasonable to assume that in an economy that is purely market-oriented, technological development will lead to a greater demand for high-tech competencies, which would lead to unemployment within the category of workers with traditional competencies associated with infrastructure projects (Sandel, 2020). Balanced development, coordination and systemic connections are therefore central concepts when pushing the economy up the value chain (Feng & Liang, 2019; Holslag, 2019).

We have illustrated the above description in Figure 3.6.

Analysis for the steps upwards in the value chain

Coordination, systemic connections, green projects and competence diversity have proven to be important concepts for moving companies and countries upwards in the value chain.[32] China's export-driven economic growth from 1978 onwards laid the economic and competence-based foundation for moving the country upwards in the value chain.[33] The final confirmation of this movement upwards in the value chain

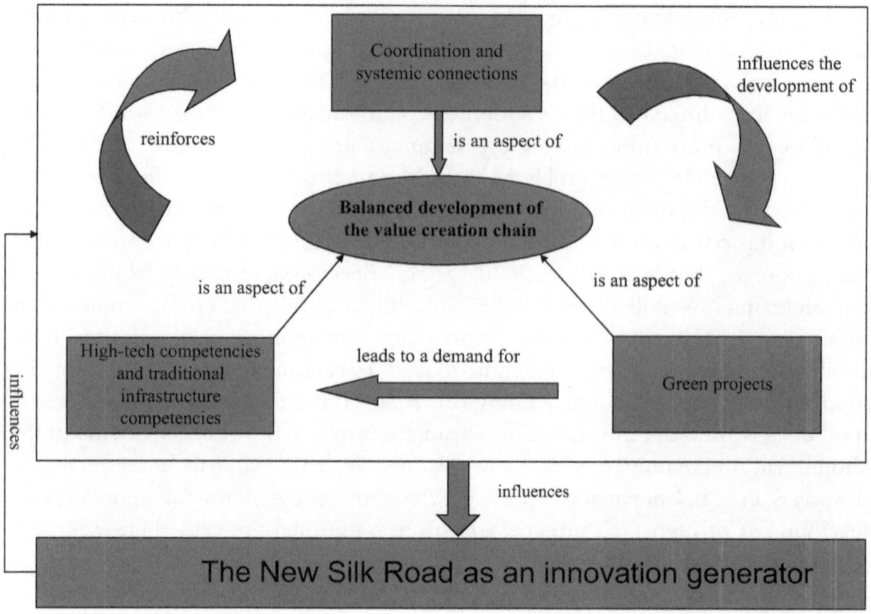

Figure 3.6 Balanced development of the value chain.

emerged around 2012, with a new economic philosophy based on a greater focus on innovation-driven growth, which we have illustrated in Figure 3.5. The most important social mechanisms for moving China upwards in the value chain are breakthroughs in the development of artificial intelligence and various applications of artificial intelligence, as well as innovative entrepreneurship. The practical purpose is to turn this technology into value creation and revenue for Chinese companies, and to increase the incomes of the Chinese people (Wang, 2016, 2017a, 2017b, 2017c).

Coordinated development, as well as systemic integration, has contributed to the creation and emergence of ten of China's foremost innovative regions: Guangdong, Beijing, Jiangsu, Shanghai, Zhejiang, Shandong, Hubei, Shaanxi, Chongqing and Shenzhen.[34] The millions of students enrolled at technological universities in China (Linehan, 2018), the Dual Circulation Development Paradigm, the many free trade and investment agreements, among others, the RCEP and the EU–China agreement, respectively, as well as the investments in the New Silk Road, bear witness to a China that is able to deliver value creation at a very high level in the value chain. In this context, the New Silk Road will be able to function as an innovation generator, not least because the projects along the Silk Road will demand a diversity of labour. In this way, there will be no need to fear that technological unemployment will become a problem. Technological unemployment and social tensions, on the other hand, emerge as a result of a lack of a balanced and coordinated development that has too great a focus on innovation-driven economic growth, with little focus on traditional infrastructure projects. It is this development we have witnessed in the United States (Frank, 2020; Sandel, 2020).

Theoretical points related to the steps upwards in the value chain

The importance of the Silk Road to China cannot be overstated. It provides an opening for China so the country can escape the economic and diplomatic pressures exerted by the United States. The seeds of these pressures were already evident in Hillary Clinton's article, "America's Pacific century", published in the *Foreign Policy* magazine in 2011. In this context, it should be remembered that in 2011 Joe Biden was vice president in the Obama administration. The point of highlighting this here is that it cannot be expected that the present US administration under Joe Biden will adopt a radically new policy towards China. One of the underlying themes of the Clinton article, and which was reinforced during the Trump administration, was that China represented a new danger to the so-called "free world".

The New Silk Road is also part of the Dual Circulation Development Paradigm, in relation to developing technological innovations based on domestic technological expertise, while exports, imports and investments along the New Silk Road will be projects that both China and the countries involved in the projects will benefit from economically (Xing, 2019). The New Silk Road promotes flexibility on many levels for China. Diplomatically, it opens up the possibility of relationships that may otherwise have been problematic. For instance, the new relationships established with the EU countries, especially Germany and France, might have been more problematic without the proposed investment deal between China and the EU (December 2020). Economically, the Silk Road enables a flexibility that may have been difficult to achieve in other ways. It is, as many critics have pointed out, the relationship with the United States, regardless of which political administration is in power that has proved to be the most difficult issue regarding Chinese technological development; in addition, there is also the possibility that the United States and its allies may attempt to involve China in a new "Cold War" situation.[35]

Without China's export-driven economic growth, it is difficult to imagine how China would be able to transform its expertise and value creation towards innovation-driven economic growth. On the other hand, if China continued to focus only on export-driven economic growth, which was formidable for many decades, it would not be able to compete in a global economy as we head towards the Fourth Industrial Revolution (Schwab, 2016).

Without a new technological and economic plan established around 2012, China might of risked remaining the "world's factory", focusing on cheap labour, and continuing to provide the rich in the West with large profits. By shifting the economic and technological emphasis to value creation at the top of the value chain, China now has the opportunity to become a leader in the development of artificial intelligence and the innovation economy at the beginning of the Fourth Industrial Revolution.

Practical utility related to the steps upwards in the value chain

Beyond doubt, the thirty years of export-driven economic growth has enabled China to become an economic superpower (Mahbubani, 2018; Mantzopoulos &

Shen, 2011: 1). China has managed to achieve this by focusing on production and distribution, which is at the very bottom of the value chain. Changing its economic philosophy, which China has focused on since 2012, is therefore not without problems.

As China gained an abundance of foreign capital, the country began to invest in infrastructure projects domestically, and in other countries, e.g. African countries and Australia (Beeson & Li, 2016; Hamilton, 2018). The New Silk Road, "Made in China 2025", the Dual Circulation Development Paradigm, and China's participation in free trade agreements and investment agreements, such as the RCEP and the EU–China agreement, respectively, came at a much later stage.

There is much to suggest that tight political control of China's economic development has been the precondition for the country's economic success (Mahbubani, 2020; Mantzopoulos & Shen, 2011: 111–141). On the other hand, there was also very tight political control under Mao Zedong's rule, but economic progress was limited. Thus, tight political control is only a necessary precondition for economic transformation and economic growth. The sufficient precondition, which we have described here, is a new economic philosophy. This new economic philosophy is based on flexibility and high-tech expertise. These two sufficient preconditions have been fulfilled in the adoption of the Dual Circulation Development Paradigm, "Made in China 2025", and by the projects along the New Silk Road, as well as the various types of trade and investment agreements that have been established. This flexibility was evident when Deng Xiaoping opened up China to foreign investment in 1978 and thus stimulated export-driven growth, and again in 2012, when Xi Jinping adopted a new economic philosophy, as mentioned above (Mahbubani, 2010, 2014, 2018, 2020).

Sub-conclusion for the steps upwards in the value chain

We have examined the following question: How do the steps upwards in the value chain influence the New Silk Road as an innovation generator?

The short answer is by using political control internally, a win–win strategy externally, and a joint coordination of the projects along the New Silk Road, so that systemic connections become a reality at all levels. In this way, different types of competencies will be in demand, at different levels, for different projects, traditional as well as high-tech.

Main conclusion for strategic awareness: the butterfly effect

In this chapter, we have addressed the following research question: How does the butterfly-effect influence the New Silk Road as an innovation generator? The butterfly-effect has been defined in relation to four social mechanisms:

1 Strategic awareness
2 Economic expansion and systemic integration
3 The Chinese Dream
4 The steps upwards in the value chain

In this chapter, we have shown that the four mechanisms that constitute the butterfly-effect are all individually and collectively of such a nature that a small change in one of them may have major consequences for the other mechanisms separately and for the economies where the consequences become apparent.

When the four mechanisms operate as one system, we have shown that this creates innovations at different levels, including the high-tech level. It seems reasonable to assume that without export-driven economic growth, China would not have been able to change its economic strategy and political philosophy around 2012, from low-end production to value-driven economic growth based on high-tech expertise. While the old globalization was based on differences in cost structures in general, and wage costs in particular, the new globalization is based on differences in competencies in general, and high-tech competence in particular. It is the struggle to take the lead in developing high-tech expertise that seems to be the most decisive factor regarding which country will take the lead in the innovation economy, as we head towards the Fourth Industrial Revolution. The innovation economy is defined in this book and this chapter as economic growth based on innovations in general and technological innovations in particular. The Fourth Industrial Revolution refers to new technologies based on artificial intelligence, intelligent robots and intelligent informats. Intelligent informats refers to robots based on artificial intelligence, which are connected to other intelligent robots around the world, primarily within a field of expertise, e.g. medical robots in general and medical robots that specialize in a particular branch of medicine. When we have referred to "steps upwards in the value chain" in this chapter, this mainly concerns steps up to high-tech production based on artificial intelligence. As the global economy evolves in the future, this value chain may of course be characterized by other factors than those we mention here.

In the innovation economy it will not be an option to preserve the status quo. The innovation economy will be characterized by the development and application of many innovations that will impact economic and social systems. In this context, it can be proposed that small innovations will create small economic crises, while large innovations will create large economic crises. In such a situation, political control is crucial in order to manage economic transformations. Without political control, economies will experience one shock after another, most probably resulting in the misuse of resources. It is against this background that it may be assumed that China, with its political system and its economic philosophy, will be able to withstand the transformations that result from the continuous processes in the innovation economy.

Notes

1 https://en.wikipedia.org/wiki/Income_inequality_in_China.
2 RCEP stands for Regional Comprehensive Economic Partnership.
3 https://en.wikipedia.org/wiki/Regional_Comprehensive_Economic_Partnership.
4 https://en.wikipedia.org/wiki/Trans-Pacific_Partnership.
5 Bougon (2017); Economy (2018); Ross & Bekkevold (2016); Wasif Khan (2019); Yang (2015).
6 https://en.wikipedia.org/wiki/Regional_Comprehensive_Economic_Partnership.

7 https://www.piie.com/system/files/documents/wp20-9.pdf.
8 https://www.bloomberg.com/news/articles/2020-10-20/sweden-bans-huawei-zte-from-new-5g-infrastructure.
9 https://global.chinadaily.com.cn/a/202012/25/WS5fe52c7ba31024ad0ba9e68a.html.
10 Ibid.
11 Hamilton (2018); Mearsheimer (2010); Schwab (2016, 2018); Wang (2017a, 2017b, 2017c); Yuan (2019); Yue & Fujian (2019).
12 https://www.chinadaily.com.cn/a/202012/11/WS5fd2c757a31024ad0ba9b2f5.html.
13 Source: International Monetary Fund (IMF) in Jianglin (2020a: 60).
14 Bougon (2017); Kuhn (2011); Mahbubani (2014); Ross & Bekkevold (2016); Wasif Khan (2019); Yang (2015); Zhang (2015).
15 https://global.chinadaily.com.cn/a/202012/30/WS5febb7c5a31024ad0ba9f690.html.
16 https://www.politico.eu/article/eu-china-investment-deal-angela-merkel-pushes-finish-line-despite-criticism/ (Date of reading: 30.12. 2020).
17 https://www.chinadaily.com.cn/a/202012/30/WS5febec51a31024ad0ba9f8de.html.
18 https://global.chinadaily.com.cn/a/202012/25/WS5fe53cb4a31024ad0ba9e6fe.html.
19 https://global.chinadaily.com.cn/a/202012/31/WS5fed04b5a31024ad0ba9faa4.html.
20 https://en.wikipedia.org/wiki/Multilateralism.
21 https://en.wikipedia.org/wiki/Geoeconomics.
22 https://en.wikipedia.org/wiki/Geopolitics.
23 https://en.wikipedia.org/wiki/China–European_Union_relations.
24 https://en.wikipedia.org/wiki/Etymology.
25 We have referred to the following books in order to establish what are the key concepts used by Xi Jinping: Angang (2014); Batzhan et al. (2020); Beeson & Li (2016); Berlie & Hung (2020); Bougon (2017); Brown (2018, 2019); Drache et al. (2019); Economy (2018); Feng & Liang (2019); Jacques (2012); Jianglin (2020a, 2020b); Lim & Lim (2020); Linggui (2020); Linehan (2018); Macaes (2020); Magnus (2018); Mahbubani (2009, 2010, 2014, 2018, 2020); Pavlicevic (2019); Ross & Bekkevold (2016); Vangeli (2017, 2018, 2019); Wah & Menkhoff (2020); Wang (2015, 2016, 2017a, 2017b, 2017c); Wasif Khan (2019); Xing (2019); Yang (2015); Yue & Fujian (2019); Yunker (2014); Zhang (2015); Zou (2018).
26 https://en.wikipedia.org/wiki/Second_Sino-Japanese_War.
27 https://en.wikipedia.org/wiki/Urbanization_in_China.
28 https://en.wikipedia.org/wiki/Megacity.
29 https://en.wikipedia.org/wiki/Income_inequality_in_China.
30 https://en.wikipedia.org/wiki/Income_inequality_in_China.
31 https://en.wikipedia.org/wiki/Mao_Zedong.
32 Boutrup (2019); Brown (2018, 2019); Economy (2018); Linehan (2018); Macaes (2020); Magnus (2018); Mahbubani (2009, 2010, 2014, 2018, 2020; Mantzopoulos & Shen (2011).
33 Boutrup (2019); Brown (2018, 2019); Economy (2018); Linehan (2018); Macaes (2020); Magnus (2018); Mahbubani (2009, 2010, 2014, 2018, 2020); Mantzopoulos & Shen (2011).
34 http://www.chinadaily.com.cn/a/202101/04/WS5ff247c2a31024ad0baa0212_1.html.
35 Allison (2018); Beeson & Li (2016); Brown (2019); Feng & Liang (2019); French (2015); Holslag (2019); Jacques (2012).

References

Adriaenssen, D. & Johannessen, J.-A. (2016). Conceptual generalizations, Methodological reflections in social science: A systemic viewpoint. *Kybernetes*, 44, 4: 588–605.

Allison, G. (2018). *Destined for war: Can America and China escape Thucydides trap?* Scribe, London.

Anderson, E.G.G. (2014). *The innovation butterfly*, Springer, London.

Angang, H. (2014). Silk Road economic belt: Strategic considerations, positioning and implementation routes. *Journal of Xinjiang Normal University*, 2: 1–10.

Batzhan, A., Alpysbayeva, S. & Kapsalyamova, Z. (2020). The Belt and Road initiative: Case of Kazakhstan. In Wah, C.Y., Menkhoff, T. & Low, L. (Eds.), *China's Belt and Road initiative: Understanding the dynamics of a global transformation*, World Scientific, London. pp. 71–97.

Beeson, M. & Li, F. (2016). China's place in regional and global governance: A new world comes into view. *Global Policy*, 7, 4: 491–499.

Berlie, J.A. & Hung, S. (2020). The Greater Bay Area and the role of Hong Kong and Macau SARs in the Belt and Road initiative. In Berlie, J.A. (Ed.), *China's globalization and the Belt and Road initiative*, Palgrave, London. pp. 77–100.

Billington, D.P. (2020). *From insight to innovation*, MIT Press, Boston, MA.

Bougon, F. (2017). *Xi Jinping*, Hurst & Company, London.

Boutrup, C. (2019). *The great tech revolution, how China is shaping our future*, Saxo Business, Copenhagen.

Brown, K. (2018). *China's dream*, Polity, London.

Brown, K. (2019). *The world according to Xi*, I.B. Tauris, London.

Carney, T.P. (2020). *Alienated America: Why some places thrive while others collapse*, Harper, New York.

Clinton, H. (2011). America's Pacific century. *Foreign Policy*, 189, 11 Oct.

Drache, D.; Kingsmith, A.T. & Qi, D. (2019). *One road many dreams: China's bold plan to remake the global economy*, Bloomsbury, New York.

Economy, E.C. (2018). *The third revolution, Xi Jinping and the new Chinese state*, Oxford University Press, Oxford.

Fang, N. & Fu, Y. (2020). *China's political system*, Springer, London.

Feng, D.H. & Liang, H.M. (2019). *Belt and Road initiative: Chinese version of Marshall Plan*, World Scientific, London.

Frank, T. (2020). *People without power*, Scribe, London.

French, H.W. (2015). *China's second continent*, Random House, London.

Hamilton, C. (2018). *Silent invasion: China's influence in Australia*, Hardie Grant Books, New York.

Holslag, J. (2019). *The Silk Road trap*, Polity, London.

Huang, Y. (2017). *Cracking the China conundrum: Why conventional economic wisdom is wrong?* Oxford University Press, Oxford.

Jacques, M. (2012). *When China rules the world*, Penguin, London.

Jianglin, Z. (2020a). Introduction. In Jianglin, Z. (Ed.), *21st century maritime Silk Road initiative, aims and objectives, implementation strategies and policy recommendations*, World Scientific, London. pp. 3–30.

Jianglin, Z. (2020b). Macroeconomic basis for the 21st century maritime Silk Road initiative. In Jianglin, Z. (Ed.), *21st century maritime Silk Road initiative, aims and objectives, implementation strategies and policy recommendations*, World Scientific, London. pp. 59–100.

Johannessen, J.-A. (2018). *Innovation leads to economic crises*, Palgrave, London.

Johannessen, J.-A. (2020). *The workplace of the future*, Routledge, London.

Johannessen, J.-A. (2021). *The innovation economy in China*, Routledge, London.

Kissinger, H. (2015). *World order*, Penguin, New York.

Kristoffersen, H. (2020). *Det nye Kina: Kinesisk handel, kultur og politikk*, Universitetsforlaget, Oslo.

Kuhn, R.L. (2011). *How China's leaders think*, Wiley, New York.

Lim, J. & Lim, D. (2020). Financing the OBOR initiative. In Wah, C.Y., Menkhoff, T. & Low, L. (Eds.), *China's Belt and Road initiative: Understanding the dynamics of a global transformation*, World Scientific, London. pp. 97–125.

Linehan, P.M. (2018). *The culture of leadership in contemporary China*, Lexington Books, London.

Linggui, W. (2020). Foreword. In Jianglin, Z. (Ed.), *21st century maritime Silk Road initiative, aims and objectives, implementation strategies and policy recommendations*, World Scientific, London. pp. v–xiii.

Macaes, B. (2020). *Belt and Road: A Chinese world order*, C. Hurst &, London.

Magnus, G. (2018). *Red flags, why Xi's China is in jeopardy*, Yale University Press, New Haven, CT.

Mahbubani, K. (2009). *The new Asian hemisphere: The irresistible shift of global power to the east*, Public Affairs, London.

Mahbubani, K. (2010). *Can Asians think?* Marshall Cavendish, Singapore.

Mahbubani, K. (2014). *Great convergence: ASIA, the West, and the logic of one world*, Public Affairs, New York.

Mahbubani, K. (2018). *Has the West lost*, Allen Lane, New York.

Mahbubani, K. (2020). *Has China won?* Public Affairs, London

Mantzopoulos, V. & Shen, R. (2011). *The Political economy of China's systemic transformation*, Palgrave, London.

Mearsheimer, J. (2010). The gathering storm: China's challenge to US power in Asia. *Chinese Journal of International Politics*, 3, 4: 381–396.

Osborn, H. (2020). *Genealogy*, Robert Hale, Ltd., New York.

Pavlicevic, D. (2019). A power shift underway in Europe? China's relationship with central and eastern Europe under the Belt and Road initiative. In Xing, L. (Ed.), *Mapping China's One Belt One Road initiative*, Palgrave, London. pp. 249–278.

Picket, K. (2017). Foreword. In Brown, R. (Ed.), *The inequality crises*, Policy Press, London. pp. vii–viii.

Piketty, T. (2014). *Capital in the twenty-first century*, The Belknap Press of Harvard University Press, Boston, MA.

Piketty, T. (2016). *Chronicles: On our troubled times*, Viking, London.

Reves, R.V. (2018). *Dream Hordes: How the American upper middle class is leaving everyone else in the dust. Why that is a problem and what to do about it*, Brooking Institution Press, Washington, DC.

Ross, R. & Bekkevold, J.I. (2016). *China in the era of Xi Jinping*, Georgetown University Press, Washington, DC.

Sandel, M.J. (2020). *The tyranny of merit: What's become of the common good?* Allen Lane, New York.

Schwab, K. (2016). *The fourth industrial revolution*, World Economic Forum, Geneva.

Schwab, K. (2018). *Shaping the fourth industrial revolution*, World Economic Forum, Geneva.

Vangeli, A. (2017). China's engagement with the sixteen countries of central, east and southeast Europe under the Belt and Road initiative. *China & World Economy*, 25, 5: 101–124.

Vangeli, A. (2018). Normative foundation of the Belt and Road initiative. In Wenhua, S., Nuotio, K. & Zhang, K. (Eds.), *Normative readings of the Belt and Road initiative*, Springer, London. pp. 59–83.

Vangeli, A. (2019). A framework for the study of One Belt One Road initiative as a medium of principle diffusion. In Xing, L. (Ed.), *Mapping China's One Belt One Road initiative*, Palgrave Macmillan, London. pp. 57–89.

Wah, C.Y. & Menkhoff, T. (2020). Introduction: Understanding the transformational power of China's Belt and Road initiative. In Wah, C.Y., Menkhoff, T. & Low, L. (Eds.), *China's Belt and Road initiative: Understanding the dynamics of a global transformation*, World Scientific, London. pp. xxiii–xxxviii.

Wang, D. (2020). *Reigning the future*, New Degree Press, New York.

Wang, Y. (2015). *One Belt One Road: Opportunities and challenges*, People's Press, Beijing.

Wang, Y. (2016). *The Belt and Road initiative: What will China offer the world in its rise*, New World Press, Beijing.

Wang, Y. (2017a). *Belt and Road initiative: China's responsibilities in its rise*, People's Press, Beijing.

Wang, Y. (2017b). *China connects the world: What behind the Belt and Road initiative*, China Intercontinental Press, Beijing.

Wang, Y. (2017c). *The world is connected: The logic of Belt and Road initiative*, The Commercial Press, Beijing.

Wasif Khan, S. (2019). *Haunted by chaos, China's grand strategy from Mao Zedong to Xi Jinping*, Harvard University Press, Cambridge, MA.

Xing, L. (2019). Understanding the multiple facets of China's "One Belt One Road" initiative. In Xing, L. (Ed.), *Mapping China's One Belt One Road initiative*, Palgrave Macmillan, London. pp. 29–56.

Yang, J. (2015). China's new diplomacy under the Xi Jinping administration. *China Quarterly of International Strategic Studies*, 1, 1: 1–17.

Yuan, F. (2019). The One Belt One Road initiative and China's multi-layered multilateralism. In Xing, L. (Ed.), *Mapping China's One Belt One Road initiative*, Palgrave, London. pp. 91–116.

Yue, Y. & Fujian, L. (2019). *The Belt and Road initiative: ASEAN countries' perspectives*, World Scientific, London.

Yunker, J. (2014). *Global Marshall plan: Theory and evidence*, Lexington, London.

Zhang, J. (2015). China's new foreign policy under Xi Jinping: Towards peaceful rise 2.0? *Global Change, Peace & Security*, 27, 1: 5–19.

Zou, L. (2018). *The political economy of China's Belt and Road initiative*, World Scientific, London.

4 Co-creation to promote knowledge processes and innovation for the countries along the New Silk Road

Key points in this chapter

General

- The co-creation effect involves synergy effects for the countries along the New Silk Road.

Systemic involvement

- Multilateralism is understood here as communication between several parties, where decisions regarding future actions are reached through dialogue and consensus. This stands in opposition to unilateralism which concerns one-sided action, often with a disregard for other parties, and often based on the use of power.
- The New Silk Road will have a strong multiplying effect on the countries it will pass through. Metaphorically, it will have the same effect as an irrigation system that provides water and nutrients to an agricultural area: production increases relatively more than it would have done without the irrigation system.
- Systemic involvement facilitates the development of the new Silk Road as an innovation generator through the development of projects based on the balance between collaboration and co-creation.

Contribution and selection

- Traditional globalization focused on competition in relation to costs in general and labour costs in particular. This led to large-scale deindustrialization in the United States and Europe.
- The new globalization focuses on competition related to competence in general and high-tech competence in particular.
- The country that manages to develop the best education system and push as many as possible through a high-tech university education will be the country that becomes the leader in the Fourth Industrial Revolution.

DOI: 10.4324/9781003316978-4

Cognitive openness

- Cognitive openness concerns a willingness to learn from others
- It is not always the case that every type of new technology that promotes productivity and earnings will be the preferred technology of those in power
- The best way to build trust in joint projects will be to show the possible results in the form of a win–win presentation, where both benefits and drawbacks are made visible.
- If we use insights from the prospect theory to examine the relationship between China and the United States, then it may be suggested that the United States will be more willing to act in order to avoid losing the position they have already achieved.
- The prospect theory can also provide a psychological explanation of Thucydides' Trap, which describes the tendency of dominant powers to resort to military force when they are threatened by an emerging power.

Systemic competence

- Systemic competence concerns being aware of the various types of competence that are used along the entire value chain of a project
- In practice, systemic competence concerns the importance of co-creation, shared futures, and win–win strategies, if success is to be achieved.
- While the value added of enterprises as a result of foreign investment grew by 2.4% in 2020, value added in high-tech production grew by 7.1%. This is a clear indication that China is fully committed to moving up the production value chain.
- We are witnessing a global transition from competition based on labour costs, to competition based on level of skills, expertise and competence.
- The Chinese economy has moved up the value chain, from producing "cheap shoes" and other consumer goods, to products based on artificial intelligence and other high-tech systems.
- With a focus on mass education, and its expansion of technological universities, China caught up with the United States in the field of education around 2012.
- By first investing in neighbouring countries, China has built a diplomatic wall around their sphere of interest.
- By expanding the New Silk Road to Europe, the Middle East and Africa, China has secured an economic bridge to avoid a possible containment by the United States.
- It is crucial for China that the projects along the New Silk Road include reciprocity, technology transfer and win–win results. If this does not occur, both the diplomatic wall and the economic bridge may be quickly eroded.
- A policy based on win–win scenarios, and a strategic intention based on shared futures, will promote systemic competence in relation to the New Silk Road as an innovation generator.

Strategic implementation

- The sustainability of the projects along the New Silk Road is oriented along six axes: economic sustainability, technological sustainability, political sustainability, diplomatic sustainability, social sustainability, and cultural sustainability.
- The implementation of the New Silk Road has coincided with the emergence of a new globalization, where mass education at university level is the social mechanism that facilitates the development of technological innovations.
- Mass education at university level in general, and technological expertise in particular, are the social mechanisms that drive forward the development of technology in the innovation economy.
- In strategic implementation, it is important to distinguish between technology as a social phenomenon and technology as a social mechanism.
- Collaborative advantages not competitive advantages can be said to constitute the basis for the entire New Silk Road mega-project.
- The basic concept in collaboration benefits is win–win, i.e. the parties involved in the projects should benefit by putting collaboration before competition.
- The strategic reasons for the New Silk Road can be understood along the following axes:

    1 The first strategic reason is to secure China an economic, political, and diplomatic corridor so as to circumvent US assertiveness in the South China Sea, and the East China Sea, especially in relation to Taiwan.
    2 The second strategic reason is to prevent the United States from gaining a monopoly with regard to economic and technological relationship-building with countries included in the New Silk Road.
    3 The third strategic reason is the importance of importing raw materials or goods that it cannot efficiently produce, or is unable to produce, itself.
    4 The fourth strategic reason is related to the need for cooperation and co-creation in relation to the development of technological innovations.

Introduction

Co-creation involves working together to promote knowledge processes and innovation. If knowledge processes and innovation are essential for value creation in the innovation economy, co-creation is an important social mechanism for initiating, maintaining and strengthening these processes. The balance between competition and cooperation, embodied in the concept of co-creation, leads to constructive criticism and the necessary scope of knowledge that exists in the network so as to promote creativity and innovation. Instead of a zero-sum situation, a positive-sum situation will be developed where everyone wins.

The co-creation effect is related to the synergy effects for the countries along the new Silk Road.

There are many aspects of co-creation. We focus on five elements here that individually and collectively constitute aspects of co-creation along the New Silk Road.[1] These elements are:

1 Systemic involvement. In practice, this means that all countries participating in the projects along the New Silk Road are involved in the projects from beginning to end. In other words, the projects have a common value for all the countries, and the projects should always have win–win intentions for the project participants.
2 Contribution and selection. In a practical context, when you decide to select something in a project or a problem as your point of focus, you have also decided not to select something else. Thus, through a selection process, you end up focusing on one aspect of the project or problem you are investigating, while ignoring other aspects. Following this logic, if a country wishes to take a leading role in the Fourth Industrial Revolution, it will have to select a particular focus. It is generally believed that such a focus will be technological innovations; such a focus presupposes a strong emphasis on mass higher education. Such a development will also constitute the basis of the new globalization.
3 Cognitive openness. In a practical context, regarding the countries along the New Silk Road, cognitive openness concerns the willingness of the participating countries to learn from each other, from history and from possible future scenarios. In this way, learning and change will become a central component of all the projects along the New Silk Road.
4 Systemic competence. In practice, regarding projects along the New Silk Road, this is related to the fact that those parties leading the various projects should continuously focus on the necessary expertise required along the entire value chain throughout a project's lifetime. In this way, the necessary expertise that the project demands during a project's lifetime will be accessible.
5 Strategic implementation. This concerns the constant balance between part and whole. In a practical context, the whole affects the parts, but the parts also affect the whole. This theoretical concept is also related to the basic principle that a chain is no stronger than its weakest link. Therefore, it is always the parts and the whole that must be considered continuously and collectively. If you carry out a project by only focusing on the parts, then you can risk losing the overview of the whole, and a link in the chain may break where you least expect it.

In our context, co-creation is especially evident in the new free trade agreement, the RCEP, which has been signed by 15 Asia-Pacific countries.[2] This agreement is not only an economic agreement, but can also be related to the growing trust between the countries in the region that is covered by the agreement. Despite the different political systems of the countries, the various historical events that have created bad blood between some of the countries, and despite tough verbal attacks against each other in the past, this agreement shows that the countries have been able to establish a basic trust so that they can make joint gains from the trade agreement. It is thus a strategic mutual trust that is expressed in this new trade agreement in the Asia-Pacific region. The strategic intention of this agreement is that the entire regional economy will flourish. *Le Monde Diplomatique* writes the following about this agreement: "With 30 percent of world GDP, 28 percent of world trade and 2.2 billion people, the RCEP is the largest agreement of its kind ever."[3] However, it is not possible to predict exactly the co-creation effect this agreement will have for the whole of the Asia-Pacific region, but it is highly probable that the agreement will have an impact on the economies of the United States and Europe.

If this free trade agreement is considered in connection with the New Silk Road, which was launched in 2013 (Yue & Fujian, 2019: 1–58), then it might be said that China is building up its economy, and thus directly and indirectly threatening the US's economic, political, and diplomatic position. In the slightly longer term, both the RCEP and the New Silk Road will contribute to China rivalling the US's economic global position (Macaes, 2020; Mahbubani, 2018, 2020). However, it should also be noted that this type of global competition may lead to Thucydides' Trap, and create a conflict between China and the United States that may spiral out of control (Allison, 2018).

When several countries invest in each other's infrastructure, production systems, and share ideas about trade, this says something about the basis for peaceful coexistence, mutual learning, and a sharing of the value created by joint projects. Over time, as the projects along the New Silk Road are implemented and completed, such as projects in Africa, the Middle East and Kazakhstan, those involved will witness that it is win–win projects that are being rolled out (Yunker, 2014; Zhang, 2015; Zou, 2018). The projects can be found in every conceivable type of production and distribution chain (Xing, 2019; Yuan, 2019). The New Silk Road and the RCEP free trade agreement, as well as China's mutual investment agreement with the EU (signed December 2020), manifest a whole new paradigm regarding China's economic policy. This concerns a transition from export-driven economic growth, based on cheap labour, to an innovation-driven economic growth, based on high-tech competence.[4]

The new paradigm also shows that the old globalization driven by differences in wage costs has been replaced by a new type of globalization based on differences in competence in general and technological competence in particular. This is where the real conflict between the United States and China lies. All the other "conflicts" and arguments are just straw men aimed at diverting attention away from the real conflict. Both parties are aware of this, and both parties know that the country that wins the battle of gaining the lead in high-tech development will also be the country that will take on the leadership role in the Fourth Industrial Revolution (Johannessen, 2021).

We have illustrated the introduction in Figure 4.1. Figure 4.1 also shows how this chapter is organized.

Systemic involvement for the countries along the New Silk Road

In this section, we will examine the following question: How does systemic involvement promote the New Silk Road as an innovation generator?

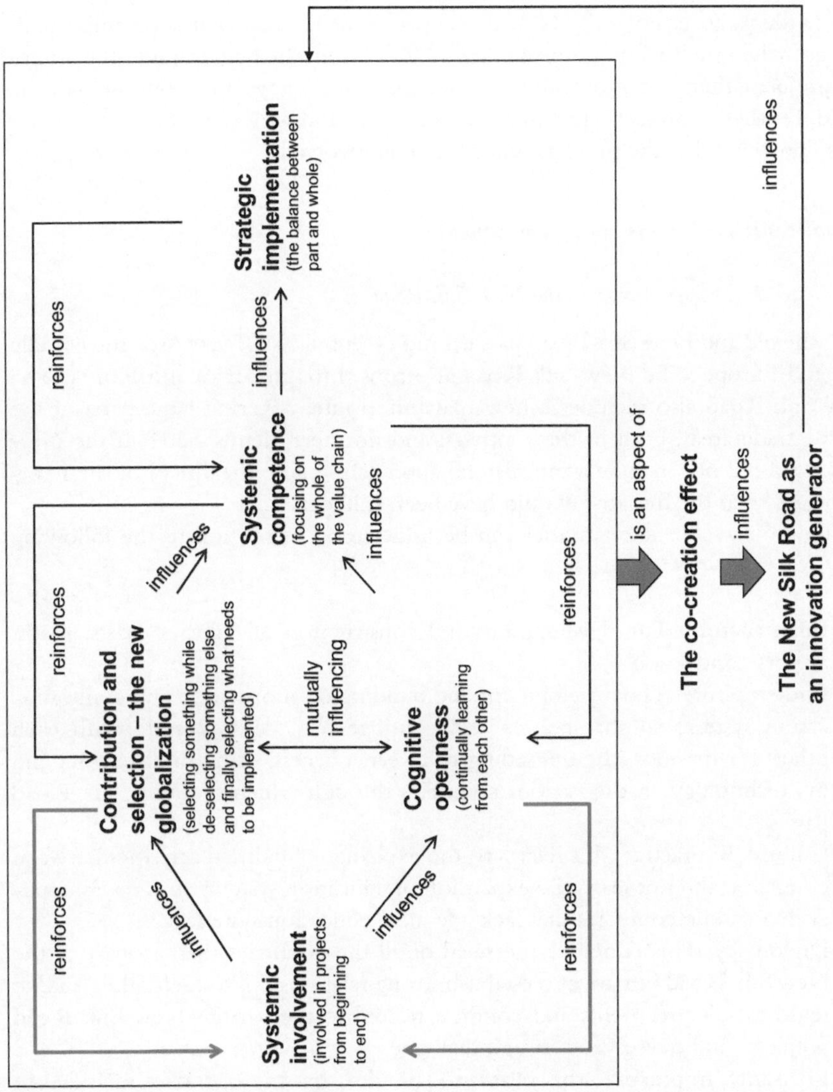

Figure 4.1 Co-creation and the New Silk Road as an innovation generator.

Multilateralism is not only concerned with power politics, it can also be related to global economic, diplomatic and social relationships. In these contexts, multilateralism can be understood as a dialogue between several parties, where decisions are reached through consensus. This stands in opposition to unilateralism, where decisions are reached by a single party, often with disregard for other parties, and often based on the use of power. Multilateralism is based on keeping the dialogue open between parties, rather than the exercise of power by a single party. In relation to the projects along the New Silk Road, systemic involvement is important, because when the various countries are involved from the beginning to the end of the projects, then the probability is high that their views and opinions will be heard. Further, if projects are based on reciprocity and win–win situations, then it is also probable that the projects will benefit all involved.

Narratives related to systemic involvement

Case letter 1: The seven axes of the New Silk Road

Both the old and New Silk Road pass through Central Asia, West Asia, the Middle East and Europe. The New Silk Road also runs through Africa and Russia. The New Silk Road also includes a new maritime route, covering large parts of the world's trade areas, both in the southern and northern hemispheres. If the New Silk Road did not include a multilateral approach, where the voices of the many are heard, then the initiative would have been stillborn.

The project's specific activities can be understood in relation to the following axes[5]:

1 Infrastructure. The development and construction of railways, ports, roads, airports, and so on.
2 Info-structure. The development and building of information and communication systems so that people and countries can communicate with each other; for instance, the upgrading of internet access, using the latest 5G and 6G technology, in the various countries through which the New Silk Road passes.
3 Culture. In practice, this relates to the exchange of cultural activities between countries, and not least, the expansion of education systems at all levels, especially in those countries that lack adequate education systems.
4 Diplomacy. This concerns the need of all the countries that are part of the New Silk Road initiative to establish strong relationships to each other, so that tensions, disagreements and conflicts related to the various New Silk Road projects can be resolved through dialogue.
5 Economy. In practice, this relates to the idea that the countries included in the New Silk Road initiative are able to generate economic benefits from participating in the initiative, which should be greater than if they had not participated. This will result in an increase in trade between the countries, which will be significantly larger than if they had not participated in the projects.

6 Technology. This relates to the importance of the transfer of technological competence in all the projects that are developed along the New Silk Road.
7 Politics. Non-intervention in the internal affairs of the other countries participating in the New Silk Road initiative.

Description for systemic involvement

One of the ideas behind the New Silk Road is that the areas in which the projects are established can be viewed as a cohesive region (Myint, 2019: 141–142). In other words, co-creation will constitute the basic principle of collaboration. However, it should be pointed out here that collaboration is qualitatively different from co-creation; that is, it is possible to collaborate without co-creating (Pieters & Jansen, 2017).

It is possible that the maritime New Silk Road has an extra multiplier effect with regard to the various projects, because the maritime route passes through existing or new ports, enabling the trading of goods in the connected areas. The various ports will in many cases also be connected to the land-based New Silk Road. Thus, the maritime New Silk Road is not only a separate component of the New Silk Road, but also connects to the land-based route. We can observe this in many of the projects that have already been completed, e.g. in Vietnam (Hoang, 2019: 233–252). We also find similar connections in Nigeria, Djibouti, Mozambique, Liberia, Ghana, Tanzania, Congo, to name a few countries in Africa (French, 2015). The port of Gwadar in Pakistan also has the same effect. This port connects the maritime New Silk Road with the land-based New Silk Road (Yuan, 2019: 91–116).

The theoretical starting point for the New Silk Road is the common economic destiny of countries in the global economy. If one of the countries falls backwards economically, this will affect the other countries. If one or more countries are pulled forward, this will have a positive effect on all the countries' economies. It is the understanding of the common destiny that lies in the concept of systemic involvement, because at all levels, and in all connections that affect the development of an economy, lies the understanding that what is the destiny of one also affects the destiny of the others. This is really no more surprising than the fact that the classical globalization competed on costs in general and labour costs in particular, which affected workers in the United States negatively while affecting workers in China positively.

In Figure 4.2, we have shown aspects of systemic involvement with regard to how this concept affects the New Silk Road as an innovation generator.

Analysis for systemic involvement

There are many indications that the New Silk Road will lead to a large degree of cooperation as well as a large degree of co-creation.[6] In general, the opportunities for global cooperation, and in particular the opportunities for cooperation between the RCEP countries, the countries along the New Silk Road and the EU countries, will mean that co-creation will be able to function as an innovation

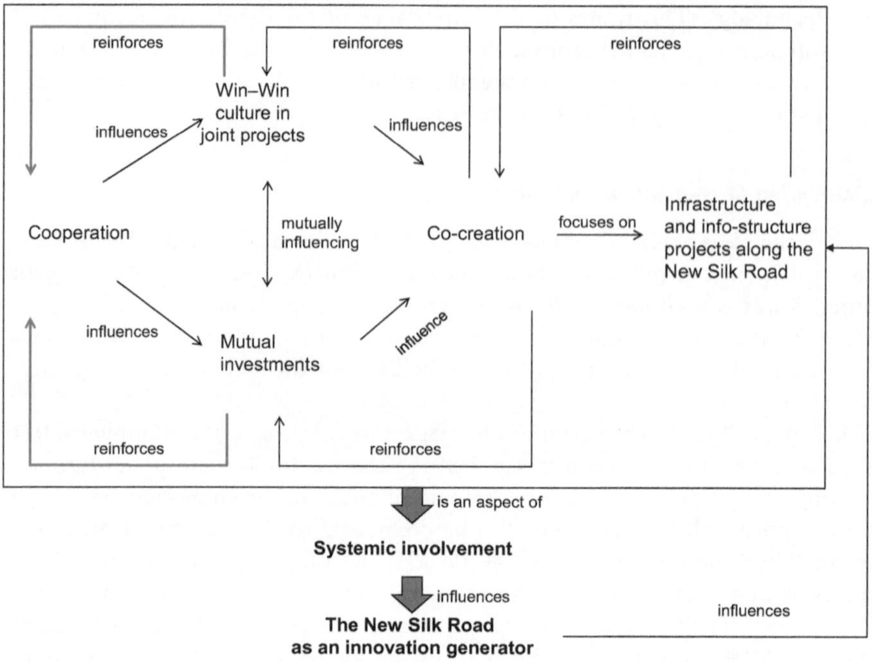

Figure 4.2 Systemic involvement: A conceptual model.

generator. The RCEP agreement and the EU–China investment agreement were both signed at the end of 2020.

The various projects that will be developed by the New Silk Road countries, the RCEP countries and European countries will have a technological and economic multiplier effect for the countries' economies. On the other hand, the countries that are not involved in these projects will slowly but surely risk ending up in a technological and economic backwater (Zou, 2018: 177–201).

It seems reasonable to assume that the same economic energy that emanated from the first three industrial revolutions will also emanate from the Fourth Industrial Revolution, where artificial intelligence will be the driving force. In practice, this means that those countries that either develop this new technology, i.e. artificial intelligence and intelligent robots, or that manage to adapt and apply this new technology, will secure a strong position at the beginning of the Fourth Industrial Revolution. To develop or adapt oneself to be able to apply new technology, there is one obvious and essential precondition that must be satisfied. This precondition is largely about university-level technological competence. In addition to this specific condition, there is an underlying condition. This underlying condition is that a country must also have a system of high-level mass education in fields other than technology. This is to ensure that the necessary competence exists for there to be an understanding of the necessity of participating at a high technological level for historical, cultural, political and social reasons. Without this underlying condition, a country may risk developing an economy that is sound in itself, but which has been built on unsound foundations. Metaphorically, this would be like building an architect-designed house on sand, with the result that a flood or heavy rain could cause the house to sink into the ground.

Theoretical points related to systemic involvement

Systemic involvement along the New Silk Road is the result of the simultaneous existence of cooperation and co-creation. While the Belt and Road Initiative (BRI) is a gigantic mega-project, thousands upon thousands of smaller projects have been planned and will be launched along the New Silk Road, both the maritime and land-based routes (Yue & Fujian, 2019). Most of the projects are funded by four of China's major state-owned banks.[7] In addition to the four banks, China has created a $40 billion fund to be used for projects along the New Silk Road (Myint, 2019: 143). Moreover, a great deal of collaboration and co-creation will be needed to implement infrastructure projects along the New Silk Road (Xing, 2019). These infrastructure projects will improve national and international transport and logistics for the countries included in the mega-project (Wang, 2017c).

We have developed a typology showing how connectivity can be achieved through systemic involvement.

Practical utility for systemic involvement

Collaboration and co-creation in the infrastructure projects is a prerequisite for triggering systemic involvement (Wah & Menkhoff, 2020). When the infrastructure projects are completed, this will increase trade in the region along the New Silk Road (Vangeli, 2017). This increased trade will also promote further investment in industry, agriculture and lay the foundation for high-tech production (Vangeli, 2019). The basic prerequisite for high-tech production is the education system (Linehan, 2018). Therefore, education, student exchange and collaboration on the development of education at a high technological level will also be

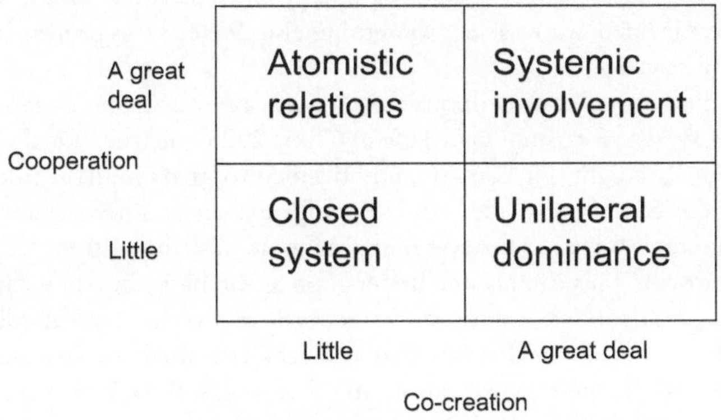

Figure 4.3 Systemic involvement: A typology.

integrated into the infrastructure projects along the New Silk Road (Vangeli, 2018; Wah & Menkhoff, 2020).

The New Silk Road will consist of six corridors[8]:

1 The new Eurasia land bridge corridor
2 The China–Mongolia–Russia corridor
3 The China–Central Asia–West Asia corridor
4 The China–Indochina corridor
5 The China–Pakistan corridor
6 The land bridge through China, Myanmar and Bangladesh[9]

If the projects along the New Silk Road are completed, and fulfil the purpose of increased trade, increased investment and cooperation in high-tech innovation development, the leaders in China will have succeeded in creating strong relationships to the countries that are part of the New Silk Road initiative, along many axes (Macaes, 2020). Among others, these axes will be related to economic development, technological development, diplomatic exchange, cultural cooperation, and people-to-people relations through various cultural connections (Mahbubani, 2014, 2018, 2020).

Sub-conclusion for systemic involvement

We have examined the following question: How does systemic involvement promote the New Silk Road as an innovation generator?

The short answer is that this will occur through the simultaneous existence of cooperation and co-creation.

The new globalization

In this section we will examine the following question: How does contribution and selection promote the New Silk Road as an innovation generator?

When you decide to select something in a problem as your point of focus, you will also have decided not to select something else. We call this process here "contribution and selection".

When China changed its economic paradigm from exporting cheap consumer goods to the West to focusing on "Made in China 2025" and the "Dual Circulation Development Paradigm", it consequently decided to give emphasis to one aspect of the Chinese economy, while reducing emphasis on another aspect. The new economic strategy focuses on developing technological innovations as a basis for economic growth. This can also be understood as the basis for a new type of globalization. In this context, education in general, and technological education in particular, is the social mechanism that can facilitate the transformation of the economy towards the new globalization. In other words, there is now less emphasis on economic growth based on low labour costs and the export of cheap Chinese consumer goods.

Narratives for the new globalization

Case letter 1: Reshoring

One of the consequences of an increased emphasis on expertise-driven economic growth and reduction in the emphasis on export-driven growth based on low-cost labour is that many countries are withdrawing their investments and companies from China. Many countries are involved in this so-called "reshoring", including Japan.[10]

Case letter 2: Dual Circulation Development Paradigm

This new paradigm guiding the Chinese economy gives greater emphasis to domestic demand. If we connect this new paradigm with "Made in China 2025", then it seems evident that the development of a new globalization is underway. The new globalization is based on differences in expertise, while the old globalization was based on differences in costs. This development requires that China focuses on developing technological innovations for its high-tech production for the domestic market, instead of importing this technology from countries such as the United States.

Case letter 3: US trade with China

US exports to China support approx. 1.2 million jobs in the United States. This was reported by Craig Allen, president of the US-China Business Council, based on a study commissioned by the U.S. China Business Council (13 January 2021).[11] According to the study, the trade war between the United States and China under the Trump administration has damaged the US's economic interests. The trade war has already cost 245,000 jobs in the United States, from 2018 to 2020, says Alex Mackle of Oxford Economics,[12] who is the main author of the study.

Description related to the new globalization

The contribution and selection process, the process where an individual, group or country selects or emphasizes something; for instance, when the United States chose to start a trade war with China in order to emphasize their views on certain matters; such a focus also has as a consequence that less emphasis is given to other issues. However, the consequence for China, among other things, was that it realized it could not depend on the United States regarding the import of high-tech products. This triggered a completely new economic policy in China, the Dual Circulation Development Paradigm.[13] The paradigm gives greater emphasis on being self-sufficient in high-tech products that are inputs in Chinese production. Trade with the United States in this area was reduced and given less emphasis by the Chinese leaders. If we consider the impact of this new paradigm in the context of the new trade agreement between 15 countries in the Asia-Pacific region (RCEP) and the new investment agreement between China and the EU, then we

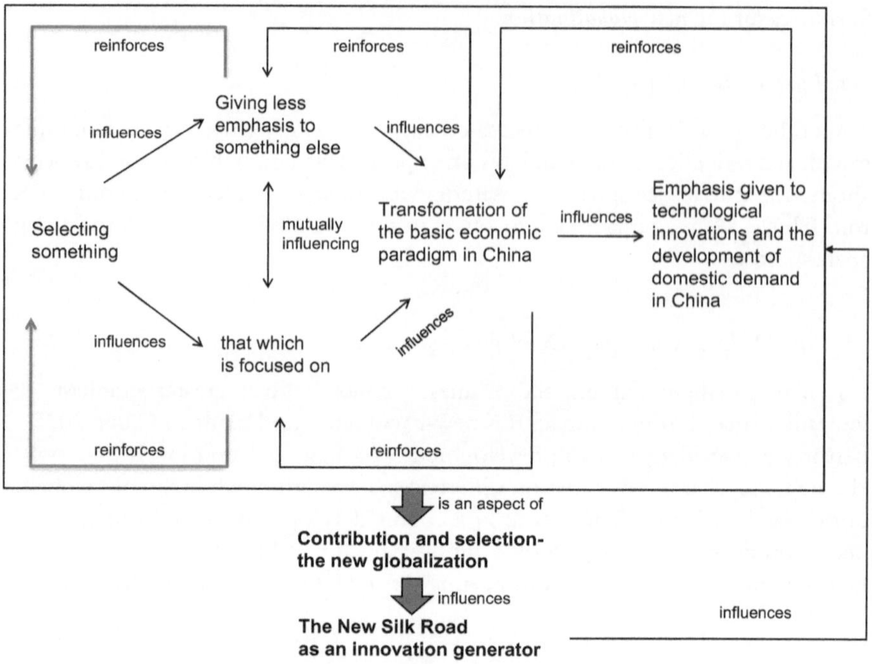

Figure 4.4 Contribution and selection.

can perceive the contours of a new economic world order, in which the United States plays a smaller role than before. Paradoxically, Trump's trade war achieved the opposite of what it set out to achieve, that is, to strengthen the US's position.

We have illustrated the contribution and selection process with regard to China in Figure 4.4.

Analysis of the new globalization

There is little doubt that China's economic progress is changing global relations (Allison, 2018). The onset of neoliberalism around the 1980s, China's opening up to foreign investment, and the fall of the Berlin Wall changed the global economic structure. In the same way, the New Silk Road and the new globalization are changing global relations again. The old globalization was driven by competition for costs, which had a negative effect on wages in the United States and Europe, but a positive effect on wages in China. The new globalization is driven by competition, which does not focus to the same extent on costs, but on competence. The consequence is that a country's education system becomes the focal point in relation to its ability to compete. With regard to systemic involvement, it is how the individual countries in general, and the United States and China in particular, develop their education systems from the start of a child's development, until he/she finishes their university education, which will be crucial for a country's competitiveness in the innovation economy (Linehan, 2018). The country that

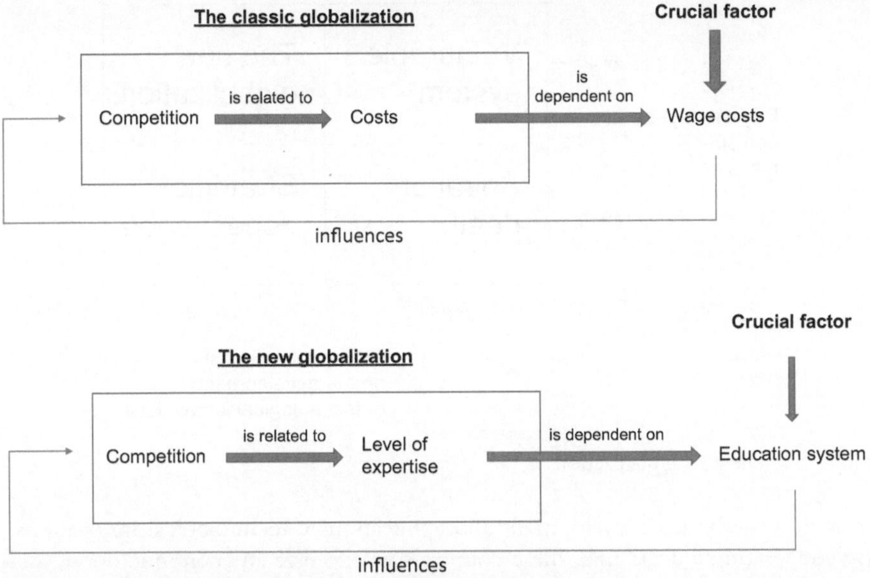

Figure 4.5 The old and the new globalization.

manages to develop the best education system, and provide a high-tech university education for as many as possible, will be the country that takes the lead in the Fourth Industrial Revolution.

Figure 4.5 illustrates the distinction between classical globalization and the new globalization, as we interpret it here. This interpretation also makes it easier to understand and explain the importance of systemic involvement from a Chinese perspective. That is, from a Chinese perspective the New Silk Road is not only a means for avoiding US encirclement, i.e. US's use of economic, military and diplomatic force in the South China Sea, but also as a link to economic systems that also question the US sincerity in its trade relations and its use of military strength. The point is that the United States has shown a unilateral dominant attitude towards many of its allies during the Trump administration, and therefore many countries, including EU countries, are genuinely interested in systemic relations at many levels with China. This becomes evident if we consider the China–EU investment agreement, which was signed on 30 December 2020, where the EU seeks strategic autonomy and will not allow itself to be dominated by the United States or by China for that matter.[14]

Theoretical points related to the new globalization

The projects along the New Silk Road will give the economies of the participant countries a vitamin injection, and when these economies flourish, this will also result in hopes and expectations of a better future. Many of the countries that the New Silk Road passes through are at a low economic and technological level; for example, in relation to the limited opportunities of gaining a high-tech education,

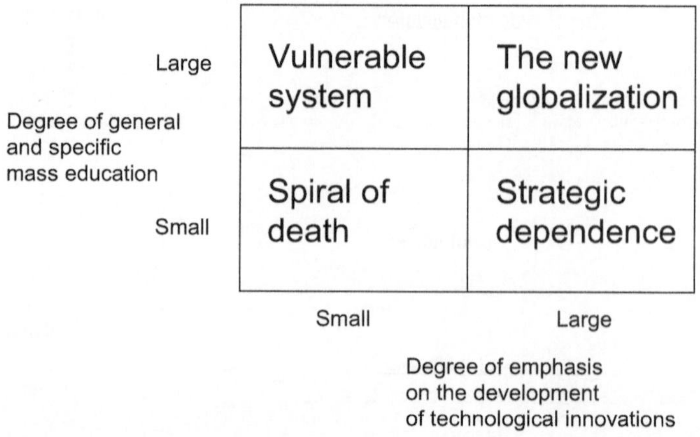

Figure 4.6 The new globalization.

as well as the limited development and application of technological innovations. By cooperating with China, these countries will receive an economic boost, and thus be able to initiate a mass education programme, where they can prepare the population for the innovation economy that is under way (Johannessen, 2021; Junxin, 2020). In the innovation economy, low labour costs will not be a decisive factor for promoting economic growth. In this context, it is important to be aware of the difference between the old and the new globalization. In the old globalization, low costs in general, and low relative wages in particular, provided countries with a competitive advantage. In the new globalization, mass education with a focus on a generally high level of expertise, and in particular, a high level of technological expertise, will be the decisive factors determining a country's competitiveness. We have illustrated the new globalization in Figure 4.6.

Practical utility for the new globalization

The vision of a common future for the countries along the New Silk Road, and the practical steps to implement this vision, will promote the understanding that the New Silk Road represents a mega-project that will provide win–win results for all the countries involved.[15]

The New Silk Road may be viewed as a new global "Marshall Plan" (Feng & Liang, 2019). The Marshall Plan was launched during the post-war period to rehabilitate the economies of the European countries by providing economic resources; the Marshall Plan was launched under the slogan "Help to self-help"; in other words, the United States would help the European countries devastated by war to help themselves ("self-help"). However, the United States also benefitted from launching the plan as American production levels increased, so one can say there was a degree of self-interest. Similarly, the New Silk Road, or the new global "Marshall Plan", aims to help other countries so they can help themselves ("self-help"), but the intention of course is that China will also benefit economically from the initiative.

On the basis of the above description, we can say that the New Silk Road countries will benefit from the help they receive with regard to the various Silk Road projects, while China will benefit by being able to open up new markets. This is especially important to China, because the United States is tearing down cooperative relationships and dissolving agreements, and urging its allies to do the same. However, this unilateral development did not begin with the Trump administration, but was already evident in the article "America's Pacific century" published in the *Foreign Policy* magazine, written by the former Secretary of State, Hillary Clinton, during the Obama presidency.

The tensions between the United States and China, regarding high-tech development, are most evident if we consider the Huawei issue. The United States have banned Huawei from developing 5G wireless network projects in the United States, and also put pressure on a number of European countries to exclude the Chinese company. The reason given is the so-called worries about national security. However, it seems no proof has been provided regarding this allegation concerning possible national security breaches; thus, logically, one could use the same argumentation against American technology companies. Of course, it is unlikely that other countries would ban American technology companies and justify this by referring to potential "security risks". Understood from this perspective, the New Silk Road can be viewed as providing China with economic, technological, diplomatic and cultural openings, especially now that China feels it is being more and more closed in by the United States and its allies.[16]

Sub-conclusion for the new globalization

In this section, we have examined the following question: How does "contribution and selection" promote the New Silk Road as an innovation generator?

The short answer is that from the viewpoint of practical politics, all the countries participating in the New Silk Road need to experience that this "new Marshall Plan" is a win–win mega-project, in which all the participant countries will be able to create a better shared future.

Cognitive openness as a willingness to learn from others

In this section, we will examine the following question: How does "cognitive openness" promote the New Silk Road as an innovation generator?

Cognitive openness concerns continuous learning from each other. Any innovation will encounter opposition from established processes, activities and procedures. This is one of the reasons why innovations always meet resistance from the forces that benefit from existing technology. In other words, it is not always the case that every type of new technology that promotes productivity and earnings will be the preferred technology of those in power (Johannessen, 2021). However, despite these challenges, if a social system or country manages to implement a strategy where the importance of learning from others is emphasized, then it is highly probable that the social system or country will greatly benefit from such a strategy.

Narratives related to cognitive openness

Case letter 1: History creates paths far into the future

History is often understood as an account of past events, but with no relevance for our lives today. On the other hand, if we examine some of the activities, attitudes and actions we are engaged in today, they may not always seem rational from a present-day perspective. One way of explaining the "irrationality" for our present-day attitudes and actions is to examine them in relation to what is termed "history's slow fields", that is, certain attitudes and actions tend to be in operation long after the functions and processes that initially created them have disappeared. The idea or rather the vision of the New Silk Road is one such concept affected by "history's slow fields". To understand the meaning of the concept, one needs to know something about its historic origins, i.e. the old Silk Road. In short, the old Silk Road was a network of trade routes connecting the East and West – the land and sea routes connecting China with the rest of Asia, the Middle East and countries in Europe. By using the concept today (2013), the New Silk Road is thus associated with its historical origins, in the sense that China is able to create mega-projects that reconnect the country with the countries that were part of the old Silk Road, and also new countries that were not part of the old Silk Road. In this way, the concept itself has an explosive force into today's reality. The old Silk Road is often associated with the travels and accounts of the Venetian merchant Marco Polo. Marco Polo was not only concerned with the trading of goods, but also the exchange of knowledge from East to West and vice versa (Hawke, 2020: 19–21). In this context, the New Silk Road is also associated with the exchange of knowledge and technology, something that is only possible when there is a high level of cognitive openness.

Case letter 2: The New Silk Road from vision to concrete plans

The New Silk Road was originally more a vision than a concrete plan. The plans came into place at a later time, once specific projects and financial instruments had been developed. The vision is still unfolding, however, just as a map unfolds. Once the map is clarified, one can start to move around the terrain. This is also the vision for the New Silk Road. First came the vision, thereafter the specific projects were explored in greater depth (Fang & Fu, 2020).

The projects that are being developed point to the west, to Asia, the Middle East, Europe and Africa. Some new branches of the project extend to a northern route towards the Barents Sea, and another extends towards some of the countries in South America.

Description of cognitive openness

The New Silk Road is not merely a Chinese expansion into the Asia-Pacific region. The projects that are initiated will also have an impact on Africa and Europe. However, one of the prerequisites for economic growth in the areas in which the New Silk Road projects are implemented is that there needs to be reciprocity between the countries, and that the projects need to be win–win projects for all the involved countries. It is this reciprocity that will be crucial, and the final proof that the New Silk Road is able to build bridges between different regions, different political systems, different religions, different cultures, etc. Among other things, this reciprocity will involve the planning and construction of infrastructure projects which will generate a demand for labour. In addition, high-tech expertise will be required, because some of the projects will be based on new technology, such as artificial intelligence and intelligent robots. Therefore, the New Silk Road is not only a bridge between regions, but will also be a bridge between the old and the new globalization.

In order for reciprocity to be established as a cornerstone in the many projects along the maritime and land-based New Silk Road, it is crucial that trust is developed between the countries involved in the various BRI and OBOR projects.[17] Perhaps the best way to build trust in the joint projects will be to show the possible results in the form of a win–win presentation, where both benefits and drawbacks are made visible. In order to achieve reciprocity, where the involved countries learn from each other, it will also be important that the countries understand and respect the differences in political governance, culture and history between the various countries. If this respect for each other's differences is not adopted as the accepted norm, then dominance and unilateral strategies may quickly develop and damage the entire mega-project (Allison, 2018; Linehan, 2018).

We have illustrated the description of cognitive openness in Figure 4.7.

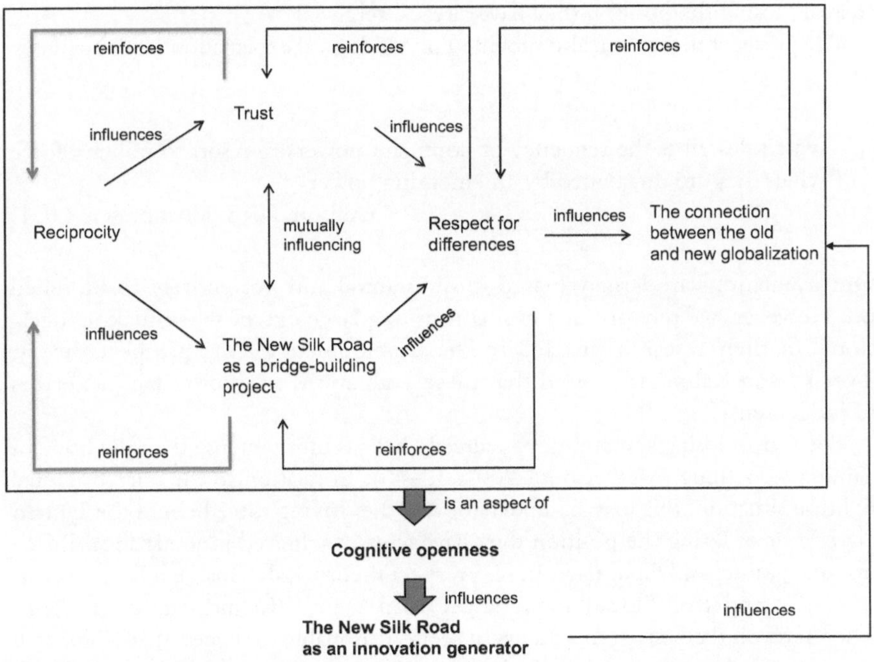

Figure 4.7 Cognitive openness.

Analysis of cognitive openness

Innovation will almost always meet resistance from those groups who feel that they have something to lose from the application of the innovation. The prospect theory can be used to explain this phenomenon.

Prospect theory has many applications in various fields and contexts. The theory was developed by Kahneman and Tversky in 1979.[18] Prospect theory shows that when participants have limited information, are taking a risk, and do not use rigorous analytical processes, their choices will often be a result of how they or others frame the situation in question (Wolfe, 2008: 6). The core of prospect theory concerns evaluations of what you want to gain and may possibly lose in relation to a decision, evaluation or action. According to prospect theory, the possibility of losing what has already been gained creates greater risk aversion than trying to gain the same; in other words, people are risk averse concerning loss, but will increase risk if there's a possibility of gaining something (Kahneman, 2011: 279–280).

Most of us are averse to losing something we have already gained; consequently, we are driven to taking risks in such situations. We often operate on the basis of intuitive rules and psychological principles that govern the framing of our choices. However, these rules and principles are not necessarily either rational or logical.[19]

We will assume here that prospect theory can also be applied to countries and not only individuals (McDermott, 2001; Vis, 2010). If we use insights from the prospect theory to examine the relationship between China and the United States, then it may be suggested that the United States will be more willing to act in order to avoid losing the position they have already achieved.

The prospect theory can also provide a psychological explanation of Thucydides' Trap,

> which describes the tendency of dominant powers to resort to military force when they are threatened by an emerging power.
>
> (Allison, 2018; Johannessen, 2021)

Our evaluations are largely biased, unsubstantial and not entirely to be relied on. However, we rely on such evaluations to a large extent when making decisions. In their research that led to the development of the prospect theory, Tversky and Kahneman found that these evaluations are more than just errors of judgement.

The fear of losing something you already have is more intense than the hope of gaining something (McDermott, 2001: 15–45). In relation to the current global political situation, this may be understood as the driving force behind the United States' fear of losing the position they have already achieved in international economics, politics and diplomacy. In his prospect theory, Kahneman explains this fear of loss saying that "losses loom larger than gains" (Kahneman, 2011: 284). Therefore, on the basis of this theory, it seems reasonable to suggest that China will attempt to balance tensions with the United States and its allies, so that China's strength is hidden so that is does not appear threatening. China's strength in the innovation economy is clearly their mass education that has produced millions of university graduates. These graduates have been educated not only in China, but also in Australia, Britain, the United States and many other countries (Johannessen, 2021; Linehan, 2018).

Theoretical points related to cognitive openness

As described above, we can use the prospect theory to understand that trust, degree of reciprocity and respect for the other's / others' differences are important in reducing resistance to change in general, and innovation in particular. If we relate this insight to the understanding of the importance of the interplay between the old and the new globalization for economic and technological development, transfer and learning between the countries included in the projects along the New Silk Road, then we can develop a typology that says something about cognitive openness and economic development. The main hypothesis is the following: A large degree of reciprocity, trust and respect for diversity among the actors involved, as well as a large degree of connection between the old and the new globalization, will in all probability develop cognitive openness.

An important factor to ensure the success of the New Silk Road will be to facilitate the transfer of high-tech knowledge between the participating countries. This will contribute to reducing the resistance to change; consequently, it will be advantageous for China to transfer high-tech expertise to the participating countries. This can be done by direct transfer; however, perhaps more importantly this can be done by helping the various countries develop their education systems, so that they can develop their own high-tech expertise (Linehan, 2018). This approach is expressed by the saying: "Give a man a fish and you feed him for a day. Teach a man to fish and you feed him for a lifetime" (Figure 4.8).

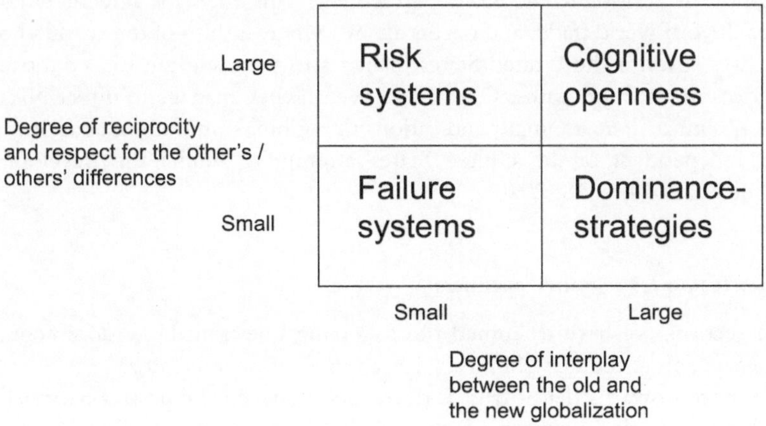

Figure 4.8 Typology: Cognitive openness.

Practical utility for cognitive openness

It is important to be aware of the fact that the New Silk Road is not limited to Asia, but extends to Africa, the Middle East and Europe. The New Silk Road also has connection points to South America and Latin America (Hawke, 2020: 21). Initially, the New Silk Road was only an idea, a strategic vision, announced by the Chinese leader Xi Jinping during an official visit to Kazakhstan in September 2013.[20] From 2013, when the idea was launched until concrete projects were developed did not take a long time. Although the New Silk Road was launched long before President Trump launched a trade war against China, it was only two years after Hillary Clinton (2011) wrote the article "America's Pacific century" outlining the US's strategic position in relation to China. Viewed in this context, the New Silk Road may be understood as an attempt by the Chinese leaders to build an economic and diplomatic bridge, on which China could side-step any attempts by the United States to contain China.

The New Silk Road is not only an "economic bridge", but also a bridge for the exchange of knowledge at different levels between China and large parts of the world. This exchange can be facilitated through Chinese investments in the West, but also Western investments in China.

The new free trade agreement between 15 countries in the Asia-Pacific region (RCEP),[21] which was signed in the autumn of 2020, as well as the new investment agreement between China and the EU, may be viewed as a further strengthening of the economic bridge that the Chinese leaders have built since the New Silk Road was launched in October 2013.

The New Silk Road, the RCEP free trade agreement, and the China–EU agreement have led to China reducing its strategic dependence on the United States. Relations between China and the United States have reached "the point of no return" (Byrre & Gallaghan, 2013). In practice, this means that the United States has a choice to join the economic and innovative development that is taking place in China, or end up on the side-lines regarding the developments that are taking place in relation to the RCEP agreement. This free trade agreement covers approx. 30% of world trade, and covers an area where a third of the world's population lives. Even if the United States manages to persuade the EU countries to form a common front against China, and even if they manage to direct NATO's focus on China, there are many indications that China's innovation economy will thrive, independent of the United States' attempt to hinder this development (Mahbubani, 2014, 2018, 2020).

Sub-conclusion for cognitive openness

In this section, we have examined the following question: How does cognitive openness promote the New Silk Road as an innovation generator?

The short answer is that if trust is developed between the project partners and an understanding that reciprocity is the only way to succeed, as well as, in practical terms, that the parties respect each other's differences at different levels, then the foundation will have been established for the necessary conditions for cognitive openness that will promote the New Silk Road as an innovation generator. The sufficient condition, on the other hand, is that the overall project also balances between projects that support the old and the new globalization.

Systemic competence along the entire value chain of the projects launched along the New Silk Road

In this section, we will examine the following question: How does systemic competence promote the New Silk Road as an innovation generator?

When we discuss systemic competence in relation to the New Silk Road and innovation in the following, it is the value chain perspective we are concerned with. In our context, systemic competence relates to the competence that will be used along the entire value chain of the projects launched along the New Silk Road. At one end of a project this may concern people with high-tech competence. At the other end, there may be expertise related to classic infrastructure projects, which do not require such a high level of competence. In practice, this means that countries that participate in OBOR projects can utilize their entire competence potential. If a country does not possess high-tech competence, then it is a precondition of the New Silk Road mega-project that it will be possible to transfer this high-tech competence from one country to another. However, the important point here is the idea behind the saying "Give a man a fish and you feed him for a day. Teach a man to fish and you feed him for a lifetime". In other words, it is better that the participating countries are given the opportunity of acquiring competence as opposed to only importing competence. This idea is enshrined in the concept "shared futures" and the win–win mechanisms that were affirmed by Xi Jinping when he announced the launching of the New Silk Road during an official visit to Kazakhstan in September 2013.[22] Zhongyuan (2020: 101–153) and Junxin (2020: 155–180) also confirm the above points.

Narratives for systemic competence

Case letter 1: China's economic growth and high-tech production

It has been evident for some time now that China's economy is almost as large as that of the United States. What is less well known, however, is the fact that the largest growth in the Chinese economy in 2020 was in the area of high-tech investments. While the value added of enterprises as a result of foreign investment grew by 2.4% in 2020, value added in high-tech production grew by 7.1%.[23] This is a clear indication that China is fully committed to moving up the production value chain.

The British Centre for Economic and Business Research (CEBR) estimates that the Chinese economy will grow by 5.7% annually for the next five years.[24] If we assume that the largest part of this growth will be manifested in the area of high-tech production, as occurred in 2020, then it is clear that China's economy is progressing at full speed up the value chain.

While in the past most of the economic growth was export-driven and based on cheap labour (from the 1980s to around 2012), today, the economic growth is, as the figures above show, moving towards high-tech production. In other words, the figures show that China is moving away from an economy based on exporting cheap consumer goods, towards becoming an economy with a greater focus on high-tech production. That is, this represents a transition from competing through low labour costs to competing through higher levels of expertise. In practice, the figures show that the new globalization based on expertise and high-tech production has moved the Chinese economy up the value chain, from producing "cheap shoes" and other consumer goods, to products based on artificial intelligence and other high-tech systems.

Description of systemic competence

Systemic competence increases in projects that demand both low-skilled workers and high-skilled workers (Myint, 2019). In such projects, the utilization of the entire competence potential is made visible. In a transition period, before the various countries have acquired the necessary high-tech expertise, it is important to facilitate the transfer of expertise between countries. However, the danger of such transfers of expertise is that it may lead to those countries without the necessary expertise becoming dependent on the country transferring the expertise. In the long run, this will lead to the "weaker" country not benefitting from collaboration, and becoming strategically dependent on the other country; such a situation will not promote the aim of shared futures and win–win projects, which is the strategic intention of the New Silk Road.[25]

Historically, China has been perceived as lying at the bottom of the global value chain without the necessary expertise to produce high-tech products. However, although this may have been the case in the 1980s, as has been shown in Case letter 1 above, this does not correspond with the prevailing reality in China today. China's competitive position in the old globalization was based on cheap labour, while its competitive position in the new globalization is based on high-tech expertise. There is much to suggest that as early as around the turn of the millennium, China could already compete with the United States in this area. The mass education and the expansion of technological universities in China also reached a point 2000–2012 where it could be compared to the United States (Linehan, 2018). The necessary prerequisite for moving a country up the global value chain is education. However, this is not sufficient. The sufficient prerequisite is linked to vertical specialization within the area of high technology. In practice, this means, as far as China is concerned, that the country specializes in technological innovations in e.g. artificial intelligence (Zhongyuan, 2020: 103–106). This is exactly what China has been doing since approx. 2012, with regard to the concepts "Made in China 2025" and the Dual Circulation Development Paradigm (Mantzopoulos & Shen, 2011; Ross & Bekkevold, 2016).

We have illustrated the description of systemic competence in Figure 4.9.

Analysis of systemic competence

The strategic intention of the New Silk Road projects is mutual learning, shared futures and win–win scenarios for the involved parties (Jinbo, 2020: 181–186).

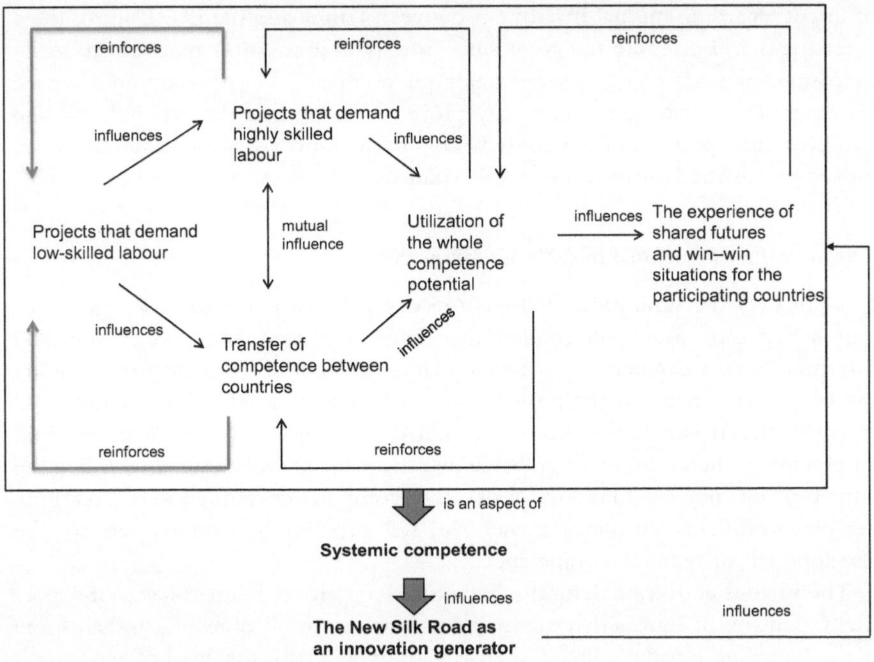

Figure 4.9 Systemic competence.

The projects that have been launched since the New Silk Road was announced in 2013 are many, and cover areas such as: finance, mutual investments, energy, science and technology, cultural exchange, transport and infrastructure, to name a few (Lim & Lim, 2020: 97–110). If we look at the projects geographically, then it is first and foremost the projects in Eurasia that are the most important. This can be explained by the fact that it is easier to develop projects near China. It can also be understood as an attempt to build a strong diplomatic wall around China's areas of interest, to prevent the United States from becoming the dominant strategic player in the region (Macaes, 2020). The development of the projects in Eurasia can also be understood as a geopolitical strategy to strengthen China in relation to the United States (Mahbubani, 2020). It is precisely the geopolitical positioning and the diplomatic wall that may prove to be China's Achilles' heel. If the partners in the projects along the New Silk Road do not perceive the projects as genuine projects in themselves, but interpret them as part of a geopolitical "game", then more countries may lose interest in the projects. It is therefore crucial for China and the New Silk Road initiative that the projects include reciprocity, technology transfer and win–win results for all the participants (Myint, 2019: 145–150).

It is possible that China has finally reached the point where it can counter US dominance effectively; this can be understood in relation to two agreements, both of which were entered into in late 2020, that is, at the end of the Trump administration. One is the free trade agreement between 15 countries in the Asia-Pacific region, the RCEP agreement.[26] The second agreement is the strategic agreement of intent regarding mutual investment between China and the EU. Both of these agreements will promote the New Silk Road as an innovation generator in terms of competence transfer between major geopolitical and geo-economic actors. However, these two agreements may prove to undermine the geo-political and geo-economic position of the United States in the innovation economy, and as we move towards the Fourth Industrial Revolution.

Theoretical points related to systemic competence

It is precisely the utilization of the entire competence potential of a country or region that can ensure full employment, even at a time when automation and robotization create insecurity in the job market in many areas. If the projects along the New Silk Road and the projects associated with the RCEP and China–EU agreements can ensure that both low-skilled and high-skilled workers can find employment, then it is highly probable that the projects will be successful. If at the same time it is possible to reduce obstacles to competence transfer, so that learning between countries can increase, then this will function as a prerequisite for the development of systemic competence.

The various countries along the New Silk Road have different levels of expertise. Countries in Europe have completely different levels of expertise than some of the New Silk Road countries, such as Laos, which has a low level of expertise.[27] Among the New Silk Road countries, Laos is perhaps the country that has the poorest education indicator (Gong & Mingjiang, 2020: 153–159). The country largely lacks access to foreign markets, has a poorly developed infrastructure and an underdeveloped economy (ibid.: 153). The country also lacks a rail system. An important investment for China here would be to develop a functioning rail system. If this is achieved, Laos will be able to reach external markets with its agricultural products.

Another country in the region that has a completely different economic and political foundation is Malaysia. The most important projects implemented as BRI projects in Malaysia are linked to railway development, energy development, and the development of several industrial parks for high-tech production (ibid.: 160–163).

The point of these two examples is to show that no matter what type of projects are implemented along the New Silk Road, it is the development and application of complementary competence aimed at using the entire competence potential, as well as the transfer of necessary competence between countries, which is important in order to promote systemic competence as an innovation generator along the New Silk Road.

We have illustrated a typology for systemic competence in Figure 4.10.

Practical utility for systemic competence

In practical politics, with regards to systemic competence, it is co-creation, shared-futures and win–win situations that is the strategic intention of the projects along the New Silk Road. However, history shows us that with regard to national

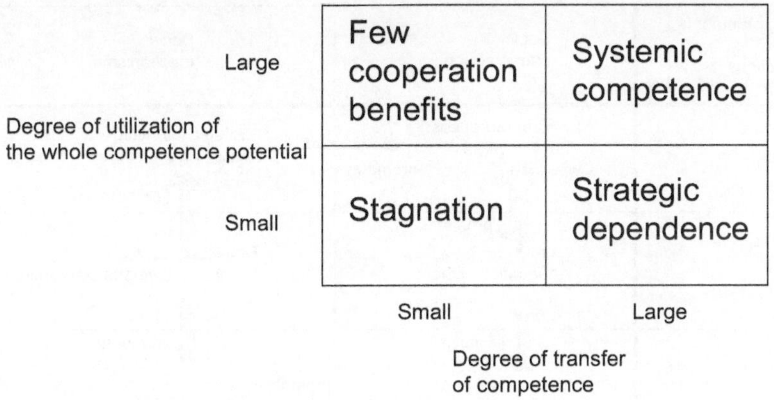

Figure 4.10 Systemic competence: A typology.

policies and the policies of large companies, that after projects are completed, there is often little or no competence left behind that the "weak" party can build on. This is why it is so important for the entire New Silk Road initiative to be able to point out that after each project is completed, competence has been developed in the countries and regions that have been involved in the project.

We can imagine a scenario where two large countries that have totally different policy preferences for the development and implementation of projects in other countries. One country is focused on win-lose thinking i.e. that even if all involved parties gain from the project in question, it is the country that invests the most that should make the largest profits. This may seem completely plausible, but the point is that it sends some clear signals down the system on how to negotiate and implement the projects. The other country in our scenario has a win–win policy as the basis for implementing projects. In our scenario, we have presented two different strategic intentions regarding policy directives. Of course, it is often the case that there may exist several policy directives, but we have presented a simplified scenario here in order to underline the point being made.

It is when the negotiations are completed and the project implementation has got off to a good start that the policy preferences will become evident. After a project has been completed it will also become evident to what extent the "weak" party has managed to develop competence in relation to the areas of competence relevant to the project in question, or whether the competence "disappears" after the project has been completed. If win-lose policy preferences prevail, then it is highly probable that dominance and competition will be the dominant logic. If the policy preferences are based on win–win, then it is highly probable that systemic competence will be developed, where co-creation and a shared-future will be the result. Therefore, it will be crucial for China and other countries that initiate such mega-projects, such as the New Silk Road, that they have clarified their strategic intentions.

In Figure 4.11, we have illustrated this description in a Boudon–Coleman diagram.

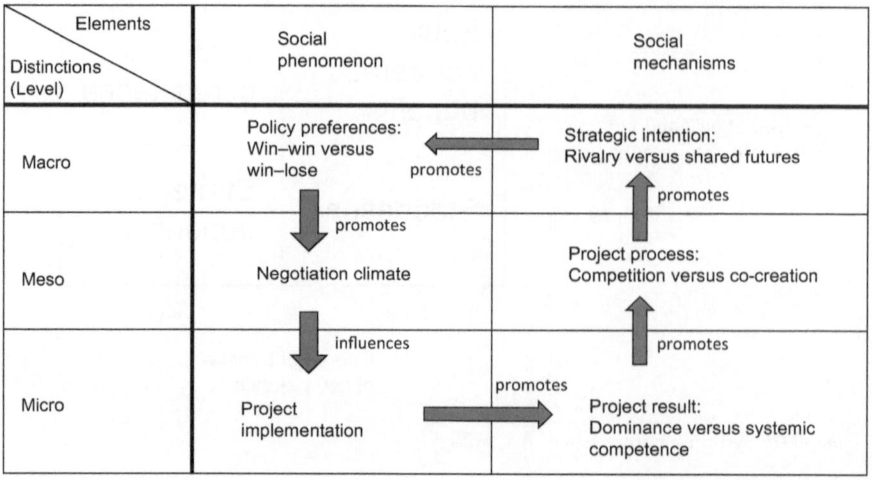

Figure 4.11 Policy preferences in mega-projects: The importance of systemic competence.

Sub-conclusion of systemic competence

In this section, we have examined the following question: How does systemic competence promote the New Silk Road as an innovation generator?

The short answer is that systemic competence promotes the New Silk Road as an innovation generator through the project preferences, and the strategic intention, which will be clarified between the parties involved in the projects. Specifically, this concerns a policy based on win–win, and a strategic intention based on a shared-future, which will make this possible.

Strategic implementation along the New Silk Road

In this section, we will examine the following question: How does strategic implementation promote the New Silk Road as an innovation generator?

The destruction of old methods of production in order to make room for new innovative methods of production is associated with Schumpeter's "creative destruction". When the old methods are destroyed, it takes time before those workers whose skills and expertise were related to the old methods are able to acquire new competence, so they can enter production based on the new technology. We refer to Schumpeter's "creative destruction" here, because it is closely related to strategic implementation and co-creation (Schumpeter, 1951, 1954, 1989). The point is that as a general rule co-creation will lead to innovation and new methods of production that replace old methods.

Narratives related to strategic implementation

Case letter 1: Strategic implementation and six types of sustainability

The New Silk Road, both along the land and maritime routes, will require cooperation and co-creation, so that the projects that are carried out are sustainable in many areas over a long period of time (Yuzhu, 2020: 211–225). Sustainability will be based on the following axes:

1 **Economic sustainability** will ensure that all project partners gain economically from participating in the project. Consequently, a win–win context should be ensured both as a positive result, but also as a process. A positive result is self-explanatory. Sustainability as a process is related to what was discussed in the previous section, namely that part of the competence that has been transferred will remain as competence after the project has been completed.
2 **Technological sustainability** is based on the principle that the technology that is used is structured around expertise that can be used later by all the project partners. In this way, the strategic implementation will ensure technology transfer and develop reciprocity in the project.
3 **Political sustainability**: In the strategic implementation, different political levels in the countries involved will come in to contact with each other. This will enable the development of political relations based on trust and mutual understanding of what a project's intention is. If at the political level it is possible to develop a common understanding of the strategic intention of a project ("why"), then it will be possible to survive many setbacks ("how"), or in the words of Nietzsche, "If We Have Our Own 'Why' of Life, We Shall Get Along with Almost Any 'How'" (1968, §12).[28]
4 **Diplomatic sustainability**: Political sustainability will form the basis of diplomatic relations. It is also the case in diplomatic relations that when you know what is the point of the relations ("why"), you will be able to cope with the many ways in which these relations may develop ("how").
5 **Social sustainability**: The social relations, or what is often referred to as: "people to people" relations, should also be developed in the strategic implementation of the projects, so that sustainability exists over a long period of time. Therefore, it will never be acceptable for relationships to be developed based on submissiveness and dominance. The mutual understanding and common acceptance of each other's differences should form the basis for the sustainability of social relations.
6 **Cultural sustainability**: The final axis for sustainability is cultural sustainability. In the same way as for the social relations, it concerns that the cultural relations should be based on the mutual acceptance of differences.

The strategic implementation of any project along the New Silk Road should be based on sustainability along all these axes.

Description of strategic implementation

Sustainability will be a key concept in ensuring the continued participation of the various countries in the projects over time. A well-functioning sustainability along the six axes mentioned in Case letter 1 will also be a necessary precondition for the development of reciprocity in the projects. The perceived and real reciprocity will be created through the collaboration that will be developed in the projects. In this context, it is important to be aware of the fact that every project is part of a larger whole. Therefore, it is always the project in its context that is decisive for the strategic implementation, and thus whether the project contributes to developing the New Silk Road as an innovation generator.

If China succeeds with the New Silk Road, both the maritime and land routes, then globalization will enter a phase that will be different from the globalization to which we have become accustomed. Metaphorically, one could say that the classic version of globalization was like a river where investments were sent downstream to producers who could manufacture consumer goods at low cost. The new version of globalization can be understood as a new river where competence is linked to hi-tech products. These products are distributed both domestically and also to other countries where they are in demand. The New Silk Road coincides with this new version of globalization, where mass education at university level is the social mechanism that promotes technological innovations. The new globalization will be characterized by the emergence of technological innovations. Mass education at university level in general, and technological competence in particular, are the social mechanisms that will drive the development of technology as a social phenomenon in the innovation economy. If we consider the co-creation effect in this perspective, then this will enable an understanding of the innovation economy along two axes: technology as a social phenomenon, and competence as a social mechanism. Such a perspective will be able to help project implementation both on an abstract level, but also in a practical context.

The reason is that any project in such a context can be evaluated along two simple axes:

1 Social phenomenon, that is, technological innovations. In this context, it is conceivable that both technology transfer but also technology development in the project will be subject to evaluation.
2 Social mechanism, that is, competence. Competence can also be evaluated in projects related to the ability of the project to transfer competence on the one hand, but also the project's ability to develop new competence. In this way, it can be established how much and what type of competence was left in the project context, after the project was completed.

We have illustrated the above description in Figure 4.12.

Analysis of strategic implementation

The New Silk Road is described by some writers as China's "Marshall Plan" for the countries and regions this economic corridor passes through (Feng & Liang, 2019). Such an understanding may of course be correct, but then from a perspective that the original Marshall Plan was developed by the US government as a "help to self-help". With the help of the Marshall Plan, Europe was able to rebuild its destroyed industries and infrastructure after World War II. However, the Marshall Plan was not an altruistic aid to Europe, but a strategic aid to build Europe, so that the United States could also reap the benefits from this aid.

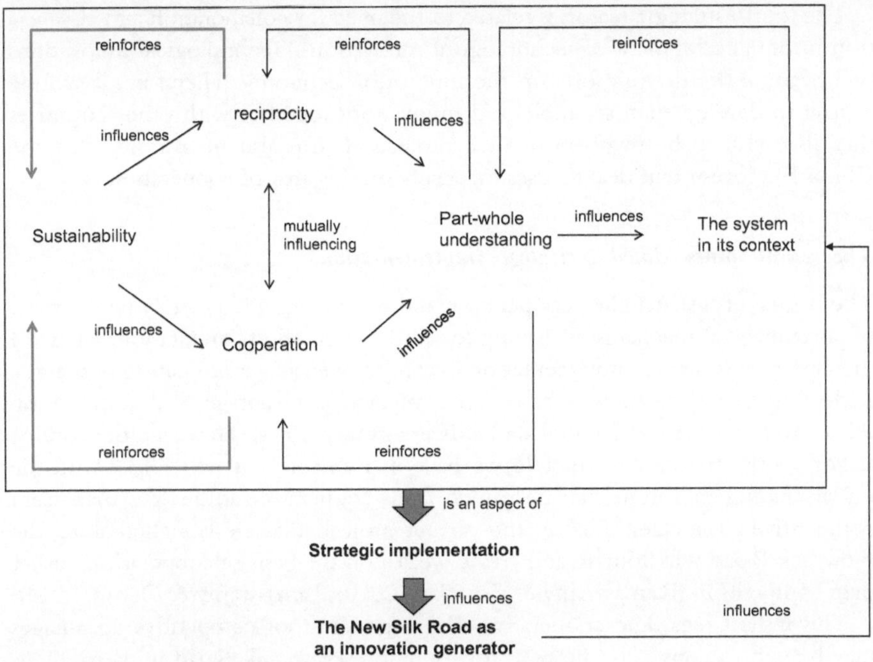

Figure 4.12 Strategic implementation: A conceptual model.

Understood in this way, the New Silk Road can also be compared to the original Marshall Plan.

What, then, is China's aim in launching and developing such a "Marshall Plan"? There are certainly many strategic reasons China's leaders may have for developing the New Silk Road as a mega-project, some of which seem obvious.

The first strategic reason is to enable China to circumvent American assertiveness in the South China Sea, but also in the East China Sea, and Taiwan in particular, by providing an economic, political and diplomatic corridor. If this is correct, as interpreted by many commentators – that the United States is increasingly focusing its interests in this region – then it is understandable that China wishes to create a corridor, a kind of back door, to provide a way out of a political, economic and diplomatic "blockade". This corridor has been strengthened by the RCEP free trade agreement, which was signed by 15 countries.[29]

The second strategic reason is to prevent the United States from dominating economic and technological relations with the countries that are part of the New Silk Road. In this connection, it is worth noting that in December 2020, the EU and China reached an agreement in principle regarding the investment deal, the Comprehensive Agreement on Investment (CAI).

The third strategic reason is the importance of importing raw materials or goods that it cannot efficiently produce, or is unable to produce, itself. For instance, this may concern the import of raw materials from countries in Africa, which have minerals that are crucial in the green economy, e.g. minerals needed in the production of computers and mobile phones, etc.

The fourth strategic reason is related to the need for collaboration and co-creation in the development of technological innovations. Technological innovations will become the driving force in the innovation economy. Therefore, it will be crucial to develop such technological innovations together with other countries that also wish to be involved in such projects. It can also be assumed that the China-EU investment deal focuses especially on this area of cooperation.

Theoretical points related to strategic implementation

The degree of sustainability, cooperation and reciprocity will possibly be the most important social mechanisms driving forward strategic implementation. Many of the aspects of strategic implementation may be viewed as a continuation of the free trade principle. Free trade is based on comparative advantage, and competition related to costs (Frey, 2019; Prahalad & Ramaswamy, 2004). However, the continuation of the free trade principle we have in mind here is rather based on the understanding that more can be gained from cooperative advantages than from competitive advantages. That is, the various projects that are launched along the New Silk Road will flourish and create wealth on the basis of cooperation, rather than competition (Ramaswamy & Gouillart, 2010; Ramaswamy & Ozcan, 2014).

This insight regarding cooperative advantages and not competitive advantages may be said to constitute the basis for the entire New Silk Road initiative. This idea will result in the development of cooperative relationships between companies and countries, and constitutes the basis if the strategic implementation of the sub-projects along the New Silk Road.

The basic concept in this cooperation is win–win, i.e. all the parties involved in the projects should benefit by putting cooperation before competition. In particular, cooperative benefits and win–win will apply to projects aimed at developing technological innovations. The reason is that innovation concerns transferring knowledge from one domain to another in order to create that which is new and innovative.

One objection to "cooperation benefits" and "win–win" is that the concepts are too theoretical and not necessarily helpful when developing and implementing concrete projects (Yuzhu, 2020: 212). In order to address this criticism, we have developed the typology in Figure 4.13. The typology may be understood as a first step to gaining a practical understanding of the concept of "strategic implementation".

Practical utility of strategic implementation

The strategic implementation of any project along the New Silk Road is constantly operating at different levels in terms of sustainability related to social phenomena. At a higher level (meta-level), this is related to political sustainability. The political sustainability is related to the parties' understanding and compliance with the projects' strategic intention. If a win–win approach constitutes one of the aspects of the strategic intention, then this should be evident in the practical context, measured along certain parameters that the parties have agreed on beforehand. Political sustainability is also linked to the understanding that multilateralism

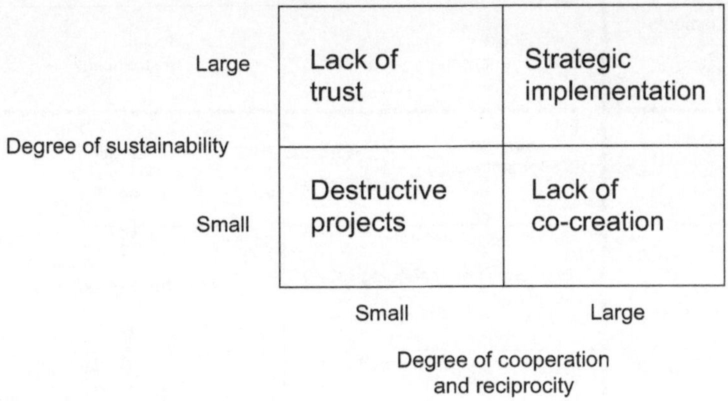

Figure 4.13 Strategic implementation: A typology.

should be a strategic intention of all the projects, and that this should be evident in the practical context. The opposite of multilateralism is unilateralism, where the strongest party benefits the most, while the weaker party takes what they are offered. Such a "winner-takes-all" thinking may soon lead to the failure of the New Silk Road projects.

At an intermediate level (meso-level) which is often equated with the organizational level in contrast to the metal-level which is the overall institutional level, two aspects of sustainability are important. These are technological sustainability and economic sustainability. The short description of these two aspects of sustainability at this level is the understanding that the parties involved are part of a shared future, where the project contributes to building competence, facilitating learning, increasing growth and enabling reciprocity in relation to economic and technological variables. These variables will differ from project to project, because different countries have different needs. For instance, this was exemplified above regarding the infrastructure project in Laos, and other types of projects in Malaysia.

The third level of sustainability is linked to the relationships that develop between the people who are involved in the projects. It is at this level that the cooperation is concretized and where different cultures meet in practical everyday situations. If these people-to-people relationships are not sustainable over time, then the projects will begin to fail, and the cooperation benefits will disappear. We may then risk being left with competitive advantages, where the strongest party benefits the most. In such a case, the whole strategic intention of the New Silk Road will disappear, resulting in detrimental consequences for China, the initiator of this mega-project.

However, there are various social mechanisms that can be used to explain the different social phenomena at the different levels of sustainability we have reviewed. These social mechanisms are also different for the different levels of sustainability mentioned above. In Figure 4.15 we have developed a Boudon–Coleman diagram to illustrate both the level of sustainability and the social mechanisms that can explain the phenomenon at the respective level.

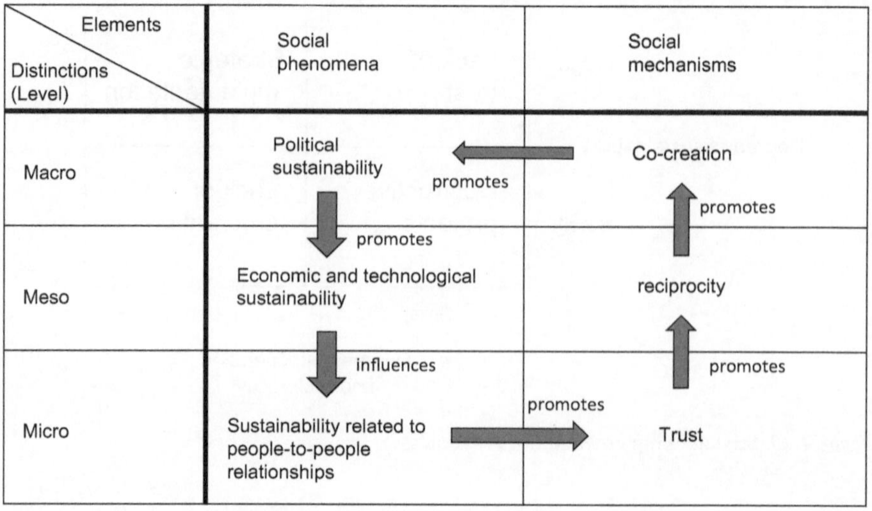

Figure 4.14 A Boudon–Coleman diagram illustrating co-creation.

Sub-conclusion for strategic implementation

We have examined the following question: How does strategic implementation promote the New Silk Road as an innovation generator?

The short answer is that a strategic understanding of the necessity of thinking in terms of sustainability at different levels should be ensured, at the same time as cooperation should ensure win–win situations for all the participants of the various projects.

Main conclusion related to co-creation to promote knowledge processes and innovation

In this chapter, we have examined the following research problem: How does the co-creation effect promote the New Silk Road as an innovation generator?

The short answer is that the co-creation effect promotes the New Silk Road as an innovation generator by means of four separate and systemically linked social mechanisms. These social mechanisms are:

1 Win–win strategy
2 Shared futures
3 Cooperation
4 Multilateralism

It seems reasonable to assume that the four social mechanisms correspond to the vision of the Chinese leaders. This vision is concretized along the land-based and maritime New Silk Road by means of the various concrete projects that are launched.

The New Silk Road also represents an overarching strategic vision for the Chinese leaders, so that China can side-step the US's economic, political and diplomatic assertiveness in the South China Sea and especially in the East China Sea and Taiwan Strait. By building a corridor towards Asia, the Middle East, Europe; Russia and Africa, China has a real opportunity to develop without the United States being able to dominate this development.

From 1980 to 2013, China has been transformed from a producer of cheap consumer goods to the West, to one that increasingly produces high-tech products both for the domestic market, but also to a growing market for countries along the New Silk Road (which was launched in 2013), as well as countries in Europe.

The period from 1980 to 2013 may be understood as the period of the old globalization, while the period from 2013 up until today may be understood as the new globalization. The old globalization was characterized by differences in labour costs between countries. The new globalization is characterized by differences in competences between countries. Low wages in the old globalization led to cheap goods being produced for the consumer market. Competence differences in the new globalization have led to the production of high-tech products and the development of technological innovations, which constitute the basis for the innovation economy.

Co-creation is both a motivating factor for the countries involved, but also a social mechanism that ensures sustainable relationships at different levels over a long period of time.

If one chooses to view the New Silk Road as an overarching plan for global interaction aimed at creating a better future for the majority, then the New Silk Road may also be viewed as a giant locomotive that is driving the world towards the Fourth Industrial Revolution based on multilateralism. This locomotive will transform the economy and political relations in China and the countries that are part of the New Silk Road.

Those countries that choose to stand on the side-lines and for various reasons are not coupled to this locomotive will have to operate along a different economic and political corridor. It is in this context that the United States is attempting to build an alternative to the New Silk Road. However, the United States has so far not attempted to launch an overall plan to achieve this. This could have been done by pursuing a Green New Deal strategy, but this is not practically possible at the moment due to the present political constellations within the United States. Thus, the countries that choose not to participate in the New Silk Road are connected to the United States, which historically was the driving force for economic development from 1945 to the 1980s. From the 1980s to 2013, the ideological thinking of the United States became fundamentally based on neoliberalism. In the United States, this ideology created a new super-rich class, while many others ended up with poorly paid jobs, and a future marked by hopelessness. On the other hand, neoliberalism led to a large-scale economic development of the Chinese economy. This economic expansion was so strong that many people in the West started to view China as a threat. This can also partly explain why the New Silk Road was launched in October 2013.

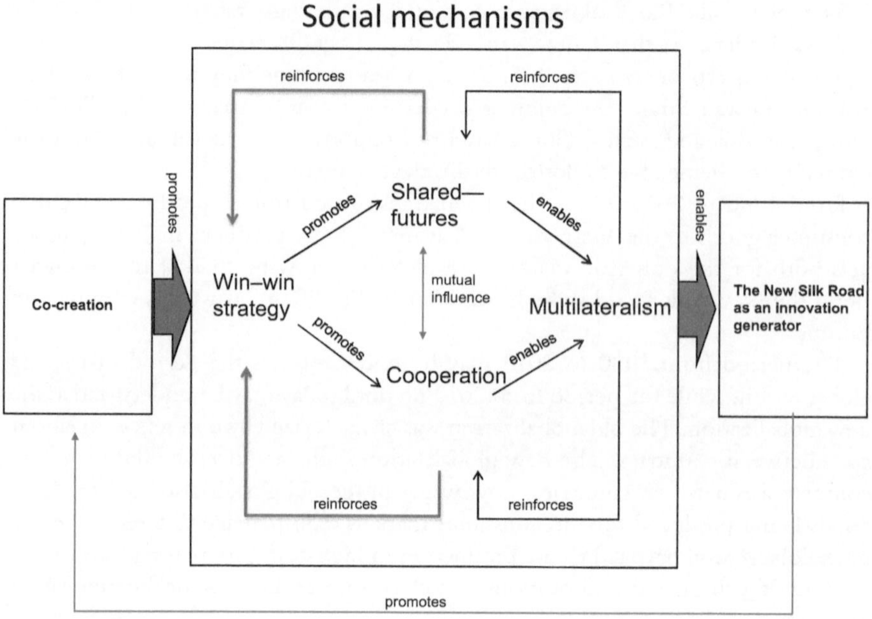

Figure 4.15 How the co-creation effect is promoting the New Silk Road as an innovation generator.

In 1978, Deng Xiaoping opened up China to foreign investment. In 2013, the launching of the New Silk Road opened up the possibility for China to make foreign investments. However, China's investments in the West is viewed as a security threat by many countries in the West, while foreign investment in China was viewed positively, because it led to large profits for a few in the West.

For China and the countries along the New Silk Road, the vision is that the projects will lead to cooperation and a shared future, based on a win–win strategy and multilateralism, i.e. where it is not a single party that dominates, but where decisions are made by all the parties involved on the basis of dialogue and reciprocity.

Figure 4.15 shows how the co-creation effect, by the means of social mechanisms, is promoting the New Silk Road as an innovation generator.

Notes

1 These elements are generated from the research of the following authors: Batzhan et al. (2020); Bougon (2017); Boutrup (2019); Drache et al. (2019); Fannin (2019); Hawke (2020); Holslag (2019); Jacques (2012); Jianglin (2020a, 2020b); Johannessen (2021); Linehan (2018); Macaes (2020); Mahbubani (2020); Pavlicevic (2019); Ross & Bekkevold (2016); Vangeli (2017, 2018, 2019); Wang (2015, 2016, 2017a, 2017b, 2017c); Wasif Khan (2019); Xing (2019); Yang (2015); Yuan (2019); Yue & Fujian (2019); Yunker (2014); Zou (2018).

2 https://en.wikipedia.org/wiki/Regional_Comprehensive_Economic_Partnership.

3 https://www.lmd.no/2021/01/frihandelsbombe-i-asia/ January, 2021; written by Martine Bulard.

4 Johannessen (2021); Vangeli (2017, 2018, 2019); Wah & Menkhoff (2020); Wang (2015, 2016, 2017a, 2017b, 2017c, 2020); Wasif Khan (2019).
5 Johannessen (2021); Vangeli (2017, 2018, 2019); Yang (2015); Wasif Khan (2019).
6 Johannessen (2021); Vangeli (2017, 2018, 2019); Wah & Menkhoff (2020); Wang (2015, 2016, 2017a, 2017b, 2017c, 2020); Yang (2015); Wasif Khan (2019).
7 The four banks are: The Bank of China, Industrial and Commercial Bank of China and the China Construction Bank, Agricultural Bank of China (MYINT, 2019: 143).
8 Johannessen (2021); Vangeli (2017, 2018, 2019); Wah & Menkhoff (2020); Wang (2015, 2016, 2017a, 2017b, 2017c, 2020); Yang (2015); Wasif Khan (2019).
9 The sixth land bridge also includes India, but there is still political opposition, and the United States is attempting to stem China's expansion by supporting alternative development in India. Therefore, it is unlikely, but still possible, that India will be drawn into the New Silk Road.
10 https://global.chinadaily.com.cn/a/202011/14/WS5faf2ad4a31024ad0ba94031.html.
11 https://www.chinadaily.com.cn/a/201909/18/WS5d81fdeda310cf3e3556c37f.html. https://news.yahoo.com/trade-war-dims-outlook-u-150943878.html?guccounter=1&guce_referrer=aHR0cHM6Ly9yLnNlYXJjaC55YWhvby5jb20vX3lsdD1Bd3JKSWt1bk9BRmdtOE1BWGd3blBneC47X3lsdT1ZMjlzYndNRWNHOXpBeklFZG5ScFpBTUVjMlZqQTNOeS9SVj0yL1JFPTE2MTA3MjE1NzYvUk89MTAvUlU9aHR0cHMlM2ElMmYlMmZuZXdzLnlhaG9vLmNvbSUyZnRyYWRlLXdhci1kaW1zLW91dGxvb2stdS0xNTA5NDM4NzguaHRtbC9SSz0yL1JTPUJkbWhuLjBCSHRoX3FGWjN4QVBRekczWVQ3OC0&guce_referrer_sig=AQAAABD35W6Ef-qMhmRAK3os3_E8v7cloW2kOU4BgXyhJnOKctjPwlhx_uXDd1dC-mfqHVFmHqIsKB49MddfXFLdXTmjLdc7K1aHSEBpTxVEbfGfG2uFvtqitg51c2x2nWiW49t_nx-4eRgkW-Rq42wjS1dccER-Yx--irSXpw7ZNI12.
12 https://www.oxfordeconomics.com.
13 https://www.europarl.europa.eu/thinktank/en/document.html?reference=EPRS_BRI(2020)659407.
14 https://global.chinadaily.com.cn/a/202101/12/WS5ffcf7f5a31024ad0baa1e89.html.
15 Angang (2014); Batzhan et al. (2020); Beeson & Li (2016); Berlie & Hung (2020); Bougon (2017); Brown (2018, 2019); Drache et al. (2019); Jianglin (2020a, 2020b); Johannessen (2021); Vangeli (2019).
16 Clinton (2011); Economy (2018); Hamilton (2018); Holslag (2019); Huang (2017); Jacques (2012); Lim & Lim (2020); Linehan (2018); Linggui (2020); Magnus (2018); Mahbubani (2009, 2010, 2014, 2018, 2020); Mearsheimer (2010).
17 BRI: Belt and Road Initiative. OBOR: One Belt One Road.
18 Kahneman & Tversky (1979: 263–292). Daniel Kahneman was awarded the Nobel Prize in Economics in 2002 for the work he did together with Amos Tversky on decision-making in relation to uncertainty, including prospect theory.
19 This is originally an idea of Schumpeter (1954: 1058), where he says about decisions that they have "a much better claim to being called a logic of choice than a psychology of value".
20 https://en.wikipedia.org/wiki/Belt_and_Road_Initiative.
21 https://en.wikipedia.org/wiki/Regional_Comprehensive_Economic_Partnership.
22 https://en.wikipedia.org/wiki/Belt_and_Road_Initiative.
23 http://english.www.gov.cn/policies/infographics/202101/19/content_WS6006bf16c6d0f72576944225.html.
24 https://global.chinadaily.com.cn/a/202101/22/WS600a21c9a31024ad0baa453a.html.
25 Angang (2014); Batzhan et al. (2020); Beeson & Li (2016); Berlie & Hung (2020); Bougon (2017); Brown (2018, 2019); Drache et al. (2019); Jianglin (2020a, 2020b); Johannessen (2021); Vangeli (2019).
26 https://en.wikipedia.org/wiki/Regional_Comprehensive_Economic_Partnership.
27 Officially called Lao People's Democratic Republic: https://en.wikipedia.org/wiki/Laos.

28 In the original German: "Hat man sein warum? des Lebens, so verträgt man sich fast mit jedem wie?".

29 https://en.wikipedia.org/wiki/Regional_Comprehensive_Economic_Partnership.

References

Allison, G. (2018). *Destined for war: Can America and China escape Thucydides' trap?* Scribe, London.

Angang, H. (2014). Silk road economic belt: Strategic considerations, positioning and implementation routes. *Journal of Xinjiang Normal University*, 2: 1–10.

Batzhan, A., Alpysbayeva, S. & Kapsalyamova, Z. (2020). The Belt and Road initiative: Case of Kazakhstan. In Wah, C.Y., Menkhoff, T. & Low, L. (Eds.), *China's Belt and Road initiative: Understanding the dynamics of a global transformation*, World Scientific, London. pp. 71–97.

Beeson, M. & Li, F. (2016). China's place in regional and global governance: A new world comes into view. *Global Policy*, 7, 4: 491–499.

Berlie, J.A. & Hung, S. (2020). The Greater Bay Area and the role of Hong Kong and Macau SARs in the Belt and Road initiative. In Berlie, J.A. (Ed.), *China's globalization and the Belt and Road initiative*, Palgrave, London. pp. 77–100.

Bougon, F. (2017). *Xi Jinping*, Hurst & Company, London.

Boutrup, C. (2019). *The great tech revolution, How China is shaping our future*, Saxo Business, Copenhagen.

Brown, K. (2018). *China's dream*, Polity, London.

Brown, K. (2019). *The world according to Xi*, I.B. Tauris, London.

Byrre, D. & Gallaghan, G. (2013). *Complexity theory and the social sciences*, Routledge, London.

Clinton, H. (2011). America's Pacific century, *Foreign Policy*, 189, 11 Oct.

Drache, D., Kingsmith, A.T. & Qi, D. (2019). *One road many dreams: China's bold plan to remake the global economy*, Bloomsbury, New York.

Economy, E.C. (2018). *The third revolution, Xi Jinping and the new Chinese state*, Oxford University Press, Oxford.

Fang, N. & Fu, Y. (2020). *China's Political system*, Springer, London.

Fannin, R.A. (2019). *Tech titans of China*, Nicholas Brealey Publishing, London.

Feng, D.H. & Liang, H.M. (2019). *Belt and Road initiative: Chinese version of Marshall Plan*, World Scientific, London.

French, H.W. (2015). *China's second continent*, Random House, London.

Frey, C.B. (2019). *The technology trap*, Princeton University Press, Princeton, NJ.

Gong, X. & Mingjiang, L. (2020). The Belt and Road initiative: Progress and prospect in southeast Asia. In Wah, C.Y., Menkhoff, T. & Low, L. (Eds.), *China's Belt and Road initiative: Understanding the dynamics of a global transformation*, World Scientific, London. pp. 151–176.

Hamilton, C. (2018). *Silent invasion: China's influence in Australia*, Hardie Grant Books, New York.

Hawke, G. (2020). Economic historical development and leadership underlying the BRI strategy. In Wah, C.Y., Menkhoff, T. & Low, L. (Eds.), *China's Belt and Road initiative: Understanding the dynamics of a global transformation*, World Scientific, London. pp. 19–43.

Hoang, N.H. (2019). The Belt and Road initiative: Vietnam's perspective. In Yue, Y. & Fujian, L. (Eds.), *The Belt and Road initiative: ASEAN countries' perspectives*, World Scientific, London. pp. 233–252.

Holslag, J. (2019). *The Silk Road trap*, Polity, London.

Huang, Y. (2017). *Cracking the China conundrum: Why conventional economic wisdom is wrong?* Oxford University Press, Oxford.

Jacques, M. (2012). *When China rules the world*, Penguin, London.

Jianglin, Z. (2020a). Introduction. In Jianglin, Z. (Ed.), *21st century maritime Silk Road initiative, aims and objectives, implementation strategies and policy recommendations*, World Scientific, London. pp. 3–30.

Jianglin, Z. (2020b). Macroeconomic basis for the 21st century maritime Silk Road initiative. In Jianglin, Z (Ed.), *21st-century maritime Silk Road initiative, aims and objectives, implementation strategies and policy recommendations*, World Scientific, London. pp. 59–100.

Jinbo, W. (2020). The 21st century maritime Silk Road and Asian Infrastructure connectivity. In Jianglin, Z. (Ed.), *21st century maritime Silk Road initiative, aims and objectives, implementation strategies and policy recommendations*, World Scientific, London. pp. 181–209.

Johannessen, J.-A. (2021). *The innovation economy in China*, Routledge, London.

Junxin, S. (2020). Global value chain and the 21st century maritime Silk Road. In Jianglin, Z. (Ed.), *21st century maritime Silk Road initiative, aims and objectives, implementation strategies and policy recommendations*, World Scientific, London. pp. 155–210.

Kahneman, D. (2011). *Thinking fast and slow*, Allen Lane, New York.

Kahneman, D. & Tversky, A. (1979). An analysis of decision under risk. *Econometrica, Journal of the Econometric Society*, 47, 2: 263–292.

Lim, J. & Lim, D. (2020). Financing the OBOR initiative. In Wah, C.Y., Menkhoff, T. & Low, L. (Eds.), *China's Belt and Road initiative: Understanding the dynamics of a global transformation*, World Scientific, London. pp. 97–125.

Linehan, P.M. (2018). *The culture of leadership in contemporary China*, Lexington Books, London.

Linggui, W. (2020). Foreword. In Jianglin, Z. (Ed.), *21st century maritime Silk Road initiative, aims and objectives, implementation strategies and policy recommendations*, World Scientific, London. pp. v–xiii.

Macaes, B. (2020). *Belt and Road: A Chinese world order*, C. Hurst, London.

Magnus, G. (2018). *Red flags, Why Xi's China is in jeopardy*, Yale University Press, New Haven, CT.

Mahbubani, K. (2009). *The new Asian hemisphere: The irresistible shift of global power to the east*, Public Affairs, London.

Mahbubani, K. (2010). *Can Asian think?* Marshall Cavendish, Singapore.

Mahbubani, K. (2014). *Great convergence: ASIA, the West, and the logic of one world*, Public Affairs, New York.

Mahbubani, K. (2018). *Has the west lost*, Allen Lane, New York.

Mahbubani, K. (2020). *Has China won?* Public Affairs, London

Mantzopoulos, V. & Shen, R. (2011). *The Political economy of China's systemic transformation*, Palgrave, London.

McDermott, R. (2001). *Risk-taking in international politics: Prospect theory in American foreign policy*, The University of Michigan Press, Ann Arbor.

Mearsheimer, J. (2010). The gathering storm: China's challenge to US power in Asia. *Chinese Journal of International Politics*, 3, 4;381–396.

Myint, K. (2019). Synergizing BRI and Myanmar's development agenda. In Yue, Y. & Fujian, L. (Eds.), *The Belt and Road initiative: ASEAN countries' perspectives*, World Scientific, London. pp. 141–164.

Pavlicevic, D. (2019). A power shift underway in Europe? China's relationship with central and eastern Europe under the Belt and Road initiative. In Xing, L. (Ed.), *Mapping China's One Belt One Road initiative*, Palgrave, London. pp. 249–278.

Pieters, M. & Jansen, S. (2017). *The 7 principles of complete co-creation*, BIS Publishers, Amsterdam.

Prahalad, K.C. & Ramaswamy, V. (2004). *The future of competition: Co-creating unique value with customers*. Harvard Business School Press, Boston, MA.

Ramaswamy, V. & Gouillart, F. (2010). *The power of co-creation: Build it with them to boost growth, productivity, and profits*. Free Press, New York.

Ramaswamy, V. & Ozcan, K. (2014). *The co-creation paradigm*, Stanford University Press, Stanford, CA.

Ross, R. & Bekkevold, J.I. (2016). *China in the era of Xi Jinping*, Georgetown University Press, Washington DC.

Schumpeter, J. (1951). *Theory of economic development*, Harvard University Press, Boston, MA.

Schumpeter, J. (1954). *History of economic analysis*, Oxford University Press, Oxford.

Schumpeter, J. (1989). *Business cycles*, Porcupine Press, New York.

Vangeli, A. (2017). China's engagement with the sixteen countries of central, east and southeast Europe under the Belt and Road initiative. *China & World Economy*, 25, 5: 101–124.

Vangeli, A. (2018). Normative foundation of the Belt and Road initiative. In Wenhua, S., Nuotio, K. & Zhang, K. (Eds.), *Normative readings of the Belt and Road initiative*, Springer, London, pp. 59–83.

Vangeli, A. (2019). A framework for the study of One Belt One Road initiative as a medium of principle diffusion. In Xing, L. (Ed.), *Mapping China's One Belt One Road initiative*, Palgrave Macmillan, London. pp. 57–89.

Vis, B. (2010). *Politics of risk-taking*, Amsterdam University Press, Amsterdam.

Wah, C.Y. & Menkhoff, T. (2020). Introduction: Understanding the transformational power of China's Belt and Road initiative. In Wah, C.Y., Menkhoff, T. & Low, L. (Eds.), *China's Belt and Road initiative: Understanding the dynamics of a global transformation*, World Scientific, London. pp. xxiii–xxxviii.

Wang, D. (2020). *Reigning the future*, New Degree Press, New York.

Wang, Y. (2015). *One Belt One Road: Opportunities and challenges*, People's Press, Beijing.

Wang, Y. (2016). *The Belt and Road initiative: What will China offer the world in its rise*, New World Press, Beijing.

Wang, Y. (2017a). *Belt and Road initiative: China's responsibilities in its rise*, People's Press, Beijing.

Wang, Y. (2017b). *China connects the world: What behind the Belt and Road initiative*, China Intercontinental Press, Beijing.

Wang, Y. (2017c). *The world is connected: The logic of Belt and Road initiative*, The Commercial Press, Beijing.

Wasif Khan, S. (2019). *Haunted by chaos, China's grand strategy from Mao Zedong to Xi Jinping*, Harvard University Press, Cambridge, Mass.

Wolfe, W.M. (2008). *Winning the war of words*, Praeger, London.

Xing, L. (2019). Understanding the multiple facets of China's "One Belt One Road" initiative. In Xing, L. (Ed.), *Mapping China's One Belt One Road initiative*, Palgrave Macmillan, London. pp. 29–56.

Yang, J. (2015). China's new diplomacy under the Xi Jinping administration. *China Quarterly of International Strategic Studies*, 1, 1: 1–17.

Yuan, F. (2019). The One Belt One Road initiative and China's multi-layered multilateralism. In Xing, L. (Ed.), *Mapping China's one belt one road initiative*, Palgrave, London. pp. 91–116.

Yue, Y. & Fujian, L. (2019). ASEAN- China cooperation under the framework of the Belt and Road initiative: A comparative study on the perspectives of China and ASEAN. In Yue, Y. & Fujian, L. (Eds.), *The Belt and Road initiative: ASEAN countries' perspectives*, World Scientific, London. pp. 1–58.

Yunker, J. (2014). *Global Marshall plan: Theory and evidence*, Lexington, London.

Yuzhu, W. (2020). New regional cooperation and integration strategy and the 21st-century maritime Silk Road initiative. In Jianglin, Z. (Ed.), *21st century maritime Silk Road initiative, aims and objectives, implementation strategies and policy recommendations*, World Scientific, London. pp. 211–225.

Zhang, J. (2015). China's new foreign policy under Xi Jinping: Towards peaceful rise 2.0? *Global Change, Peace & Security*, 27, 1: 5–19.

Zhongyuan, Z. (2020). Microeconomic basis for the 21st century maritime Silk Road initiative: From the perspective of a value chain. In Jianglin, Z. (Ed.), *21st century maritime Silk Road initiative, aims and objectives, implementation strategies and policy recommendations*, World Scientific, London. pp. 101–154.

Zou, L. (2018). *The political economy of China's Belt and Road initiative*, World Scientific, London.

5 Feed forward

The transition from the old globalization to the new globalization

Key points in this chapter

General

- The connections between the infrastructure projects and info-structure projects along the New Silk Road will ensure the transition from the old globalization to the new globalization.

Global expectations

- As of 2021, 40 African countries have signed various agreements related to New Silk Road projects.
- Apart from launching and developing the New Silk Road with the intention of stimulating the economies of China and other participating countries, it seems reasonable to assume that the Chinese leaders also have additional intentions.
- It is most probable the ideological and political differences that hinder cooperation between the United States and China, because cooperation would benefit both countries economic development.
- It seems reasonable to assume that two main categories of projects will be developed and implemented: infrastructure projects and info-structure projects. This has become evident with regard to the many New Silk Road projects that have already been launched in various countries.
- If the New Silk Road projects demand varying levels of competence and expertise, then the so-called "automation debate", regarding the danger of mass unemployment, will become a non-topic in the development of a fully-fledged innovation economy.
- One consequence of the double commitment to both infrastructure and info-structure projects along the New Silk Road will be the emergence of two categories of entrepreneurship projects. These will be based on "classical" entrepreneurship and innovative entrepreneurship.
- When both of these types of entrepreneurship projects operate side by side, the market will be in a state of constant change.

DOI: 10.4324/9781003316978-5

Shared futures

- The New Silk Road can be understood as a global "Marshall Plan".
- 5G and 6G networks will enable global production, distribution and consumption to reach new levels.
- 5G networks, and later 6G networks, will enable the development from intelligent robots to intelligent informats on a global scale.
- When new knowledge is developed in one location, all the intelligent robots and intelligent informats will immediately be able to share in this new knowledge. Such an interconnection via 5G and 6G networks will facilitate improvements in various fields, such as the health sector, where it will improve medical operative expertise that will save lives.
- More than 800 million people have been lifted out of poverty in China since 1978. This has led to other countries viewing the Chinese political system in a more positive light, which is reflected in China's success in establishing and signing the RCEP free trade agreement.
- The New Silk Road and all the projects it has triggered has led to many countries entering into trade and investment agreements with China, including the 14 other countries in the Asia-Pacific region in the autumn of 2020 (RCEP), and the agreement of intent regarding mutual investment between China and the EU (December 2020).
- China's strengthened global position has also led to strong opposition against China gaining more economic influence in the West.
- The strategy of the leaders before Xi Jinping may be expressed by the axiom, "Hide your strength, bide your time". However, when Xi Jinping became president in 2012, China began to show its strength as we move towards the Fourth Industrial Revolution.
- We know from economic history that innovations, almost without exception, lead to social tensions and conflicts. The New Silk Road will be no exception in this regard.

Win–win ideology

- A win–win ideology emphasizes cooperative and co-creation advantages at the expense of competitive advantages.
- When competition gives way to cooperation and co-creation, it will be possible to address global challenges more effectively.
- There is much to suggest that cooperation will be a more effective strategy in the innovation economy, than the competition that prevailed in the industrial economy.
- Metaphorically, the New Silk Road may be viewed as a new global "Marshall Plan".
- Our perspective is that China needs to offer the United States some strategic advantages, in order to prevent the entire New Silk Road initiative from culminating in Thucydides' Trap.

- If we assume that the innovation economy is driven by cooperative advantages, and not so much by competitive advantages, then some countries will be better equipped than others to become leaders in the innovation economy.
- In addition to cooperation and co-creation benefits, those countries and regions that have a large degree of interconnected systems at all levels will be more likely to develop innovations.
- The greater the degree of interconnected systems at all levels, and the greater number of over-arching institutions that can promote co-creation, the greater the likelihood that a win–win ideology will be supported and developed.
- Innovations are mainly a result of cooperation and co-creation. Therefore, cooperative advantages will be preferred to competitive advantages in the innovation economy.
- Some cultures are more cooperation and co-creation oriented than other cultures. These cultures have comparative cooperative advantages.
- If China is unable to solve the Thucydides' Trap problem, and the problem regarding which role the USA will have in the innovation economy, then it is probable that conflicts will arise and the win–win ideology of the New Silk Road will suffer, resulting in a win-lose ideology gaining precedence.

The new mindset

- The new mindset in our context means that rule-based systems will dominate, at the same time as there is a large degree of systemic cooperation and co-creation.
- By the new mindset, we mean there is a focus on dialogue and collective solutions rather than competition, dominance and unilateral approaches.
- The new mindset in our context represents a transition from unilateralism to multilateralism.
- In multilateral relationships, dialogue between parties is crucial when making decisions.
- Unilateralism refers to decisions and actions that do not take into consideration the interests of the other parties, and actions are often based on the strength of the unilateral party.
- The New Silk Road may be understood as a way of integrating China into the emerging innovation economy.
- The launching and the development of the New Silk Road may be understood in relation to the growing tensions between the United States and China in the innovation economy.
- It is a paradox that the stronger China becomes economically and technologically, the greater will be the counterforces that will attempt to reduce China's growing strength.
- The counterforces may emerge in the form of Thucydides' Trap or by the "contamination trap".
- The "New Silk Road" acts as a metaphor giving the network of projects involved in the initiative a common direction.

- The primary strategic intention of the New Silk Road is economic growth.
- The New Silk Road has four secondary strategic intentions: to increase cultural understanding, to foster people-to-people relations, to enhance diplomatic relations and to develop innovative co-creation.
- The new "grand strategy" is demonstrated in relation to the investments made in the New Silk Road, the Dual Circulation Development Paradigm and Made in China 2025.
- Since 2013, a new mindset has changed China's global position. This new mindset is a transition from China "hiding its strength, and biding its time" (which characterized the period from 1978 to 2013), to 2013 onwards, when China started to show its strength as it takes on an assertive role in the global economy.

New globalization

- The major problems and challenges in today's world are mainly global.
- Global sustainability is the common denominator of the new globalization
- The old globalization was characterized by competition based on low costs.
- The old globalization led to de-industrialization in the industrialized countries and increased industrialization in the countries with low costs, such as low labour costs.
- The new globalization is based on competition for competence in general, and high-tech competence in particular.
- The development of high-tech innovation necessitates the use of a cooperative model.
- The new globalization has gained two centres of power. The first is China and the countries connected through the New Silk Road, and the RCEP free trade agreement. The second is a technology alliance led by the United States.
- The degree of high-tech competence, and the degree of technological innovations, will determine how the new globalization emerges.
- There are four institutional innovations in China, which may be decisive for how China manifests its economic strength in the new globalization. These four institutional innovations are: The New Silk Road, the RCEP free trade agreement, Made in China 2025, and the Dual Circulation Development Paradigm.
- China has a two-sided lead in the new globalization. First, China has more students completing high-tech education than all the countries in the West considered together. Second, the wage levels of the high-skilled workers in China is much lower than for the same group in the West.

Main conclusion

- The main philosophical idea behind the vision of the New Silk Road is that when you share with others, you will receive more in return.

Introduction

In our context in this chapter, the feedforward effect refers to expectations regarding the national sub-production of the countries along the New Silk Road. Feedforward relates to the future through an expectation mechanism. It is the expectations we have for the future that will affect our actions in the present (Richardson, 1991). Of course, expectations are not the same as implementation, but the expectations provide guidelines for the specific plans, projects and their implementation.

The expectations that the Chinese leadership have of the New Silk Road can be read in the various speeches, communiques, and other communications made by Xi Jinping and other Chinese leaders.[1]

The strategic vision in relation to the social mechanism feedforward for the New Silk Road can be formulated in relation to five elements:

1 **Global expectations**: Regarding this element, cooperation is more important than competition (Batzhan et al., 2020; Bougon, 2017; Wang, 2015, 2016, 2017a, 2017b, 2017c).
2 **Shared futures**: This concerns relations that are based on opportunities and not "threats" (Boutrup, 2019; Drache et al., 2019; Fannin, 2019; Wasif Khan, 2019; Xing, 2019).
3 **Win–win economy**: This relates to thinking based on "what benefits the other party or parties involved in the project?" (Hawke, 2020; Holslag, 2019; Jacques, 2012; Yang, 2015; Yuan, 2019; Yunker, 2014; Zou, 2018).
4 **New mindset**: Here the focus is on collective decisions rather than unilateral ones. This also involves a ruled-based global system, as opposed to a system based on power, dominance and position. In other words, the new mindset is based on systemic global collaboration (Jianglin, 2020a, 2020b; Johannessen, 2021a; Linehan, 2018; Macaes, 2020; Mahbubani, 2020)
5 **New globalization**: This is characterized by the development of technological innovations and high-tech production. The old globalization from the 1980s until approx. 2013 was characterized by wage differences, whereas, the new globalization is characterized by differences in competency (Pavlicevic, 2019; Ross & Bekkevold, 2016; Vangeli, 2017, 2018, 2019; Yue & Fujian, 2019).

The common denominator for the projects that are being initiated is that they will ensure the physical and communication connections between countries along the New Silk Road. These infrastructure projects and info-structure projects[2] will ensure the demand for competence along the entire value chain, i.e. employing both low-skilled and high-skilled workers.

Competence as an "irrigation system" in the future economy is crucial due to global competition. This is an important reason why high-tech knowledge is a necessary prerequisite for wealth creation in the knowledge society. The new technology includes, amongst others, micro-electronics, telecommunications, computers, bio-engineering, new materials and molecular engineering as well as various types of networks, such as Internet. The new technology enables us to produce, communicate, organize, distribute and consume in different ways than before. For instance, the network architecture of Internet is not controlled by any single body, but consists of autonomous systems. In this context, sophisticated systems of intelligence that are networked become a form of collective intelligence.

The new technology promotes a communication and network logic. This logic can be understood as a transition from infrastructure to info-structure (information structure). While infrastructure provided the industrial society with an analytical tool, the info-structure provides the knowledge society with an analytical tool.

The info-structure is the processes that enable the development, transfer, analysis, storage, coordination and handling of data, information and knowledge. The info-structure forms the basis for communication processes and thus also the development of new cooperation networks. It is precisely the development of the new info-structure that enables the development of new cooperation networks, and new forms of organization and management. While the infrastructure enables the transport of goods, services and energy, the info-structure enables coordination and integration on a hitherto unknown scale. It is precisely through the info-structure that the interactions in the knowledge society develop in the global economy.

The info-structure consists of ten critical processes (Miller, 1978):

- Information control
- Information channels and networks for communication
- Information gathering
- Information analysis
- Information strategy
- Information structuring and systematization
- Information coordination
- Information storage and retrieval
- Information culture
- Information transmission.

The connections between the infrastructure projects and info-structure projects along the New Silk Road will ensure the transition from the old globalization to the new globalization. This can be explained by the fact that global expectations, the new mindset, shared futures and win–win concepts will function as mechanisms enabling the development and transfer of expertise to the countries along the New Silk Road, which will help to bring them one step closer to being able to compete in the new globalization.

The Chinese leaders have repeatedly pointed out that the New Silk Road is not in competition with the other agreements China has in the region, e.g. the projects within ASEAN, Shanghai Cooperation Organization, etc. (Horesh, 2018: 1).

We have summarized the introduction in the conceptual model in Figure 5.1. Figure 5.1 also shows how this chapter is organized.

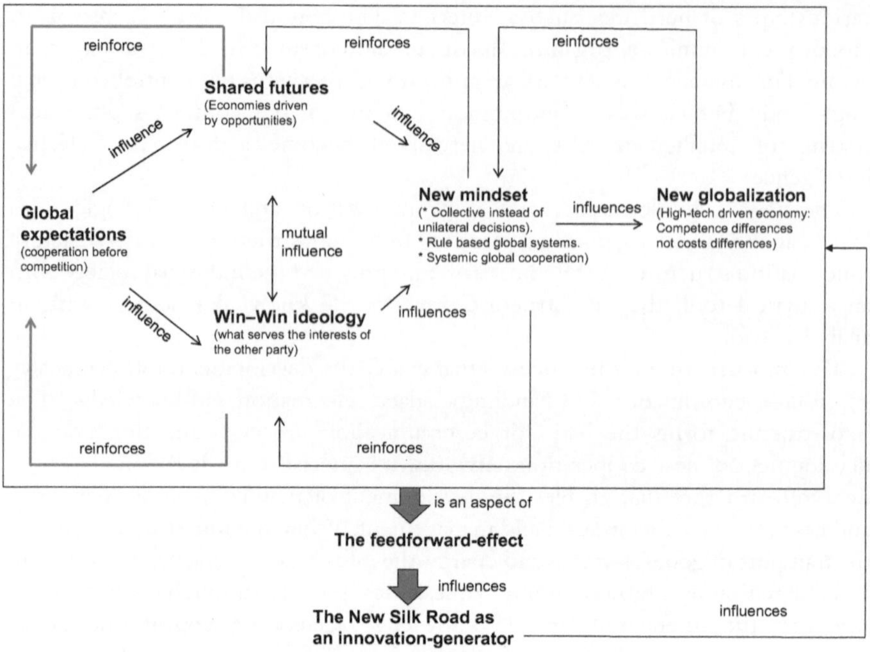

Figure 5.1 Feedforward.

Global expectations for joining the New Silk Road

In this section, we will examine the following question: How do global expectations promote the New Silk Road as an innovation generator?

Global expectations are evident in all the countries on different continents that have signed agreements concerning mutual projects along the maritime and land-based New Silk Road (Wah & Menkhoff, 2020). To take the Middle East as an example, arch-enemies such as Israel and Iran have entered into agreements for participation in sub-projects that are part of the New Silk Road (Horesh, 2018: 2). The Middle East is important to China for many reasons. The oil and transport routes from the Middle East to China are clear areas of interest (Scobell, 2018: 9–24). Another reason is the geopolitical importance of the Middle East to other great powers, e.g. USA, EU and Russia. In addition to the Middle East, Africa is also an important destination for the New Silk Road, both the land-based and the maritime Silk Road (French, 2015).

Narratives related to global expectations

Case letter 1: China–Africa

Between 2013 and 2018, Africa received 44.65% of China's total foreign aid.[3] This clearly shows how the Chinese leaders view Africa. China is especially interested in minerals which can be found in abundance on the African continent. These are important to China's current and future industries for the development of batteries for cars, telephones and computers.

However, China's investments in Africa are not only focused on the extraction of minerals; during the same period (2013–2018), Africa also received about 45% of human resource development aid from China.[4] Chinese leaders have stated on several occasions that the humanitarian aid from China is intended to reduce poverty in the areas where the aid is provided. To help many African countries eradicate poverty, China provides emergency aid for disaster relief. To develop skills and thus promote future employment, China supports several educational projects in Africa (French, 2015). Part of the humanitarian aid also goes to agriculture projects, and to alleviate the effects of climate change.[5]

Although the Chinese humanitarian aid to Africa is substantial, it is the projects linked to the New Silk Road that receive the most attention from the Chinese leaders. This is shown by the fact that as of 2021, there are 40 African countries that have signed agreements related to the New Silk Road.[6]

However, it should be noted that it was not the New Silk Road project that triggered the first cooperation projects between China and Africa. As early as October 2000, i.e. 13 years before the New Silk Road was launched, "the Forum on China-Africa Cooperation was established".[7]

In connection with investment and humanitarian aid, China has developed robust student exchange programs so that African students can receive a higher university education in China (French, 2015; Linehan, 2018).[8]

Description of global expectations

Global expectations will naturally vary from country to country, and from region to region. In Africa, for example, humanitarian aid and student exchange programmes will be emphasized, while in the case of Europe, it is unlikely that these two factors will be important regarding relations to China. *In December 2020, EU* and *China* reached an agreement in principle regarding an *investment* treaty. The various EU countries will most probably have different areas of focus regarding investments. For instance, Germany, France, and Sweden will most probably be interested in mutual investments in the auto industry, while other countries, such as Denmark may focus on investing in green energy from wind turbines.

Many projects have been implemented by Chinese entrepreneurs in the mining industry in Africa (French, 2015), while, relations between Australia and China focus on mutual investment in the coal industry, as well as educational programmes in Australia that attract a large number of Chinese students (Hamilton, 2018). For large parts of Asia, free trade agreements will be an important global expectation linked to relations with China. This is reflected in the new free trade agreement RCEP (15 November 2020).[9] The 15 signatory countries account for approx. 30% of the world's population and approx. 30% of global GDP,[10] making it the largest free trade agreement ever concluded.

Apart from launching and developing the New Silk Road with the intention of stimulating the economies of China and other participating countries, it seems reasonable to assume that the Chinese leaders also have additional intentions. One should not be blind to the fact that China's leaders are interested in bringing Asia in general, and China in particular, back to the centre of economic and innovative development in the world (Cohn, 2019).

One way to do this is to stem the influence and possible dominance of the United States in the regions through which the New Silk Road passes (Winston, 2021). This assumption is also made in an article in the *Time* magazine (18 November 2020).[11] Against this background, it seems reasonable to assume that the New Silk Road, RCEP, the China–EU agreement and other investment agreements that China has entered into have other purposes than purely economic ones. We also assume that the US military build-up in the South China Sea, and the East China Sea, can to some extent be understood against this background. Similarly, the banning of the Chinese tech giant Huawei by the United States and its allies regarding the development of 5G wireless network projects in Western countries can also be understood against the same background. The reason given for banning the Chinese company is the concern about national security, that is, Huawei can be required to hand over data to the Chinese government if the government requires it, because of Chinese national security laws. However, the U.S. anti-terrorism laws also give the American government the authority to obtain information from American companies, if the information poses a security threat. In other words, the governments of both China and the USA can demand that technology companies provide them with information if the information poses a national security threat. However, it is only the Chinese companies that have been banned.

We have illustrated the above description in Figure 5.2.

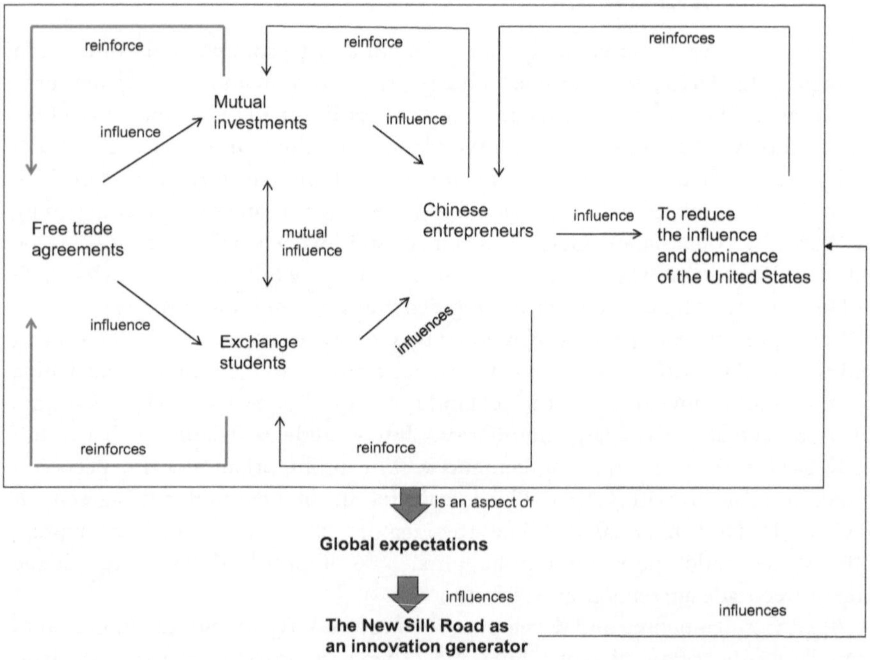

Figure 5.2 Global expectations: A conceptual model.

Analysis of global expectations

The idea that the United States should join the Chinese New Silk Road initiative does not seem likely to become a reality (Feng & Liang, 2019: 57). On the other hand, it is more uncertain whether China is deliberately trying to exclude the United States from participating in the New Silk Road initiative. However, cooperation between China and the United States related to technological development and trade would benefit both countries greatly (Anderson, 2014; Berlie & Hung, 2020). The reason is that both countries have a high level of expertise in technology, and could have in collaboration developed innovations related to artificial intelligence (Billington, 2020). The reasons preventing such collaboration seem to be ideological and political (Brown, 2018; Sandel, 2020).

The New Silk Road has great potential for entrepreneurial development based on technological innovations.[12] We have witnessed innovative entrepreneurship in the many technology companies in both the USA and China, which has been developed over the last 20 years (Billington, 2020). If the two countries had collaborated to develop innovative entrepreneurship, it seems reasonable to assume that this would have further accelerated innovative entrepreneurship in the global economy (Billington, 2020; Boutrup, 2019).

There is an obvious opportunity for cooperation between the USA and China regarding the many Chinese exchange students in the USA (Cohn, 2019; Linehan, 2018). However, there does not appear to be any interest in exploiting this potential to launch entrepreneurial activities based on technological innovations (Jain, 2021; Popper et al., 2021). These entrepreneurial businesses are developed either in the United States or in China. It seems that competition is preferable to collaboration (Winston, 2021). There is also little indication that a free trade agreement between the United States and China will be developed in the near future. It seems to be rather the case that the trade war launched by the Trump administration against China in 2018 will continue under the Biden administration.

There is much to suggest that the future of United States' relationship with China will be influenced by ideological and political factors (Winston, 2021). For much of the post-war period, the United States has used human rights as its trump card against various countries in international politics. Today, the US has weaponized human rights issues against China, such as China's actions in Hong Kong, and China's treatment of the Uyghur Muslims of Xinjiang. However, it should be remembered that these criticisms, concerning human rights in China, are made by a country that has on numerous occasions abetted the overthrow of democratically elected governments in order to replace them with military dictatorships, such as the overthrow of the democratically elected government in Iran in 1953, and the overthrow of the democratically elected government in Chile in 1973. Moreover, the USA exploits its so-called anti-terror laws to detain people for years without trial at the Guantanamo Bay detention centre. Therefore, when the United States launches an ideological crusade against China concerning human rights and the plight of the Muslim Uyghurs in Xinjiang, and the democratic rights of the people of Hong Kong, then this seems to be a hollow and hypocritical argument considering the United States' record regarding human rights in their own country, and how the United States has intervened in the affairs of sovereign states on numerous occasions by using military force, and in the process deny the people of these states their basic democratic rights.

Theoretical points related to global expectations

Mutual investments and free trade agreements will mainly determine the global expectations related to China (Popper et al., 2021), such as the RCEP,[13] the free trade agreement between 15 Asia-Pacific countries. The agreement is expected to increase the wealth creation in the region, and lead to mutual investments, and provide mass employment for both low-skilled and high-skilled workers.

The Comprehensive Agreement on Investment (CAI), an investment deal between China and the EU, has been proposed (as of December 2020, agreement had been reached in principle). The agreement is not a free trade agreement, but focuses on mutual market access for EU and Chinese investors. European companies that are already established in China will be able to benefit from the agreement, and the agreement will in all probability lead to more investments by the EU in China. The agreement applies to many areas, including the auto industry, telecommunications, raw materials, etc.[14]

It is probable that the U.S. will continue to negatively influence the EU regarding its cooperation with China, by focusing on national security issues and human rights' issues, amongst others. However, it seems less likely now than during the Trump administration that the EU will allow itself to be politically dominated by the US. There is much to suggest that the EU has developed a new policy in the global world, termed "strategic autonomy".[15]

We have developed a typology in Figure 5.3 to illustrate "global expectations".

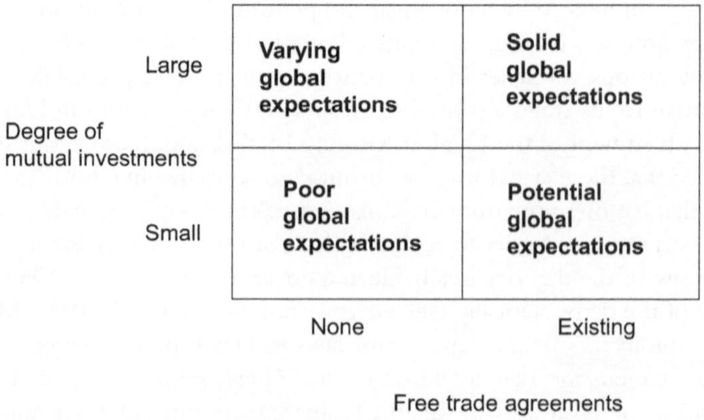

Figure 5.3 Global expectations: A typology.

Practical utility for global expectations

Free trade agreements and mutual investment agreements such as the RCEP and the China–EU agreement will most probably promote the development of various projects (Berlie & Hung, 2020). It seems reasonable to assume that two main categories of projects will be developed and implemented; firstly, traditional infrastructure projects; we have witnessed the implementation of such projects in many countries along the New Silk Road.[16] These projects have increased the demand for low-skilled, semi-skilled and high-skilled labour. Secondly, info-structure projects will be developed, which constitute the ten main information and communication processes in any social system, as described above. The implementation of info-structure projects will increase the demand for workers with high-tech expertise especially, but also semi-skilled workers.

In other words, this division of project categories into infrastructure and info-structure projects will result in a demand for labour of varying skills and expertise. Moreover, the implementation of giant projects, such as the New Silk Road, which may be viewed as a global "Marshall Plan", will result in an increased demand for various categories of labour. In turn, this will probably lead to the "automation debate", concerning the danger of mass unemployment during the Fourth Industrial Revolution, becoming a non-topic (Feng & Liang, 2019; Winston, 2021). The debate does not take into account the fact that the major giant projects that are being implemented, which will demand different types of labour, unskilled, semi-skilled and high-skilled. If the future projects along the New Silk Road are successful, increasing the demand for different categories of labour, then the "automation and unemployment debate", which often assumes developments will head towards mass unemployment, will become redundant in the fully-developed innovation economy (Johannessen, 2020a).

One consequence of the large-scale implementation of both infrastructure and info-structure projects along the New Silk Road will be the emergence of two categories of entrepreneurship projects. The first category is the classic entrepreneurs who fill the market where innovations have created a gap in the market. The second category is the entrepreneurs who create new projects by applying innovations. We term the latter category innovative entrepreneurship. When both of these types of entrepreneurships operate side by side, the market will be in constant change. This will create an economic dynamic along the New Silk Road, which will create temporary crises, when innovations enter the market, but which will also create economic progress when the classic entrepreneurs enter the market (Johannessen, 2020b).

In Figure 5.4, we have illustrated the above description, analysis and presentation in a Boudon–Coleman diagram.

Sub-conclusion for global expectations

In this section, we have examined the following question: How do global expectations promote the New Silk Road as and innovation generator?

The short answer is that this will occur through mutual investments, with and without free trade agreements, which will increase the demand for different types of labour.

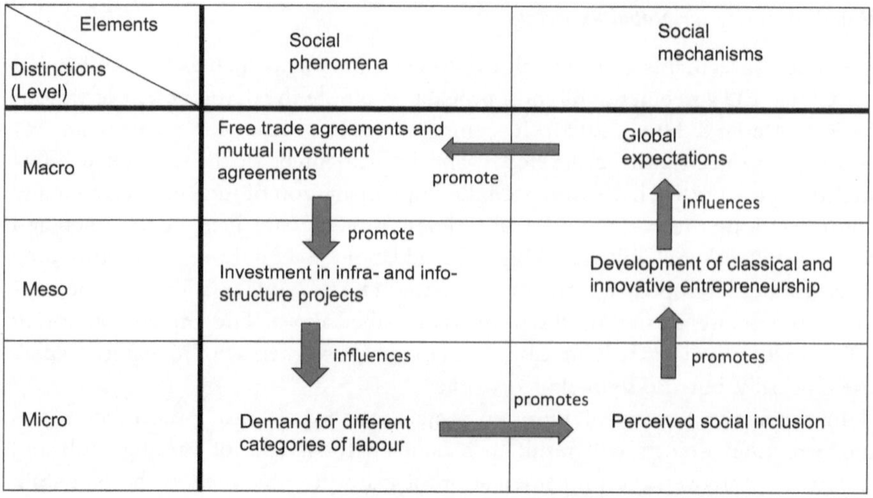

Figure 5.4 Global expectations: A Boudon–Coleman diagram.

Shared futures for the countries along the New Silk Road

In this section we will examine the following question: How do shared futures promote the New Silk Road as an innovation generator?

The New Silk Road, which also goes by the name of OBOR (One Belt One Road) and BRI (Belt and Road Initiative) has visionary goals for Asia, the Middle East, Africa and Europe (Shiyan et al., 2020: 1). The shared future of this mega-region shows some of the potential that the New Silk Road has. Such a vision will inevitably encounter challenges of an economic and technological nature, but also an opposition that runs along ideological, diplomatic and political lines (Allison, 2018; Winston, 2021). We have recently witnessed US diplomatic efforts to prevent European countries from using Huawei as a partner in the development of 5G networks.

Narratives related to shared futures

Case letter 1: 5G network

What can 5G networks do that 3G and 4G networks can't? For most users, it is the speed of data when they are using their computers and smartphones that will increase with better and faster networks. However, 5G, and also now under experimentation 6G networks, has a completely different application than just increasing the speed of data for the average consumer. The 5G networks improve production, distribution, control, monitoring of various processes, quality development of products, and innovation processes. With the implementation of 5G and 6G networks, production, distribution and consumption will be globalised and be able to reach new levels.

Intelligent processes in production will be easier to develop and implement when the networks are such that almost no time-lag exists. The feedback will be immediate, so that the visions of intelligent machines can move on to the vision of connecting intelligent machines globally in a network, where all information one place in the network is instantly updated to all other places in the network. This represents a transition from intelligent robots to intelligent informats.

5G networks and later 6G networks will enable a development from intelligent robots to intelligent informats on a global scale. An intelligent robot is based on artificial intelligence and operates using algorithms. Thus, intelligent robots can use artificial intelligence to learn from their mistakes, and self-adjust to make better future decisions and actions. Intelligent informats are intelligent robots that are connected to a network of similar robots. If we imagine a medical intelligent robot that specializes in surgical procedures, then an intelligent informat in the same medical field will be connected to the other intelligent medical robots in the field. When new knowledge is developed in this field, all the intelligent robots will immediately be able to share in this new knowledge. Such interconnections via 5G and 6G networks will improve medical operational expertise that will save lives.

Description of shared futures

The economic growth in China over the last twenty years has led to speculation as to whether China is overtaking the United States as an economic power. This has led to geopolitical challenges for the West, and especially for the United States (Zhengqi, 2020: 221–240). Moreover, the World Bank has estimated that more than 800 million people have been lifted out of poverty since 1978, which has also led to other countries viewing the Chinese political and economic system in a positive light,[17] which is reflected in China's success in establishing and signing the RCEP free trade agreement.

The New Silk Road viewed from this perspective has led many countries to negotiate and sign trade and investment agreements with China, including the investment agreement with the EU, the Comprehensive Agreement on Investment, which was concluded in principle 30 December 2020. However, China's strengthened global position has also led to strong opposition against China gaining more economic influence in the West. This is most evident when we consider the American-led opposition to new technology from China, e.g. Huawei.[18]

The strategy of the leaders before Xi Jinping may be expressed by the axiom, "Hide your strength, bide your time" (Ferdinand, 2016). However, Xi Jinping has abandoned this doctrine. China's foreign policy ambitions under Xi Jinping become evident when we consider the huge New Silk Road initiative (Popper et al., 2021; Winston, 2021). This has resulted in the United States adopting a more aggressive policy towards China, for instance, US's assertiveness in the South China Sea, but also its diplomatic efforts to influence its allies to curb China's economic and political expansion.

The projects that have been initiated, and many others that are being planned, show that the various cooperation projects take into account the different economic levels of the various countries. In Laos, for example, an infrastructure project, a functioning rail system, is being built to connect the rural areas with the cities and with the outside world (Gong & Mingjiang, 2020: 153). Other countries need to implement development projects at a higher economic level, such as Malaysia (Gong & Mingjiang, 2020: 160–163).

China's new foreign policy has led to many collaborative projects resulting in economic development and progress in other countries, such as in Africa (French, 2015). This has also been shown in the Middle East (Ehteshami & Horesh, 2018). However, China's improved regional and geopolitical position has also led to strong opposition, especially from the United States (Allison, 2018; Winston, 2021).

We have illustrated the above description in Figure 5.5.

Analysis of shared futures

The New Silk Road may be viewed as Xi Jinping's way of telling the West that China has entered the geopolitical scene, as a great power, both economically, politically and diplomatically. What the New Silk Road has not yet shown is China as a military-strategic challenge to the West. However, as early as 2011 during the Obama administration, when the former Secretary of State, Hillary Clinton, wrote the article "America's Pacific century" published in the *Foreign Policy* magazine, it was evident that the US viewed China as a strategic threat and a challenge to its dominant global position (Clinton, 2011). However, the emergence of China as a great power, as made evident by its implementation of its huge global initiative, the New Silk Road, may lead to "Thucydides' Trap", a term

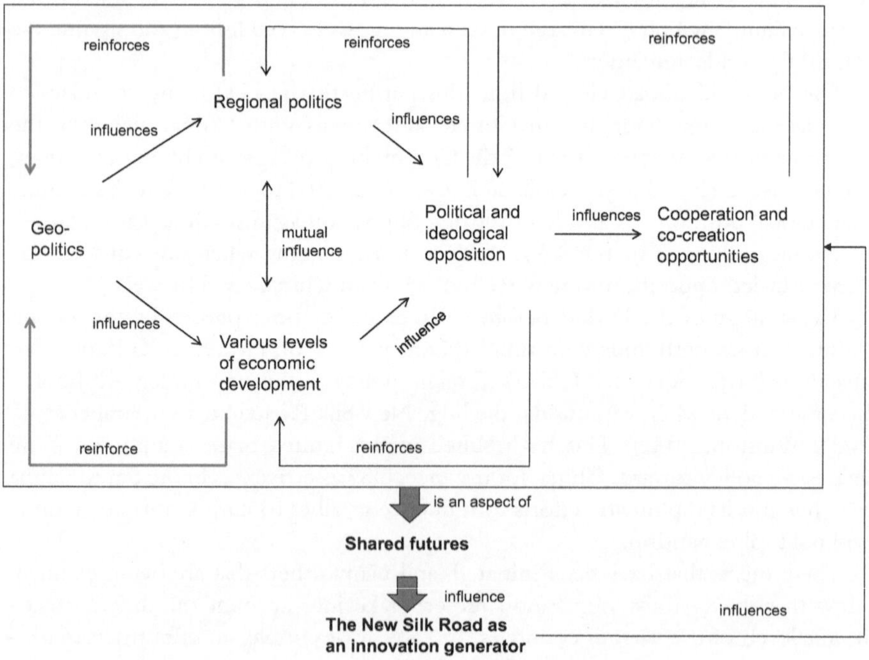

Figure 5.5 Shared futures.

coined by the political scientist Graham Allison (2018). Thucydides (2009) was an Athenian historian who wrote about the 5th-century BC war between Sparta and Athens, in which the two powers were battling for hegemony in the classical Greek World.[19] Sparta was the dominant power of the Greek world at that time, but feared the rise of Athens. To prevent the further rise of Athens, which would challenge the Spartan hegemony, the Spartans went to war with the Athenians ("the Peloponnesian War"). According to Thucydides, the war between Sparta and Athens was inevitable due to the fact that the dominant power (Sparta) was challenged by the rising power (Athens). Today, the term is often used by commentators when referring to a potential military conflict between the US (dominant power) and China (rising power). It is in this context that the US fears the rise of China and is pursuing a preventive strategy to prevent or impose restrictions on China's economic expansion. It is against this background one can understood why the United States, and its allies in Europe, are banning the use of Huawei in their 5G networks. The United States and the European countries that are banning Huawei have explained their actions by referring to national security issues; that is, Huawei can be required to hand over data to the Chinese military, because of Chinese national security laws. This may be true, but US anti-terrorism laws also give the US military authority to obtain information from Western telecommunications companies, if the information poses a national threat.

Showing one's strength is not always a wise choice, because then one's opponents will know where to launch an attack. This can lead to a loss of strength, precisely because the opponents will know where to attack. On the other hand, it is a long Chinese tradition as far back as Mao Tse-tung's leadership that being attacked is a "good thing", because then you know who are your enemies and who are your friends.[20] It is conceivable that such a consideration has been behind the strategic change Xi Jinping made in 2013 when he launched the New Silk Road as a vision in a speech in Kazakhstan. He also put forward the idea of the maritime Silk Road later that year in Malaysia (Jianglin, 2020a: 3). Thus, he showed China's strength economically, technologically and diplomatically.

Theoretical points related to shared futures

With the many investments in the various projects along the New Silk Road, the political landscape has changed character. The political and ideological opposition to various OBOR projects comes from many places. One example is the economic corridor between China and Pakistan, which is a project along the New Silk Road. This project expands the railway system in parts of Kashmir. Kashmir has long been a conflict zone between India and Pakistan. Therefore, India has strongly opposed this project (Shiyan et al., 2020: 4–5). When such objections are brought to the table, the opportunities for cooperation and co-creation between China and India are reduced, because the risk of the investments becomes great. One can say that in such situations it is at best turbulent shared futures that exist.

We have previously observed that even though the EU and China have concluded in principle the negotiations on the Comprehensive Agreement on Investment (CAI) both the US and some EU countries are pushing to reduce contact with Chinese companies that supply high-tech products, such as Huawei. Although there is political and ideological opposition to the EU–China investment agreement, the opportunities for cooperation and co-creation are still great. Although there may be obstacles and opposition to various projects, resulting in uncertainties, the future opportunities for China–EU are nevertheless feasible. One can only imagine what could happen to the German auto industry, if the Chinese market suddenly disappeared. This was made evident at the World Economic Forum in Davos in 2020, when Herbert Diess, the chairman and CEO of Volkswagen, emphasized the importance of further and extensive cooperation and co-creation between China and Germany. Peter Altmaier, the German minister of economic affairs and energy, supported this view. This view, as well as the Comprehensive Agreement on Investment, or CAI, between the European Union and China concluded at the end of 2020, came at a time when China replaced the US as the EU's largest trade partner. At the same meeting in Davos, German Chancellor Angela Merkel also spoke positively about the new agreement between China and the EU.[21]

We have developed a typology for different shared futures in Figure 5.6.

Practical utility of shared futures

The geopolitical developments will be decisive for how the regional economies develop in the future as we move towards the Fourth Industrial Revolution. If geopolitical developments are dominated by one great power, then regional economic development will take one direction, while there will be a different development if multilateralism[22] becomes predominant.

New innovations, technological or institutional, will almost without exception meet challenges. According to Thucydides' Trap, the largest challenges will occur when an emerging power threatens the dominant power (Allison, 2018). It is in this context, that the growing tensions between the United States, as the dominant power, and China as the emerging power, can be understood.

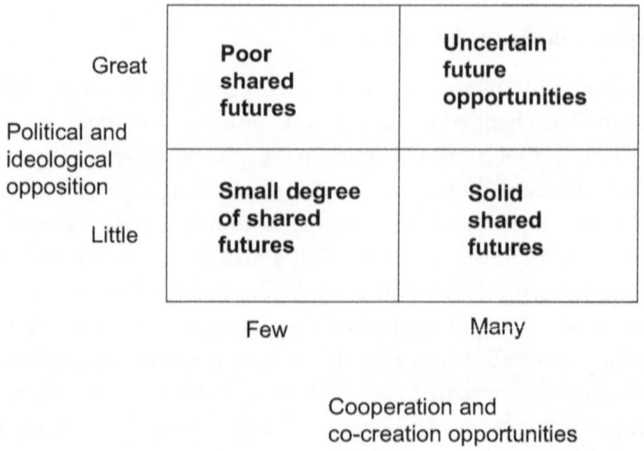

Figure 5.6 Shared futures: A typology.

If global relations are characterized by the assertiveness of a dominant geopolitical power, or by multilateralism, where a balance is maintained through dialogue, then either way, this will affect the opportunities for cooperation both regionally and globally. Given that the cooperation is based on a win–win strategy, the probability is high that cooperation will also result in co-creation projects.

Regardless, such co-creation projects will meet with opposition, both for political and ideological reasons. From China's perspective it is therefore positive that the German business leaders and the German Chancellor, as well as Ursula von der Leyen, the President of the European Commission, are positive regarding the EU's co-operation and co-creation projects with China. Moreover, this may contribute to reducing tensions between China and the United States, or at least between the EU and China.

We know from economic history that innovations almost without exception lead to social tensions and conflicts (Johannessen, 2018, 2020a, 2020b). The New Silk Road will be no exception in this regard. This innovative initiative includes both an institutional innovation, technological institutional innovation, and a market innovation (Johannessen, 2018). If we consider the various OBOR projects as a whole, they will change the economic, diplomatic and trade policies in the countries that the New Silk Road passes through (Hawke, 2020: 19–23; Zhengqi, 2020: 221–241).

When the various projects along the New Silk Road are implemented, the strategic inter-dependence between the countries will increase. This will function as a social mechanism that will help to prevent conflicts between the countries, because everyone will lose if conflicts develop, because the inter-dependencies between the countries are great. In this way, economic inter-dependence, as a strategic intention, can reduce conflicts between countries. This strengthens the positive development of shared futures with an increasing reciprocity in the economic ties that the projects along the New Silk Road contribute to.

We have illustrated the description, analysis and the presentation above in a Boudon–Coleman diagram in Figure 5.7.

Sub-conclusion for shared futures

In this section, we have examined the following question: How do shared futures promote the New Silk Road as an innovation generator?

The short answer is that the global geopolitical situation and the political and ideological opposition that develops as a result of the geopolitical situation will affect the co-operation and co-creation climate, and thus provide guidelines for the shared futures of the New Silk Road as an innovation generator.

Win–win ideology along the New Silk Road

In this section, we will examine the following question: How do win–win projects promote the New Silk Road as an innovation generator?

A win–win strategy in economic projects is a situation where all the parties are accommodated, where all the parties benefit, and where the end result is good for

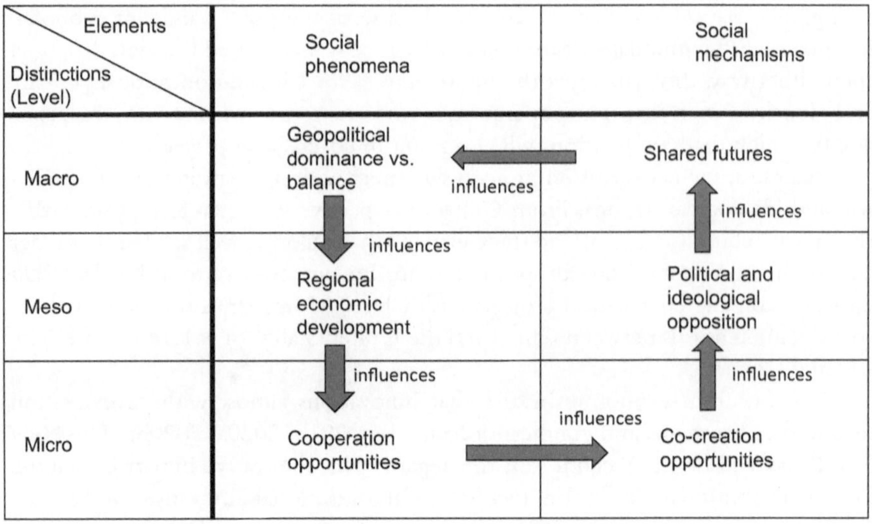

Figure 5.7 Shared futures: A Boudon–Coleman diagram.

everyone involved.[23] Cooperation and co-creation, with the clear strategic intention that all parties should gain from participation, seems to point the way forward for the economic, diplomatic and relational situation the world now finds itself in (Brown, 2019; Byrre & Gallaghan, 2013). Competition may be advantageous in some situations, but it is often cooperation and co-creation that is in the best interests of all parties (Billington, 2020; Valdmanis, 2021). This understanding – that cooperation should take precedence over competition, and that a win–win strategy is the desired strategy, seems to be the perception most Asia-Pacific countries had when they signed the world's largest free trade agreement, the RCEP, in the autumn of 2020. Cooperation and a win–win strategy also seems to be the desired strategy of the 130 countries and organizations that have signed agreements linked to the New Silk Road initiative (Huang, 2017; Junxin, 2020: 155–180).

Narratives related to a win–win ideology

Case letter 1: Cooperation, co-creation and win–win take precedence over competition

The global economy is designed in such a way that the production process of a specific product often concerns a global production chain involving collaboration between various countries and organizations, which ultimately creates the final product. However, this insight is nothing new, and may be traced as far back as to the ideas of Adam Smith.[24]

The entire value creation process is driven by a focus on costs, quality, competence, innovations and design. It is these five social mechanisms that determine where the individual parts of a product will be produced. Finally, the product is assembled after an overall assessment. The product may be assembled close to the market, or where the costs, quality and competence are such that it produces the best result.

Part of the product may be developed in China, if cost differences are important. On the other hand, if quality is a crucial factor, part of the product may be developed in Korea or Japan. If design is important, then part of the product may be produced in France or Denmark. Expertise differences can also determine where parts of the product are developed. If, for example, it is a product related to a technological innovation within the field of artificial intelligence, then an American or Chinese company may be preferable. If the product is dependent on technological innovations, then it is conceivable that the parts to which the technological innovation is related will be produced in countries such as China, Japan, Korea or the USA. The point of this case letter is to show that the global economy depends on cooperation and co-creation in relation to a number of parameters in order to develop even the simplest product.

All the political and ideological obstacles that are laid out as stumbling blocks to prevent cooperation and co-creation are negative for global economic development. There is much to suggest that the challenges in the global system today, not just the global economy, have moved up to such a level of complexity that competition only reduces scope and opportunity, while cooperation, co-creation and a win–win attitude can provide optimal solutions. For instance, this applies to global issues such as, pandemics and other health crises, the growing economic inequality, poverty, famine disasters, climate challenges and adapting to a green economy. It is only when competition gives way to cooperation and co-creation that global challenges can be solved. Therefore, it is conceivable that cooperative advantages are a more suitable concept in the innovation economy, than the competitive advantages that prevailed in the industrial economy.

Description of a win–win ideology

The win–win ideology put forward by several Chinese leaders in connection with the New Silk Road is constituted by some very specific aspects (Yuzhu, 2020). We highlight five aspects here, but do not suggest that these are the only ones. We contend here, and in the Analysis, that these aspects are a necessary condition to enable the win–win ideology to contribute to promoting the New Silk Road as an innovation generator.

The first aspect of a win–win ideology is to emphasize the importance of cooperation as opposed to competition (Prahalad & Ramaswamy, 2004). In some contexts, competition can be important, but in the innovation economy, cooperation will be more important. While competition was important in an economy where cost differences were the main driving force, in the innovation economy, competence differences will be the most important factor in driving the economy forward (Anderson, 2014; Billington, 2020). In order to achieve this, it will be crucial that the various systems are interconnected in such a way that information and knowledge are spread efficiently (Byrre & Gallaghan, 2013). In this way, it will require less effort to facilitate the development and dispersal of innovations in and between various systems at different levels. In order for this to occur smoothly, it will be crucial that supranational institutions can resolve any conflicts and facilitate trade and production between countries, and within countries (Billington, 2020).

If such supranational institutions can be utilised to resolve tensions and conflicts, then wealth creation can be maintained sustainably, both in the individual countries, but also between the countries (Cohn, 2019; Economy, 2018).

Metaphorically, we might think of the New Silk Road as China's new global "Marshall Plan" (Feng & Liang, 2019). If the New Silk Road is to be implemented successfully on a global scale then it will not only function as an innovation generator, but also as a wealth creation generator for the countries involved in the various projects (Ferdinand, 2016; Gong & Mingjiang, 2020).

We have pointed out several times in this book, and in our book *The Innovation Economy in China* (Johannessen, 2021a), the importance of "Thucydides' Trap", to which Allison (2018) has devoted a large part of his research. Thucydides' Trap refers to the tendency of dominant powers to resort to military force when they are threatened by an emerging power. The United States has been the dominant global power since 1945, especially after the fall of the Soviet Union in 1991. Today, the diplomatic and ideological measures of the rising power, China, are perceived as a threat to the future global dominance of the United States. The political slogan, "Make America Great Again" (MAGA), used by the former president, Donald Trump, can be understood against this background. President Biden's "America is back and ready to lead the world again" is not substantially any different from Trump's "Make America Great Again", despite the seemingly ideological differences of the two presidents. However, this is not so difficult to understand if we consider this in the light of the article "America's Pacific century", written by the former secretary of state Hillary Clinton, and published in the magazine, *Foreign Policy* in 2011. If we consider the political slogans of the two presidents in conjunction with the Obama administration's view that the US needs to have an assertive Asia-Pacific regional strategy to deal with China's rise and re-establish America's regional hegemony (as expressed in the Clinton article), then Thucydides' Trap is more than just a political metaphor; it is rather a realpolitik reality regarding US–China relations. We focus on this here, because the win–win ideology may be thrown out with the bathwater, if the Chinese leaders are not able to take strategic action to remedy the "psychological crisis" the United States finds itself in due to its diminishing global role (Carney, 2020: Frank, 2020). Our perspective is that China needs to offer the United States some strategic advantages, to prevent the entire New Silk Road project from culminating in Thucydides' Trap.

We have illustrated the above discussion in Figure 5.8.

Analysis of a win–win ideology

We will apply the concept of "comparative advantage"[25] here to the distinction between competition and cooperation. As described above, in a win–win approach, cooperation is preferable to competition. If we then assume that some cultures or countries, without being specific, have a cultural advantage with regard to competition, while others have a cultural advantage with regard to cooperation, we can say that some have a competitive advantage while others have a cooperative advantage. If we further assume that the innovation economy will be driven by

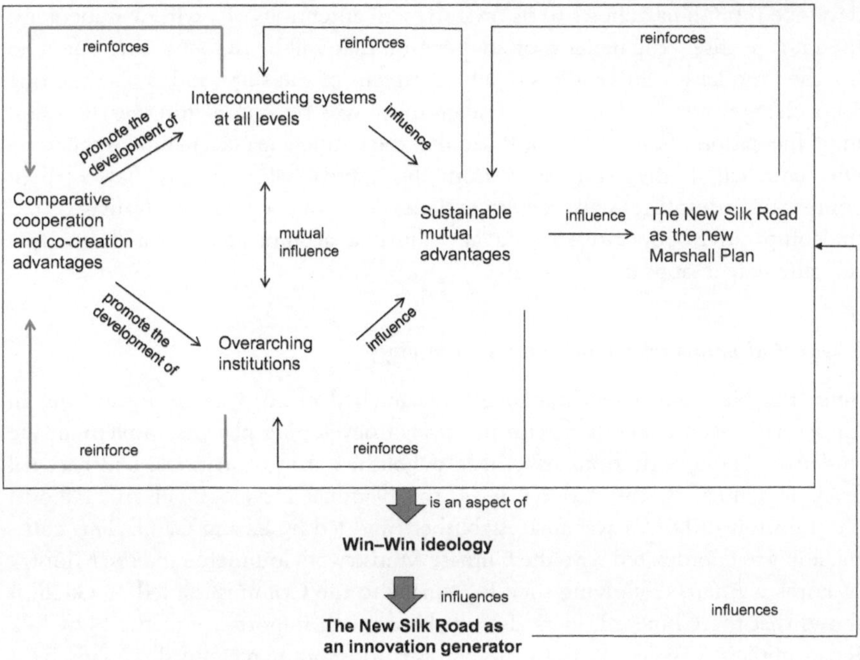

Figure 5.8 Win–win ideology.

cooperative advantages, and not so much by competitive advantages, then some cultures or countries will be better equipped than others to succeed in the innovation economy (Anderson, 2014; Johannessen, 2020a, 2020b).

In addition to co-operation and co-creation benefits, those countries and regions that have a high degree of interconnected systems at all levels will be more likely to develop the creative new, i.e. innovations, because innovations always occur along the boundaries between knowledge domains (Anderson, 2014; Billington, 2020). It is precisely this interconnection that is the intention of the New Silk Road, both along the land-based and the maritime silk roads (Yue & Fujian, 2019; Zhongyuan, 2020: 101–110).

Where conflicts arise, it will be crucial that these are resolved through international laws and regulations, which, historically, are best regulated by supranational organizations, such as the World Trade Organization. For instance, the conflict between China and India could be detrimental to the development of the New Silk Road (Xiaoxue, 2020: 227–258).

In China, from 2013, when the New Silk Road project was launched, a number of national bodies have been set up to connect with international institutions, to ensure the sustainability of the projects and a win–win ideology that benefits all the parties involved. The probability that China will benefit from the New Silk Road initiative is due to many factors. At a general level, China will have great advantages, because it has the "model power",[26] in other words, the defining power regarding what the New Silk Road initiative constitutes, and how it should be developed. If China adheres to its own strategic intentions of a win–win ideology, then it is precisely the benefits of cooperation that will be in focus. The one who has the "model power" is the so-called "captain of the ship" and is also the one who changes course if needed. Therefore, it will be crucial for the successful implementation of the New Silk Road that the Chinese leaders maintain the win–win approach. If they stray away from this approach for various reasons, then competitive advantages will creep in at the expense of cooperative advantages, and the comparative cooperative advantages China has accumulated culturally and historically may disappear.

Theoretical points related to a win–win ideology

Since the New Silk Road initiative was launched in 2013, many institutions in China have been established with the task of developing plans to implement the initiative. These institutions have been established at local, regional and national levels in China. At the national level, the National Development and Reform Commission (NDRC) was first established, and led by Zhang Gaoli. This commission was coordinated with the Chinese Ministry of Commerce and the Ministry of Foreign Affairs. By giving such legitimacy to the Commission led by Gaoli, it shows that the Chinese leaders also attribute much importance to the New Silk Road initiative. Assigning both the Ministry of Commerce and the Ministry of Foreign Affairs as coordinating institutions shows that the Chinese leaders view the New Silk Road initiative as something more than just an economic project. The Ministry of Foreign Affairs and the Ministry of Commerce have always been active in relation to the Commission led by Gaoli. In this way, all the activities in the New Silk Road initiative are connected to an external focus. This gives China a foreign policy advantage in a global world, which has economic challenges at various levels.

Africa is struggling to improve its economic performance. The Middle East faces various types of problems, some of which can be solved by projects triggered by the New Silk Road, while other challenges require a greater degree of diplomatic negotiations, in which China and its allies can contribute. Europe is struggling with an economic transformation problem, among other things, related to the automotive industry in Germany, France, Italy and Sweden. In this context, the New Silk Road can function as a positive force, something the chairman of Volkswagen, Herbert Diess, stated in Davos in 2020,[27] and which is also indicated by the China–EU agreement that was concluded in principle on 30 December 2020 indicates.

The New Silk Road has become a top priority in many of China's national, regional and local institutions. The degree of interconnections at various levels and in different systems is revealed through what are called the five interconnections related to the New Silk Road. This is the interconnections of policy, infrastructure, trade, finance and people. A review of the five interconnections shows that there exists a complex network of local, regional and national institutions that are all based on promoting a win–win ideology, for the projects internally in China, and also for the projects that are developed and implemented along the New Silk

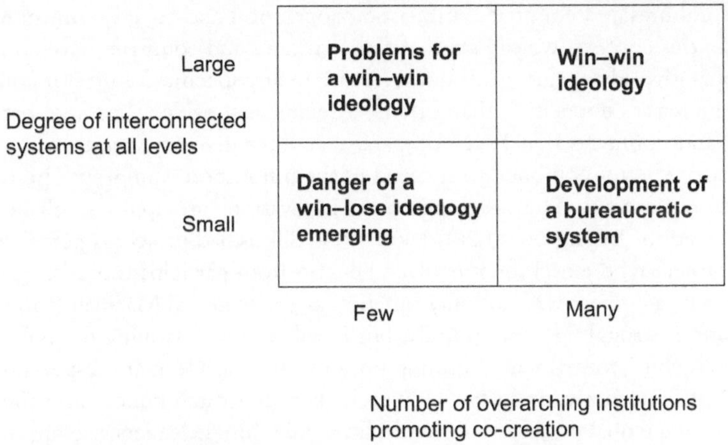

Figure 5.9 Win–win ideology: A typology.

Road in other countries, among others, the development projects for the European automotive industry, both in Europe and in China.[28]

We have developed a typology related to the win–win ideology and the New Silk Road in Figure 5.9.

The proposition that can be drawn from the typology in Figure 5.9 is as follows:

> The greater the degree of interconnected systems at all levels, and the larger number of overarching institutions that promote co-creation, the greater the probability will be that a win–win ideology will be supported and developed.

Practical utility of a win–win ideology

Since its launch in 2013, the New Silk Road has become the dominant social phenomenon on the international agenda, says Hoang (2019: 234). The reasoning is related to the many project agreements that have been signed in South-East Asia, Central Asia, the Gulf region, Africa and Europe, and the many projects that have already been initiated. Reciprocity and a win–win ideology characterize all these projects. This emerged from the Davos forum in 2020, where Herbert Diess, chairman of the Volkswagen Group, Peter Altmaier, the German minister of economic affairs, and the German Chancellor Angela Merkel all supported the idea of expanded cooperation with Chinese companies.[29] This support was concretized by the Comprehensive Agreement on Investment (CAI) between the European Union and China which was agreed on in principle at the end of 2020.[30]

Competition has always been important for economies and countries. The innovation economy is no exception. Competition will be crucial to success. However, although the old globalization was characterized by competition regarding costs in general, and wage costs in particular, collaboration and co-creation will be more important in the innovation economy than competition.[31]

Some cultures and countries emphasise cooperation and co-creation more than others. In this context, we can say that these cultures and countries have comparative cooperative advantages. Without referring to any specific cultures or countries that are better at cooperating than others, it seems reasonable to assume that those cultures and countries that have comparative cooperative advantages will also be those that are better equipped to succeed in the innovation economy. The reasoning is straightforward. The development of innovations presupposes collaboration and co-creation (Billington, 2020). If the New Silk Road project is perceived as a mutual project where everyone involved benefits from participation in the project, then this mega-project will not only function as a new global Marshall Plan for the many nations struggling economically, but it will also be a driving force for those countries seeking to maintain a leading position, such as Germany, especially with regard to its automotive industry. However, there is a catch concerning the New Silk Road as a global project – no matter how the Chinese leaders attempt to present the New Silk Road, the United States will view the project as a threat to their global economic, diplomatic and military position (Allison, 2018). As mentioned previously, this may quickly lead to Thucydides' Trap, which has been the subject of much research by Allison (2018). The extent to which the New Silk Road is perceived by the United States' allies as a win–win opportunity may be the result of negotiated solutions within the western alliance. By "western alliance", we mean not only NATO, but all the global institutions that aim to improve relations between Western nations. If China is unable to solve the Thucydides' Trap problem, and the problem regarding which role the USA will have in the innovation economy, then it is probable that conflicts will arise and the win–win ideology of the New Silk Road will suffer, resulting in a win-lose ideology gaining precedence.

We have illustrated the above description, analysis, and theoretical reflections in a Boudon–Coleman diagram in Figure 5.10.

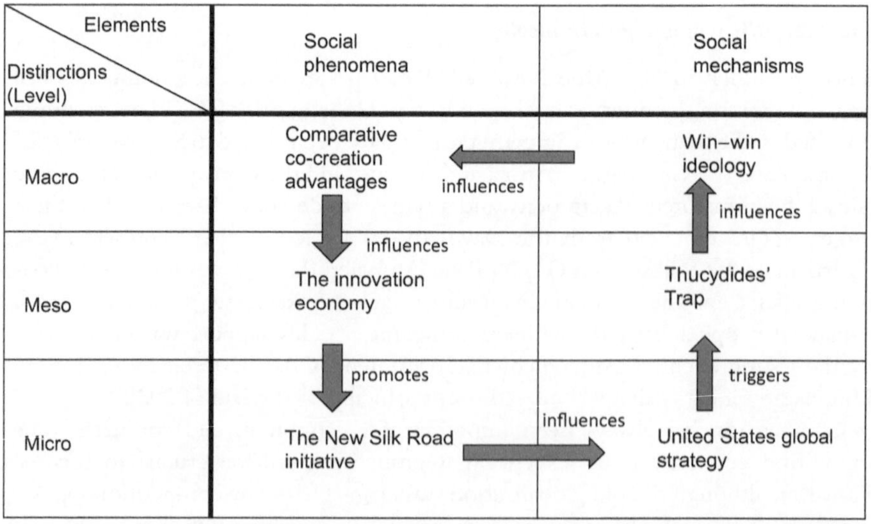

Figure 5.10 Win–win ideology: A Boudon–Coleman diagram.

Sub-conclusion related to a win–win ideology

In this section, we have examined the following question: How do win–win projects promote the New Silk Road as an innovation generator?

The short answer is that a win–win ideology will promote cooperation and co-creation so that innovations can be created and drive the innovation economy forwards.

New mindset is a focus on dialogue and collective solutions rather than competition

In this section, we will examine the following question: How does the new mindset promote the New Silk Road as an innovation generator?

By New Mindset, we mean there is a focus on dialogue and collective solutions rather than competition, dominance and unilateral approaches. Countries that have adjusted to the new mindset are interested in following rule-based systems, even if they have enough strength, both economically and militarily, to be the dominant party. New mindset is thus a transition from unilateralism to multilateralism. In multilateral relationships, dialogue between parties is crucial when making decisions. Unilateralism refers to decisions and actions that do not take into consideration the interests of the other parties, and actions are often based on the strength of the unilateral party. It is in this context that we can say that the new mindset is based on systemic global cooperation and co-creation, and aims to promote economic development, for example, in the countries participating in the New Silk Road initiative (Zhongyuan, 2020).

Narratives related to new mindset

Case letter 1: Many roads that lead to the same goal

There are many roads that lead to the same goal. The goal of the New Silk Road is sustainable economic growth in the participating countries (Zhengqi, 2020). For China, the New Silk Road has many strategic intentions. One of these is to stabilize the economies of the countries bordering China (Jianglin, 2020a: 261). The New Silk Road initiative is generated, shaped and driven by China, so it should come as no surprise that one of the strategic intentions is that the Chinese economy will be developed through the various projects that are initiated (Yuzhu, 2020).

However, there is an overarching strategic intention implicit in the New Silk Road. This is the struggle for markets, commodities and diplomatic allies, at a time when geopolitical power is changing (Mahbubani, 2018, 2020). The changes are emerging in many areas. This applies in particular to the changes from the old globalization based on competition due to wage differences, to a new globalization based on differences in competence in general, and technological competence in particular. Against this background, the New Silk Road will enable China to integrate into the emerging innovation economy. In this innovation economy, the

United States has taken the lead, but China is in a good second place, and its economy is surging ahead.[32]

The growing tension between the United States and China provides us with an understanding why the development of the New Silk Road is so important to China. The competition and rising discord between the nations also help us to understand the importance to China of the new mindset, as an integral element of its new global "Marshall Plan" (Feng & Liang, 2019). That is, a new mindset in the global economy which is based on a rule-based system administered by supranational institutions, and involving cooperating countries with a collective strategic intention of win–win with regard to projects, agreements and relationships (Yunker, 2014).

It is a paradox that the stronger China becomes economically and diplomatically, the greater will be the counterforces that will emerge in an attempt to reduce China's growing strength. We can witness such counterforces in the current efforts of the US, in its assertiveness in the South China Sea, its commitment to Taiwan and Hong Kong, and its highlighting of China's treatment of Uighur Muslims in Xinjiang, with regard to human rights.

Description of a new mindset

Both the land-based and the maritime New Silk Road are financed by Chinese banks and funds (Miller, 2017). However, there is a growing need for private investors to invest in sub-projects along the New Silk Road (Lim & Lim, 2020: 97–124). The "New Silk Road" acts as a

> metaphor giving the network of projects involved in the initiative a common direction. In order for such a complex network to be able to function towards the same goal, collective efforts by means of cooperation and co-creation are crucial. This will also require a supranational rule-based system to function efficiently.
>
> (Drache et al., 2019)

According to the Chinese leaders, such a rule-based system presupposes that dialogue is the instrument that forms the basis for decisions (Brown, 2018). In addition to this, China emphasizes that the World Trade Organization, as a supranational institution, ensures that free world trade is strengthened.[33] For China, multilateralism is the instrument that will ensure that no nation, due to its strength, should dominate and set standards for rules and procedures for free world trade (Angang, 2014). Global economic development should also be ensured through systemic global interaction and co-creation (Brown, 2019). This may sound like an ideal aim, but it can be ensured through supranational institutions and a common understanding that a rule based system should form the basis for free trade between countries (Mahbubani, 2018, 2020).

In contrast to free world trade and dialogue as a decision-making instrument, the United States under the Trump administration explicitly put protectionism and "America first" on its political agenda in opposition to multilateralism.

There are many risks that China may be exposed to in its launching and development of the mega New Silk Road project. If the entire project is completed successfully, both the maritime part and the land-based part, then this will constitute the largest ever global mega-project of its kind. However, this is also where the risk lies. By launching and developing such a mega-project, China and not the United States will be viewed as being the driving force behind economic transformation in Asia, the Middle East and Africa. This in itself could trigger counter-forces, especially in the United States. The rationale is simple and linked to Thucydides' Trap (Allison, 2018). As China grows and continues to develop such a mega-project, the United States is downgraded, relatively speaking, as the leader in the global world (Mahbubani, 2018).

Another danger is what we choose to term "the contamination trap". If the US and the EU continue their finger pointing against China regarding human rights concerning the Uighur Muslims in Xinjiang province in China, then this could have a "contamination effect" with regard to other countries that China has relations to. In practice, it may be precisely this contamination effect that could result in other countries distancing themselves from China's projects, because they may begin to fear what the "real" motive is behind the Chinese projects. It may be suggested that the US is using such a "contamination strategy" to disseminate the idea that if China can do this to its own people, what can they not do to other countries in Asia, Africa, the Middle East, etc., if they get control of these areas economically. The contamination strategy can be as effective as the economic warfare used by the United States against the Soviet Union. The Chinese countermove may be two-sided. First, the importance of establishing a new mindset, Second, China needs to improve its image abroad by resolving the Uighur Muslims issue and the Hong Kong problem.

We have illustrated the above description in Figure 5.11.

Analysis of a new mindset

The new mindset, which characterizes the development and implementation of the New Silk Road initiative, will in all probability lead to economic growth. This growth will occur not only in the countries participating in the Silk Road sub-projects, but in the Chinese economy as a whole, not unlike what happened to the US economy as a result of the Marshall Plan after World War II (Feng & Liang, 2019; Jianglin, 2020c: 262; Jinbo, 2020: 181–209).

The open ruled-based system will facilitate dialogue in the decision-making process, in contrast to decision-making characterized by the dominance of one single party. However, this presupposes strong global institutions, which have the authority to make decisions that regulate the involved parties (Linggui, 2020: Mahbubani, 2018, 2020).

Chinese diplomacy has also changed its position in the development and implementation of the New Silk Road. It can be expressed as follows: "You can only forgive when you are strong" (rather than when you are weak). Over the last twenty years, China has developed into one of the strongest players in the global economy, geo-political field and global diplomacy (Mahbubani, 2009, 2020). With this

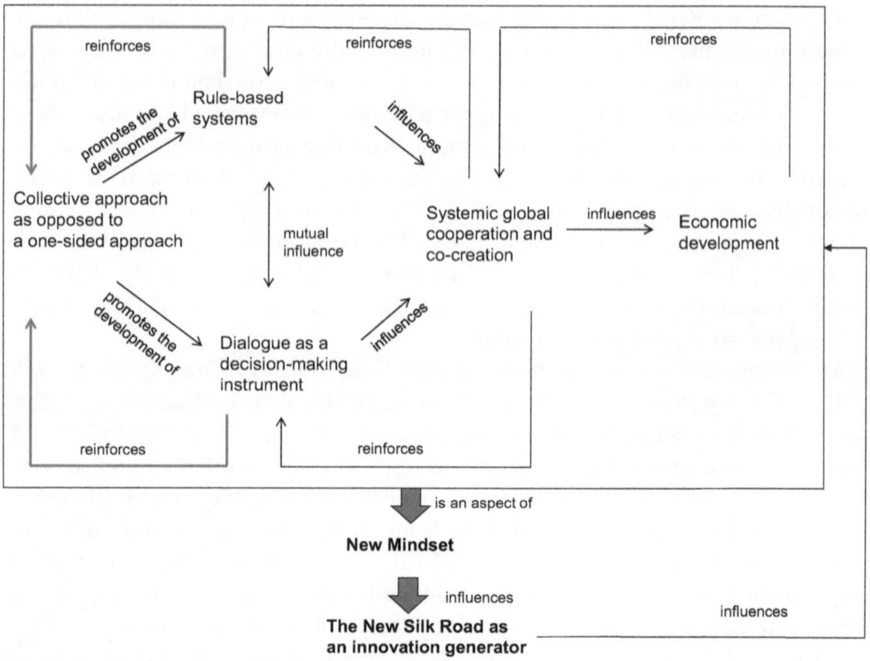

Figure 5.11 The new mindset.

strength, they can also afford to show weakness (Mahbubani, 2014). Weakness in this context is to show appeasement. However, the point here is that appeasement may be compared to when a judo master backs off until an opportune moment arises when an effective move can be executed. This is reminiscent of Chinese policy towards the outside world up until 2013, when Xi Jinping took over the leadership. The foreign policy before Xi Jinping is encapsulated in the phrase used by Deng Xiaoping, "hide your strength, bide your time".[34] The intention is that when you grow in strength, you should not seem threatening to a potential competitor, because you are not strong enough to take up the fight. It is better to wait until the time is ripe and the outside world sees your real strength. It is this strength Xi Jinping is now showing with the launching and implementation of the New Silk Road and China's new diplomacy policy (Mahbubani, 2010). China's strength lies in its economic, diplomatic and military capacity (Economy, 2018; Ferdinand, 2016).

The collaborative initiative that the New Silk Road constitutes is thus based on China's strength. It is this strength that the United States has now also become aware of (Allison, 2018; Zhang, 2015). It is precisely the emergence of this strength that has resulted in the United States beginning to view China as a potential competitor, and also a possible future enemy.[35]

Theoretical points related to a new mindset

The alternative to rule based systems is that a dominant power or a dominant alliance decides which rules apply. Such a concentration of power can then also change the rules as they see fit, so that the rules are best suited to them. Regarding systemic global cooperation and co-creation, it is precisely the connections between systems at all levels that will promote wealth creation (Ramaswamy & Ozcan, 2014).

If there is a small degree of cooperation and co-creation, and there are no connections between systems and levels, then a master-slave relationship may develop, or similar types of dominance strategies (Ramaswamy & Gouillart, 2010). In this context, the new mindset means that relationships are to a large extent guided by rule-based systems, at the same time as there is a large degree of systemic cooperation and co-creation.

The primary strategic intention of the New Silk Road is economic growth for China and the participating countries (Skiyan et al., 2020). On the other hand, there are also secondary strategic intentions (Vangeli, 2017). In some contexts, these secondary strategic intentions may be just as important as the primary strategic intention. There are four secondary strategic intentions (Jianglin, 2020c: 261–275).

The first secondary strategic intention is the importance of increasing cultural understanding between the countries, with regard to each other's distinctiveness and historical development (Vangeli, 2019). The second is the importance of fostering people-to-people relations, where people get to know each other and gain an understanding of each other's history and biography (Vangeli, 2018). The third is the importance of strengthening diplomacy; that is, China and the countries participating in the New Silk Road projects are developing relations at different levels, which are strengthening the ties between the countries (Wah & Menkhoff, 2020). The fourth secondary intention is the importance of developing innovative co-creation. This means that the countries participating in the various projects will be co-creators of innovative solutions on an equal level, while applying their distinctive expertise. Such innovative co-creation connects the countries more strongly to each other and also results in strengthening ties, which can also have an effect on the other three secondary intentions (Wang, 2015, 2016).

Both the primary and the four secondary strategic intentions of the New Silk Road connect the countries along this economic corridor in completely different ways (Wang, 2017a, 2017b). The reason is that the different countries have different conditions, different challenges and opportunities to participate in the various projects (Myint, 2019). Therefore, the empirical data from the various projects also show that there are various paths that lead to the same goal (Wang, 2017c). The goal is primarily economic growth and increased trade (Xing, 2019). The four secondary intentions can be understood as social mechanisms to achieve the goal. Although the goal is unambiguous, the different countries will have different goals, precisely because they take different paths towards the same main goal, economic growth. The different paths taken by the different countries will depend on their historical and cultural preconditions (Xing, 2019). Therefore, it can be said that there is one common goal, but different sub-goals for the different countries participating in the initiative. Regardless of the preconditions, it is crucial for the achievement of the goal that the economic corridor is guided by what we have

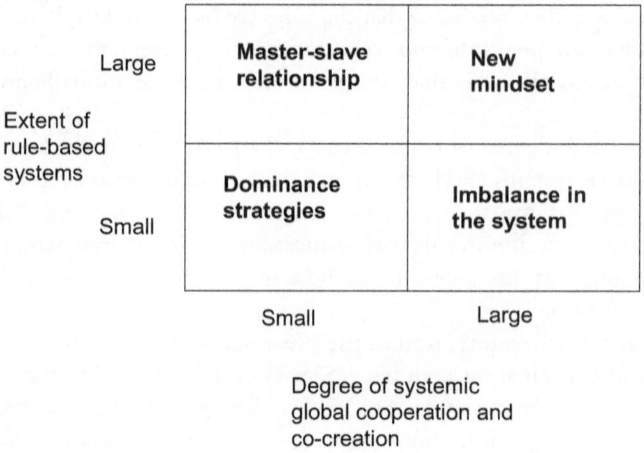

Figure 5.12 The new mindset: A typology.

termed here the new mindset, because this will ensure the necessary preconditions for economic growth (Yuan, 2019; Yue & Fujian, 2019).

Figure 5.12 illustrates the new mindset as discussed above.

Practical utility of a new mindset

The New Silk Road can be understood as a way to develop and share economic growth at a time when there is a strong political trend towards nationalism and protectionism (Frank, 2020). To achieve this, the New Silk Road projects are coordinated through policies in the countries that have signed agreements regarding participation (Gong & Mingjiang, 2020: 151–176). Furthermore, there is also coordination of the various infrastructure projects, so that resources can be used as efficiently as possible (Jianglin, 2020c: 263). In addition, it emerges that an important social mechanism for economic growth, cultural integration, people-to-people integration, innovation integration and diplomatic integration, is an unhindered trade between countries both along the New Silk Road, but also with other countries bordering this economic corridor. This became very clear with the signing of the new free trade agreement, the RCEP (15 November 2020).[36] Almost at the same time as the RCEP was signed, China and the EU reached an agreement of intent regarding mutual investment (December 2020).[37]

This development shows that China has jettisoned Deng Xiaoping's strategic policy of "Hide your strength, bide your time". The situation today is quite the opposite; when Xi Jinping implemented the New Silk Road in 2013 as part of China's "grand strategy", China's new strategy may be said to be to "show its strength". This new strategy is based on the fact that the original strategy of "hide your strength, bide your time" has paid off. During the period from 1978, when China was "hiding its strength", until around 2013, when China started to "show its strength", the country was able to lay the foundation for the position it has achieved today. By "hiding its strength", China had, like a judo master, to take one step back, by accepting the demands of foreign capital. This enabled foreign capital to profit from China's low labour costs and low costs due to China's lax environmental regulations. At the same time, this enabled China to accumulate a vast capital reserve from these foreign investments.

Amongst other things, this enabled China to invest heavily in education in general, and specifically in the development of technological universities. This is illustrated by the fact that there were 6 million students enrolled at Chinese universities in 2008, while nine years later, in 2017, this figure had increased to 20 million students (Linehan, 2018). Thus, by "hiding its strength", China has accumulated capital and resources in the necessary areas that will enable it to become one of the world's largest economies. This accumulation of capital has been utilised in the financial system, but also in the educational system, that is, to enable China to gain competence in general, and technological expertise in particular (Jain, 2021). If we assume that the largest input factor in the innovation economy is human capital and intellectual capital, i.e. competence and expertise, then it is clear that China has already managed to educate large parts of its population. The New Silk Road can be understood as a new way of thinking for the Chinese leaders. From 2013, China was able to show its strength, which largely consists of the country's expertise in various areas, not least in technology in general and artificial intelligence in particular. The new grand strategy shows itself by the investments made in the New Silk Road, the Dual Circulation Development Paradigm and Made in China 2025, to name a few initiatives. In addition, we also see the new grand strategy appear in the RCEP and in the China–EU agreement of intent. From 2013 to 2020, a new mindset emerged, that is, "showing its strength" has become an important part of China's new policy.

We have illustrated the description, analysis, reflections and presentation in a Boudon–Coleman diagram in Figure 5.13.

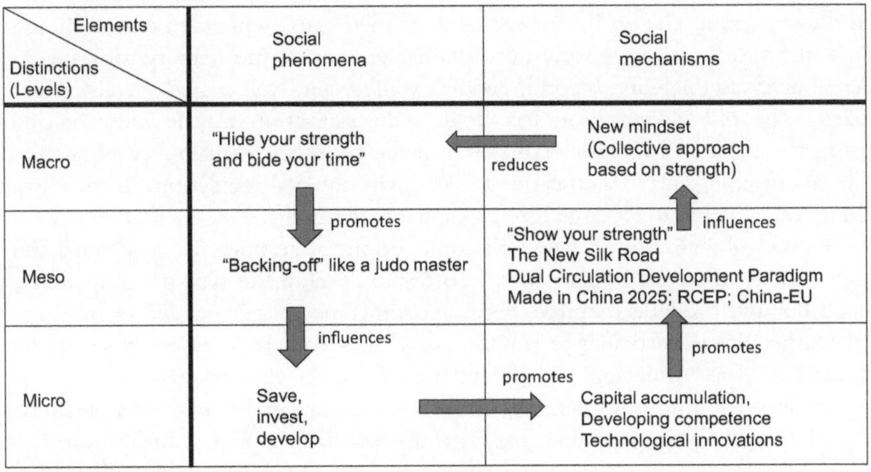

Figure 5.13 The new mindset: A Boudon–Coleman diagram.

Sub-conclusion related to a new mindset

In this section, we have examined the following question: How does the new mindset promote the New Silk Road as an innovation generator?

The short answer is that the new mindset promotes the New Silk Road as an innovation generator through economic growth, increased trade, and four social mechanisms. These four social mechanisms are: cultural integration, people-to-people integration, innovative integration and diplomatic integration.

The new globalization

In this section, we will examine the following question: How does new globalization promote the New Silk Road as an innovation generator?

The major problems and challenges in today's world are mainly global. This concerns the inequality crisis, the climate crisis, the health crisis, the extremism crisis, etc. None of these crises can be solved without thinking globally. Neither can any of the crises be solved without thinking in terms of sustainability. Global sustainability is thus the common denominator for the new globalization. In order to achieve global sustainability, global co-operation is necessary; this global cooperation needs to transcend ideological and religious tensions and conflicts if it is to be successful. In plain language, this presupposes that China and the United States, as well as their alliance partners, are able to cooperate more, and to a lesser extent focus on competition and conflicts between themselves and their alliance partners.

Narratives related to a new globalization

Case letter 1: Alliances and the new globalization

The old globalization was characterized by competition based on low costs. This led to downward pressure on the wage levels in the western industrialized world. At the same time, the profits for capital were increasing, which led to two things. First, the various projects were not sustainable, because profitability took precedence over sustainability; second, people's welfare and well-being was not prioritized. The old globalization led to de-industrialization in the industrialized countries and increased industrialization in the countries with low costs, such as low labour costs, and low costs due to lax environmental regulations. In this way, China was able to attract large foreign capital investments.

The new globalization is based on competition for competence in general and high-tech competence in particular. In order to develop this type of competence, a collaborative model is required, because competence in general and technological competence in particular presupposes that knowledge is developed through the clashing of ideas (Anderson, 2014; Popper et al., 2021). It is through such a clashing of ideas that innovations emerge. It is these innovations in general and technological innovations in particular that form the basis for the new globalization.

To promote the development of competencies and expertise, China launched and implemented the economic alliance, the New Silk Road. The United States started later than China in terms of developing alliances to foster the development of technological innovations. However, in February 2021, the President of the United States, Jo Biden, had spearheaded a technology alliance with allied countries to stem China's technological development. This technology alliance could be the United States' response to the New Silk Road initiative, and stem China's technological development. The new technology alliance, led by the United States, is intended to build a supply chain outside China, for computer chips, battery technology, medical equipment, rare raw materials, etc.[38]

The new globalization has gained two centres of power. The first is China and the countries connected through the New Silk Road, and the RCEP free trade agreement. The second is a technology alliance led by the United States.

It seems reasonable to assume that the new globalization may lead to a division of the world by creating two strong alliances, which are in open conflict with each other. It is not difficult to envision that the US's new technology alliance, combined with its NATO military alliance and its ideology alliance can lead to an increase in tensions between the two leading global economies. It does not take much to imagine a division of the world through the new globalization, with China in one alliance and the United States in the other alliance.

Description of a new globalization

Globalization is not a new phenomenon. Jeffrey D. Sachs (2020) outlines seven steps in the globalization of the planet, ranging from the Palaeolithic age (70,000–10,000 BC), to the digital age (21st century). We take a much more focused look at globalization and refer to the old globalization as the period from the 1980s to around 2013. This is the period from when China opened up to foreign investment, until the New Silk Road was introduced as a concept. Regardless of how one defines the period of globalization, it is innovations of various types that drive globalization forward. The four industrial revolutions from 1750 onwards, starting with the First Industrial Revolution that had the steam engine as its driving force, to the Fourth Industrial Revolution with artificial intelligence as its driving force, technological innovations have been the main focal point accelerating change (Johannessen, 2020a). However, it is not only technological innovations that drive these change processes, but also institutional innovations. The New Silk Road is such an institutional innovation. Globalization in the 1980s was largely driven by institutional innovations. First, there were political innovations where the opening up of China to foreign capital was perhaps the most important; then there was a new economic ideology, neoliberalism, which drove American investment in China.

As China's economic development progressed, the country was able to focus on mass education in general and technological education in particular. The diffusion of innovations from the United States and Europe were important to China at the beginning of this development, as it had been important to Japan forty years earlier. China gradually developed its own technology, and became a leader in several technological fields. When China started to show its strength, as reflected by the mass education of over one billion people, then the United States began to realise the power of the forces they had unleashed (Clinton, 2011; Kissinger, 2015). This eventually led to barriers being set up against China's technological development. In practice, there was a focus on the dangers to national security rather than efficiency and costs, something which impacted Huawei as the first Chinese company to be subjected to restrictions. Eventually, other Chinese companies were also subjected to the same negative and hostile treatment. The new US administration with Jo Biden as president in 2021 adopted a more strategic hindrance to the development of Chinese technology by forming a technology alliance excluding Chinese influence. The new globalization, with technological innovations as drivers, shifted from a multilateral strategy to a strategy based on two major alliances competing for the development of technological innovations in the Fourth Industrial Revolution. The two alliances that are emerging around 2021 are the US-led alliance and the China-led alliance. This constitutes the backdrop for the new globalization as we move towards the Fourth Industrial Revolution.

We have illustrated the above description in Figure 5.14.

Analysis of a new globalization

There is much to suggest that economic development does not happen as a continual or linear trend. From a metaphorical perspective, economic development is more like the steps on a staircase. At each level, one can envisage continual or linear economic development. Sometimes this economic development is going in

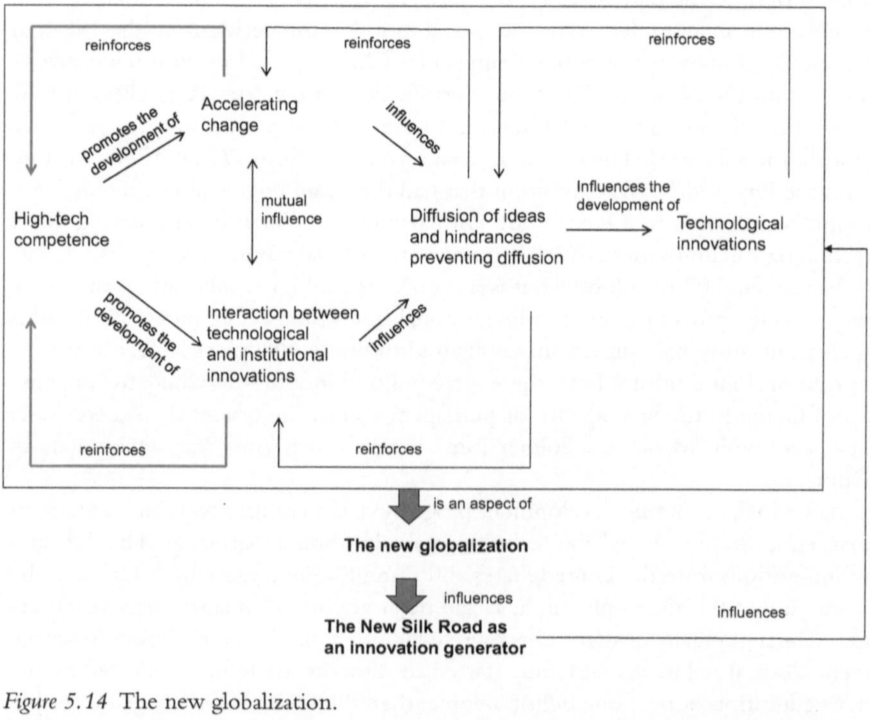

Figure 5.14 The new globalization.

an upwards direction, at other times it is going downwards, while at other times the trends resemble a sine wave. Our point is that when one starts to progress towards the next step, this will occur as the result of innovation, to a greater or lesser extent. This innovation may be technological or institutional. In other words, in this metaphor, an innovation occurs that brings economic growth and development up to the next level on the staircase. We know that this is a simplified, and thus not completely accurate, understanding of innovation and economic growth, but the metaphor gives a rough indication of what is happening, at least from a long-term perspective.

Innovations lead to changes that affect existing production, distribution and consumption methods. Minor innovations can lead to minor economic and social crises, because production changes and people's skills related to the old method of production are no longer in demand. Major innovations can lead to major economic and social crises, because entire industries become outdated and extinct, resulting in large-scale unemployment for those workers whose skills become outdated. It is also the case throughout economic history that innovations can lead to tensions, conflicts and even wars. This can be understood in relation to Thucydides' (2009) Trap that Allison (2018) has written about with regards to China's economic and technological growth which poses a "threat" to the USA. It is in this context that Chinese strategic awareness has resulted in the launching of the New Silk Road and the projects along it, providing China with a back door to enable the Chinese economy to thrive despite the US alliance against China. This strategic awareness has also led China to orient itself towards agreements in the Asia-Pacific region, e.g. the RCEP agreement, which is the world's largest free trade agreement. We also see the same strategic awareness in the agreement of intent between China and the EU regarding mutual investment (December 2020), as well as the concepts Made in China 2025 and the Dual Circulation Development Paradigm.

The interplay between technological and institutional innovations characterizes globalization in the innovation economy. High-tech expertise and technological innovations seem to go hand in hand with institutional innovations. Regarding China, the New Silk Road and all the cooperation agreements that this involves, constitute a major institutional innovation. The same applies to China's ratification of the RCEP agreement, which is the world's largest free trade agreement.

At the global level, the innovation economy will face three crucial challenges that need to be solved if the new globalization is to ensure welfare and well-being for the majority. The first challenge is the growing economic inequality that has developed from the 1980s onwards (Picket, 2017; Piketty, 2014, 2016). If this challenge is not addressed, there is a danger that the world will move towards more authoritarian and feudal structures (Kotkin 2020). The second challenge is the environmental and climate threat (Scheidel, 2017; Streeck, 2017). If this challenge is not resolved, it will not be of much help to resolve the other challenges facing the world. The third challenge is related to the core of the new globalization, that is, the struggle to become a leader in the new globalization (Allison, 2018). In short, this is the battle to become a leader in the fields that will dominate the Fourth Industrial Revolution, that is, artificial intelligence and intelligent robots. This explains the barriers that have been raised to Chinese development. This is evident from the growing assertiveness of the United States to once again try to take the lead in the fight for global leadership. In this context, there is not that much difference between Trump's slogan: "Make America Great Again" and President Biden's slogan that "America is back and ready to lead the world again".

Theoretical points related to a new globalization

The degree of high-tech competence, and the degree of technological innovations, will determine how the new globalization emerges. It is beyond doubt that the United States has been and still is the leading nation regarding technological innovations (Frey, 2019). On the other hand, we also know that the internal conflicts in the United States are very great (Frank, 2004, 2020), and that they are negatively affecting the country's social cohesion (Carney, 2020). However, under the Trump administration, the US managed to lead a joint struggle to impede a growing economic and technological China (Mahbubani, 2018, 2020).

There are four institutional innovations in China, which may be decisive for how China manifests its economic strength in the new globalization. The first of these is the New Silk Road, which will enable China to connect to countries in Asia, the Middle East and Europe. The question is whether the US will manage to split the EU and bring about a technological alliance against China. If the United States manages such a manoeuvre, then the part of the New Silk Road that is aimed at Europe will be reduced in strength. However, some parts of the European New Silk Road will not be completely destroyed, because China has already implemented several projects. One of these many projects is the port of Piraeus, and the railway that is being constructed from Piraeus, via Belgrade to Budapest.[39] Regardless of the European New Silk Road projects that have already been implemented, a US-led alliance against Chinese technology development could hamper and be detrimental to China's technological development in the innovation economy.

The second institutional innovation is China's new connections to the ASEAN countries through the RCEP free trade agreement, which it signed in the autumn of 2020. The 15 signatory countries account for approx. 30% of the world's population and approx. 30% of global GDP.[40] This free trade agreement alone indicates that the United States will have problems competing with China's economic and technological impact as we move towards the Fourth Industrial Revolution.

The third institutional innovation "Made in China 2025"[41] is a national strategy aimed at developing Chinese technology, so the country will not be dependent on US technology, and enable it to develop its own high-tech products. The strategic intention of "Made in China 2025" is to transform China from being the world's factory, where production resources are cheap labour, to the world's leading nation in high-tech production (Berlie & Hung, 2020).[42] This national plan aims to make China increasingly independent of foreign technology in general, and American technology in particular. The plan is also linked to the large-scale mass education at all levels that China has developed (Linehan, 2018).

The fourth institutional innovation is the Dual Circulation Development Paradigm. The strategy of this new paradigm is to reorient China's economy by increasing domestic consumption, while reducing or balancing this against international trade and investment. It is assumed that the development of Chinese high-tech production will be greatly aided by an increasing domestic consumption.[43]

If we connect the four institutional innovations, we arrive at a picture of a growing and confident China that is increasing its degree of high-tech competence, at the same time as it is making every effort to increase the degree of high-tech innovations.

We have illustrated the above description, analysis and the theoretical presentation in a typology in Figure 5.15.

Practical utility of a new globalization

The old globalization, with competition for wage costs, led to large economic growth in China, and resulted in 850 million people being lifted out of extreme poverty. This was officially celebrated in China on 26 February 2021.[44]

In the West, the old globalization has led to two important phenomena. Firstly, a deindustrialization of traditional industry. Secondly, there has been a development towards a knowledge economy, where education is a crucial input factor to ensure well-paid jobs. The downside of this development is that there are fewer well-paid jobs in industry for people without any special education. This has created tensions in society, pitting the unemployed against the intellectual elite – those people with secure and well-paid jobs in the knowledge economy.

Further, extreme economic inequality has emerged in the West, as a result of the old globalization (Sachs, 2020: 196–187). Those who own capital have become rich, while those who do not own capital have not kept up with economic development (Picket, 2017). In China, a very strong private sector has also emerged, where there are more billionaires than in the USA (Johannessen, 2021a; Magnus, 2018).

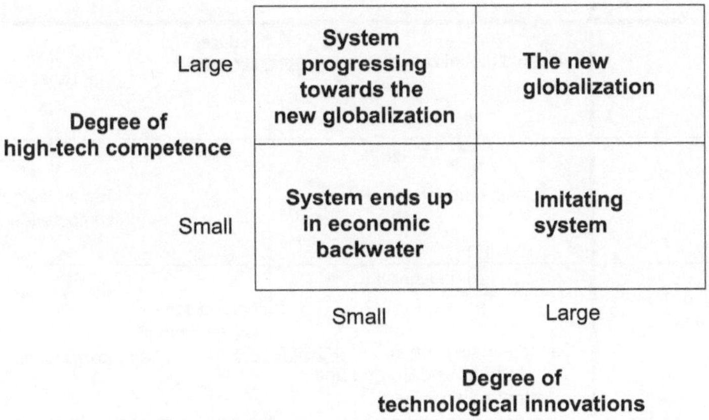

Figure 5.15 The new globalization: A typology.

While the old globalization competed on wage costs, in the new globalization competition is mainly related to competence in general and technological competence in particular. It is in this context that the Chinese economy has an advantage with its huge population and relatively open opportunities for higher education (Linehan, 2018). In other words, the millions of students enrolled at China's universities will ensure the future necessary technological competence needed to develop technological innovations that will promote the new globalization.

An important point of the new globalization is that wage costs will not be insignificant, even though they will be relatively less important for investment than in the old globalization. This is where China has a two-sided strategy in the new globalization. First, China has more students completing high-tech education than other countries. In other words, the large number of university graduates will constitute the most important resource as we move towards the Fourth Industrial Revolution. Second, the wage levels of the high-skilled workers in China is much lower than for the same group in the US. Against this background, it seems reasonable to assume that China will be the country that emerges strengthened from competition with the United States with regard to leadership in the Fourth Industrial Revolution.

We have illustrated the description, analysis, theoretical reflection and presentation of the practical utility in a Boudon–Coleman diagram in Figure 5.16.

Sub-conclusion related to a new globalization

In this section, we have examined the following question: How does the new globalization promote the New Silk Road as an innovation generator?

The short answer is that the new globalization promotes the New Silk Road as an innovation generator through collective development and application of

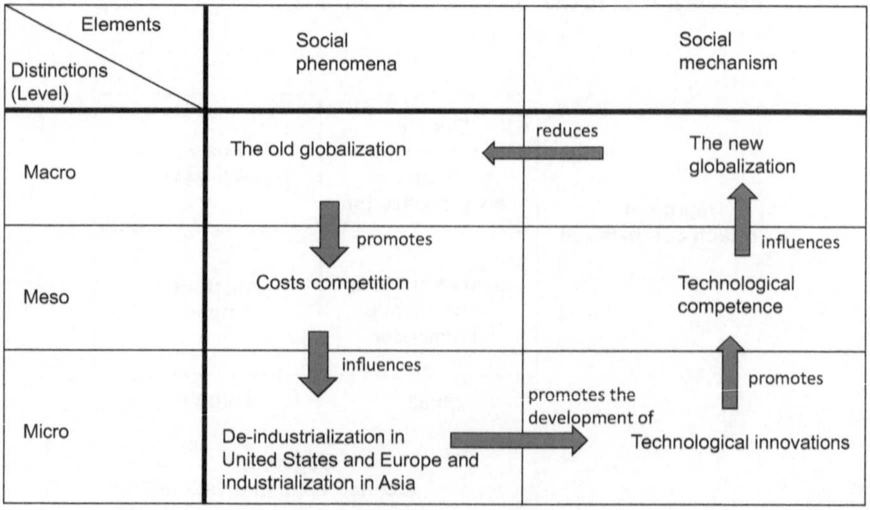

Figure 5.16 Practical utility: A Boudon–Coleman diagram.

high-tech expertise and technological innovations in various projects along the New Silk Road.

Main conclusion related to the transition from the old globalization to the new globalization

In this chapter, we have examined the following question: How does the feedforward effect promote the New Silk Road as an innovation generator? The feedforward effect is regarded here as an expectation mechanism, that is our expectations of the future affect our actions in the present.

In this chapter, we have divided the feedforward effect into five elements. These five elements are: global expectations, shared futures, a win–win ideology, new mindset and the new globalization. These five elements systemically promote the New Silk Road as an innovation generator.

It is argued in this chapter, that there is much that indicates that the feedforward mechanism will promote the New Silk Road, both the land-based and the maritime silk roads, as an innovation generator.

It is important to be aware of the fact it is not economic growth per se that creates prosperity and well-being for the population. It is rather a question of how economic growth is distributed that will determine the welfare in individual countries, and prosperity for individual citizens. Economic growth does not necessarily have to exploit resources to the limit, and consequently adversely affect the climate and the environment. If economic growth is increased in line with the variables set by the UN's sustainability goals, then it is possible to have economic growth that is not harmful to people, the environment and the climate. It is against this background that one can understand the expectations of mass education and high-tech innovation along the New Silk Road. In this economic growth, which is sustainable, economic, social, climate and environmental threshold values are integrated. These threshold values, which indicate the lower and upper limits in a control area, are organized and set in relation to the UN's sustainability goals for the individual national standards. Sustainable economic development is always the goal of the New Silk Road and is the basis for technological innovations and the mass education on which these innovations are based.

The organization of the new globalization along the New Silk Road has the vision to promote economic growth within sustainable economic development. This concerns shared futures through global expectations via the new globalization, which will create a new mindset and a win–win ideology for everyone involved along the New Silk Road, which is the overarching goal of economic growth and economic development along the New Silk Road. If profits for the capital owners and economic inequality result from this economic development, then it seems likely that many of the 130 countries that have signed agreements related to the New Silk Road will withdraw. It is when the individual countries experience a win–win consequence that the projects will be completed, and new projects along the New Silk Road will be launched.

The main philosophical idea behind the New Silk Road concept is that when you share with others, you will receive more in return. This is the driving force in

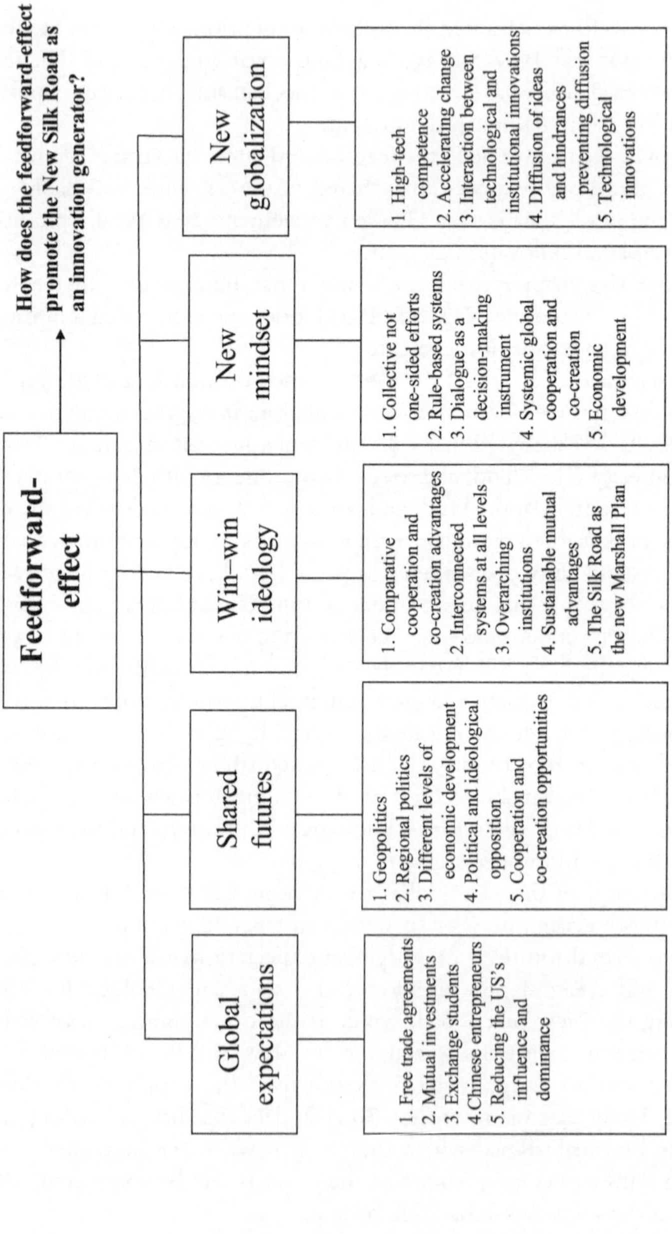

Figure 5.17 How does the feedforward effect promote the New Silk Road as an innovation generator?

the new mindset of the Chinese leaders from 2013, when the New Silk Road was launched as a concept.

The descriptions, analyses, mini-theories and presentations in this chapter are summarized in Figure 5.17. Figure 5.17 also shows an integrated answer to the research problem in this chapter: How does the feedforward effect promote the New Silk Road as an innovation generator?

Notes

1 The following are some of the most important sources we have used regarding the expectations of the Chinese leaders: Batzhan et al. (2020); Bougon (2017); Boutrup (2019); Drache et al. (2019); Fannin (2019); Hawke (2020); Holslag (2019); Jacques (2012); Jianglin (2020a, 2020b); Linehan (2018); Macaes (2020); Mahbubani (2020); Pavlicevic (2019); Ross & Bekkevold (2016); Vangeli (2017, 2018, 2019); Wang (2015, 2016, 2017a, 2017b, 2017c); Wasif Khan (2019); Xing (2019); Yang (2015); Yuan (2019); Yue & Fujian (2019); Yunker (2014); Zou (2018).

2 We deliberately make a distinction between infrastructure projects and info-structure projects so as to point out that traditional infrastructure projects are to a large extent based on low-skilled labour. The info-structure projects are all those projects that expand and develop information and communication processes; to a great extent, these projects require high-skilled labour.

3 https://global.chinadaily.com.cn/a/202102/04/WS601b4baaa31024ad0baa7283.html.

4 Ibid.

5 Ibid.

6 Ibid.

7 https://en.wikipedia.org/wiki/Forum_on_China–Africa_Cooperation.

8 Ibid.

9 https://en.wikipedia.org/wiki/Regional_Comprehensive_Economic_Partnership.

10 Ibid.

11 *Time* magazine sourced from reference 12 in: https://en.wikipedia.org/wiki/Regional_Comprehensive_Economic_Partnership (Date of reading: 6.2. 2021).

12 Anderson (2014); Billington (2020); Johannessen (2020b, 2020d, 2021a, 2022); Johannessen & Sætersdal (2020).

13 https://en.wikipedia.org/wiki/Regional_Comprehensive_Economic_Partnership.

14 https://trade.ec.europa.eu/doclib/press/index.cfm?id=2233.

15 https://www.politico.eu/article/europe-trade-wants-strategic-autonomy-decide-what-means/.
https://en.wikipedia.org/wiki/Strategic_autonomy.

16 Batzhan et al. (2020); Bougon (2017); Boutrup (2019); Drache et al. (2019); Fannin (2019); Hawke (2020); Holslag (2019); Jacques (2012); Jianglin (2020a, 2020b); Johannessen (2021a); Linehan (2018); Macaes (2020); Mahbubani (2020); Pavlicevic (2019); Ross & Bekkevold (2016); Vangeli (2017, 2018, 2019); Wang (2015, 2016, 2017a, 2017b, 2017c); Wasif Khan (2019); Xing (2019); Yang (2015); Yuan (2019); Yue & Fujian (2019); Yunker (2014); Zou (2018).

17 https://www.worldbank.org/en/country/china/overview.

18 https://www.cnbc.com/2019/05/16/why-huaweis-problems-with-the-us-government-have-been-so-bad.html.

19 https://en.wikipedia.org/wiki/Peloponnesian_War.

20 https://www.marxists.org/reference/archive/mao/selected-works/volume-6/mswv6_32.htm.

21 https://global.chinadaily.com.cn/a/202101/27/WS6010bf61a31024ad0baa556b.html.

22 In multilateral negotiations decisions are made by all the parties involved on the basis of dialogue between the parties. Unilateralism, or unilateral action, is executed independently of other parties, and is often based on power.

23 https://en.wikipedia.org/wiki/Win-win_game.
24 https://en.wikipedia.org/wiki/Adam_Smith.
25 https://en.wikipedia.org/wiki/Comparative_advantage.
26 "Modellmakt", a concept associated with the work of Stein Bråten, the Norwegian sociologist.
27 https://global.chinadaily.com.cn/a/202101/27/WS6010bf61a31024ad0baa556b.html.
28 Ibid.
29 https://global.chinadaily.com.cn/a/202101/27/WS6010bf61a31024ad0baa556b.html.
30 https://trade.ec.europa.eu/doclib/press/index.cfm?id=2233.
31 Anderson (2014); Billington (2020); Johannessen (2020b, 2020c, 2020d, 2020e, 2021b, 2022); Johannessen & Sætersdal (2020).
32 Allison (2018); Beeson & Li (2016); Jain (2021); Johannessen (2021a); Popper et al. (2021); Mahbubani (2010, 2014, 2018, 2020); Winston (2021).
33 https://global.chinadaily.com.cn/a/202101/30/WS6014aeb3a31024ad0baa628e.html.
34 Deng Xiaoping's point was that China should hide its strength so as not to provoke countries in the outside world, and wait for the right time to show the outside world its strength (https://en.wikipedia.org/wiki/Deng_Xiaoping).
35 Allison (2018); Jain (2021); Johannessen (2021a); Mahbubani (2018, 2020); Popper et al. (2021); Winston (2021).
36 https://en.wikipedia.org/wiki/Regional_Comprehensive_Economic_Partnership.
37 https://trade.ec.europa.eu/doclib/press/index.cfm?id=2233.
38 https://www.msn.com/en-us/news/politics/a-new-biden-executive-order-promises-to-restore-scientific-integrity-to-the-us-government-in-a-slapdown-of-the-trump-white-house/ar-BB1d8AR3.
39 https://en.wikipedia.org/wiki/Port_of_Piraeus.
40 https://en.wikipedia.org/wiki/Regional_Comprehensive_Economic_Partnership.
41 https://en.wikipedia.org/wiki/Made_in_China_2025.
42 https://www.chinadaily.com.cn/a/202011/27/WS5feadde5a31024ad0ba9f582.html.
43 https://global.chinadaily.com.cn/a/202011/27/WS5fc03a18a31024ad0ba96be0.html. https://global.chinadaily.com.cn/a/202012/28/WS5fe90e99a31024ad0ba9ec90.html.
44 https://www.scmp.com/news/china/politics/article/3123174/xi-jinping-declares-extreme-poverty-has-been-wiped-out-china.

References

Allison, G. (2018). *Destined for war: Can America and China escape Thucydides' trap?*, Scribe, London.

Anderson, E.G.G. (2014). *The innovation butterfly*, Springer, London.

Angang, H. (2014). Silk road economic belt: Strategic considerations, positioning and implementation routes. *Journal of Xinjiang Normal University*, 2: 1–10.

Batzhan, A., Alpysbayeva, S. & Kapsalyamova, Z. (2020). The Belt and Road initiative: Case of Kazakhstan. In Wah, C.Y., Menkhoff, T. & Low, L. (Eds.), *China's Belt and Road initiative: Understanding the dynamics of a global transformation*, World Scientific, London. pp. 71–97.

Beeson, M. & Li, F. (2016). China's place in regional and global governance: A new world comes into view. *Global Policy*, 7, 4: 491–499.

Berlie, J.A. & Hung, S. (2020). The Greater Bay Area and the role of Hong Kong and Macau SARs in the Belt and Road initiative. In Berlie, J.A. (Ed.), *China's globalization and the Belt and Road initiative*, Palgrave, London. pp. 77–100.

Billington, D.P. (2020). *From insight to innovation*, MIT Press, Boston, MA.

Bougon, F. (2017). *Xi Jinping*, Hurst & Company, London.

Boutrup, C. (2019). *The great tech revolution, how China is shaping our future*, Saxo Business, Copenhagen.

Brown, K. (2018). *China's dream*, Polity, London.

Brown, K. (2019). *The world according to Xi*, I.B. Tauris, London.

Byrre, D. & Gallaghan, G. (2013). *Complexity theory and the social sciences*, Routledge, London.

Carney, T.P. (2020). *Alienated America: Why some places thrive while others collapse*, Harper, New York.

Clinton, H. (2011). America's Pacific century. *Foreign Policy*, 189, 11 Oct.

Cohn, S.M. (2019). *Competing economic paradigm in China*, Routledge, London.

Drache, D., Kingsmith, A.T. & Qi, D. (2019). *One road many dreams: China's bold plan to remake the global economy*, Bloomsbury, New York.

Economy, E.C. (2018). *The third revolution, Xi Jinping and the new Chinese state*, Oxford University Press, Oxford.

Ehteshami, A. & Horesh, N. (2018). *China's presence in the Middle East*, Routledge, London

Fannin, R.A. (2019). *Tech titans of china*, Nicholas Brealey Publishing, London.

Feng, D.H. & Liang, H.M. (2019). *Belt and Road initiative: Chinese version of Marshall Plan*, World Scientific, London.

Ferdinand, P. (2016). The China dream and One Belt One Road: Chinese foreign policy under Xi Jinping. *International Affairs*, 92, 4: 941–957.

Frank, T. (2004). *What's the matter with Kansas? How conservatives won the Heart of America*, Metropolitan Press, New York.

Frank, T. (2020). *People without power*, Scribe, London.

French, H.W. (2015). *China's second continent*, Random House, London.

Frey, C.B. (2019). *The technology trap*, Princeton University Press, Princeton, NJ.

Gong, X. & Mingjiang, L. (2020). The Belt and Road initiative: Progress and prospect in Southeast Asia. In Wah, C.Y., Menkhoff, T. & Low, L. (Eds.), *China's Belt and Road initiative: Understanding the dynamics of a global transformation*, World Scientific, London. pp. 151–176.

Hamilton, C. (2018). *Silent invasion: China's influence in Australia*, Hardie Grant Books, New York.

Hawke, G. (2020). Economic historical development and leadership underlying the BRI strategy. In Wah, C.Y., Menkhoff, T. & Low, L. (Eds.), *China's Belt and Road initiative: Understanding the dynamics of a global transformation*, World Scientific, London. pp. 19–43.

Hoang, N.H. (2019). The Belt and Road initiative: Vietnam's perspective. In Yue, Y. & Fujian, L. (Eds.), *The Belt and Road initiative: ASEAN countries' perspectives*, World Scientific, London. pp. 233–252.

Holslag, J. (2019). *The Silk Road trap*, Polity, London.

Horesh, N. (2018). Introduction-China's one Belt, one road vision. In Ehteshami, A. & Horesh, N. (Eds.), *China's presence in the Middle East*, Routledge, London. pp. 1–7.

Huang, Y. (2017). *Cracking the China conundrum: Why conventional economic wisdom is wrong?* Oxford University Press, Oxford.

Jacques, M. (2012). *When China rules the world*, Penguin, London.

Jain, R. (2021). *China's soft power and higher education in South Asia*, Routledge, London.

Jianglin, Z. (2020a). Introduction. In Jianglin, Z. (Ed.), *21st-century maritime Silk Road initiative, aims and objectives, implementation strategies and policy recommendations*, World Scientific, London. pp. 3–30.

Jianglin, Z. (2020b). Macroeconomic basis for the 21st century maritime Silk Road initiative. In Jianglin, Z. (Ed.), *21st century maritime Silk Road initiative, aims and objectives, implementation strategies and policy recommendations*, World Scientific, London. pp. 59–100.

Jianglin, Z. (2020c). By different paths to common outcomes: The Belt and Road initiatives. In Jianglin, Z. (Ed.), *21st century maritime Silk Road initiative, aims and objectives, implementation strategies and policy recommendations*, World Scientific, London. pp 261–275.

Jinbo, W. (2020). The 21st century maritime Silk Road and Asian infrastructure connectivity. In Jianglin, Z. (Ed.), *21st century Maritime Silk Road initiative, aims and objectives, implementation strategies and policy recommendations*, World Scientific, London. pp. 181–209.

Johannessen, J.-A. (2018). *Innovation leads to economic crises*, Palgrave, London.

Johannessen, J.-A. (2020a). *The workplace of the future*, Routledge, London.

Johannessen, J.-A. (2020b). *Automation, innovation and economic crises: Survival the fourth industrial revolution*, Routledge, London.

Johannessen, J.-A. (2020c). *Knowledge management philosophy: Communication as a strategic asset in knowledge management*, Emerald, London.

Johannessen, J.-A. (2020d). *Knowledge management for leadership and communication: AI, innovation and the digital economy*, Emerald, London.

Johannessen, J.-A. (2020e). *Artificial intelligence, automation and the future of competence at work*, Routledge.

Johannessen, J.-A. (2021a). *The innovation economy in China*, Routledge, London.

Johannessen, J.-A. (2021b). *Artificial intelligence, automation and ethics in the innovation economy: Intelligent robots reflecting about unintelligent people*, Routledge, London.

Johannessen, J.-A. (2022). *Artificial intelligence and creativity: Implications for* automation and the innovation economy, Routledge, London.

Johannessen, J.-A. & Sætersdal, H. (2020). *Automation, innovation and work: The impact of technologic, economic and social singularity*, Routledge, London.

Junxin, S. (2020). Global value chain and the 21st century maritime Silk Road. In Jianglin, Z. (Ed.), *21st century maritime Silk Road initiative, aims and objectives, implementation strategies and policy recommendations*, World Scientific, London. pp. 155–210.

Kissinger, H. (2015). *World order*, Penguin, New York.

Kotkin, J. (2020). *The coming of neo-feudalism: A warning to the global middle class*, Encounter Books, New York.

Lim, J. & Lim, D. (2020). Financing the OBOR initiative. In Wah, C.Y., Menkhoff, T. & Low, L. (Eds.), *China's Belt and Road initiative: Understanding the dynamics of a global transformation*, World Scientific, London. Pp. 97–125.

Linehan, P.M. (2018). *The culture of leadership in contemporary China*, Lexington Books, London.

Linggui, W. (2020). Foreword. In Jianglin, Z. (Ed.), *21st century maritime Silk Road initiative, aims and objectives, implementation strategies and policy recommendations*, World Scientific, London. Pp. v–xiii.

Macaes, B. (2020). *Belt and Road: A Chinese world order*, C. Hurst, London.

Magnus, G. (2018). *Red flags, Why Xi's China is in jeopardy*, Yale University Press, New Haven, CT.

Mahbubani, K. (2009). *The new Asian hemisphere: The irresistible shift of global power to the east*, Public Affairs, London.

Mahbubani, K. (2010). *Can Asians think?* Marshall Cavendish, Singapore.

Mahbubani, K. (2014). *Great convergence: ASIA, the West, and the logic of one world*, Public Affairs, New York.

Mahbubani, K. (2018). *Has the west lost*, Allen Lane, New York.

Mahbubani, K. (2020). *Has China won?* Public Affairs, London

Miller, J.G. (1978). *Living systems*, McGraw-Hill, New York.

Miller, T. (2017). *China's Asian dream: Empire building along the New Silk Road*, Zed Books, London.

Myint, K. (2019). Synergizing BRI and Myanmar's development agenda. In Yue, Y. & Fujian, L. (Eds.), *The Belt and Road initiative: ASEAN countries' perspectives*, World Scientific, London. Pp. 141–164.

Pavlicevic, D. (2019). A power shift underway in Europe? China's relationship with central and eastern Europe under the Belt and Road initiative. In Xing, L. (Ed.), *Mapping China's One Belt One Road initiative*, Palgrave, London. Pp. 249–278.

Picket, K. (2017). Foreword. In Brown, R. (Ed.), *The inequality crises*, Policy Press, London. Pp. vii–viii.

Piketty, T. (2014). *Capital in the twenty-first century*, The Belknap Press of Harvard University Press, Boston, MA.

Piketty, T. (2016). *Chronicles: On our troubled times*, Viking, London.

Popper, S.W., Blumenthal, M.S. & Eugeniu, H. (2021). *China's propensity for innovation in the 21st century: Identifying indicators of future outcomes*, RAND Corporation, New York.

Prahalad, K.C. & Ramaswamy, V. (2004). *The future of competition: Co-creating unique value with customers*. Harvard Business School Press, Boston, MA.

Ramaswamy, V. & Gouillart, F. (2010). *The power of co-creation: Build it with them to boost growth, productivity, and profits*. Free Press, New York.

Ramaswamy, V. & Ozcan, K. (2014). *The co-creation paradigm*, Stanford University Press, Stanford.

Richardson, G.P. (1991). *Feedback thought in social science and systems theory*, University of Pennsylvania Press, Philadelphia, PA.

Ross, R. & Bekkevold, J.I. (2016). *China in the era of Xi Jinping*, Georgetown University Press, Washington, DC.

Sachs, J.D. (2020). *The ages of globalization*, Colombia University Press, New York.

Sandel, M.J. (2020). *The tyranny of merit: What's become of the common good?* Allen Lane, New York.

Scheidel, W. (2017). *The great leveler*, Princeton University Press, Princeton, NJ.

Scobell, A. (2018). Why the Middle East matters to China. In Ehteshami, A. & Horesh, N (Eds.), *China's presence in the Middle East*, Routledge, London. Pp. 9–24.

Shiyan, D., Xiangquanm W. & Yang, Y. (2020). External challenges arising from BRI development and approaches for solutions. In Wah, C.Y., Menkhoff, T. & Low, L. (Eds.), *China's Belt and Road initiative: Understanding the dynamics of a global transformation*, World Scientific, London. Pp. 1–18.

Streeck, W. (2017). *How will capitalism end?* Verso, London.

Thucydides. (2009). *The Peloponnesian war*, OUP, Oxford.

Valdmanis, W. (2021). *Accountable: How can we save capitalism*, Penguin, London.

Vangeli, A. (2017). China's engagement with the sixteen countries of central, east and south-east Europe under the Belt and Road initiative. *China & World Economy*, 25, 5: 101–124.

Vangeli, A. (2018). Normative foundation of the Belt and Road initiative. In Wenhua, S., Nuotio, K. & Zhang, K. (Eds.), *Normative readings of the Belt and Road initiative*, Springer, London, pp. 59–83.

Vangeli, A. (2019). A framework for the study of One Belt One Road initiative as a medium of principle diffusion. In Xing, L. (Ed.), *Mapping China's One Belt One Road initiative*, Palgrave Macmillan, London. Pp. 57–89.

Wah, C.Y. & Menkhoff, T. (2020). Introduction: Understanding the transformational power of China's Belt and Road initiative. In Wah, C.Y., Menkhoff, T. & Low, L. (Eds.), *China's Belt and Road initiative: Understanding the dynamics of a global transformation*, World Scientific, London. Pp. xxiii–xxxviii.

Wang, Y. (2015). *One Belt One Road: Opportunities and challenges*, People's Press, Beijing.

Wang, Y. (2016). *The Belt and Road initiative: What will China offer the world in its rise*, New World Press, Beijing.

Wang, Y. (2017a). *Belt and Road initiative: China's responsibilities in its rise*, People's Press, Beijing.

Wang, Y. (2017b). *China connects the world: What behind the Belt and Road initiative*, China Intercontinental Press, Beijing.

Wang, Y. (2017c). *The world is connected: The logic of Belt and Road initiative*, The Commercial Press, Beijing.

Wasif Khan, S. (2019). *Haunted by chaos, China's grand strategy from Mao Zedong to Xi Jinping*, Harvard University Press, Cambridge, Mass.

Winston, M. (2021). *The digital war: How China's tech power shapes the future of AI blockchain and cyberspace*, Wiley, New York.

Xiaoxue, L. (2020). India and the 21st century maritime Silk Road. In Jianglin, Z. (Ed.), *21st-century maritime Silk Road initiative, aims and objectives, implementation strategies and policy recommendations*, World Scientific, London. pp. 227–258.

Xing, L. (2019). Understanding the multiple facets of China's "One Belt One Road" initiative. In Xing, L. (Ed.), *Mapping China's One Belt One Road initiative*, Palgrave Macmillan, London. pp. 29–56.

Yang, J. (2015). China's new diplomacy under the Xi Jinping administration. *China Quarterly of International Strategic Studies*, 1,1: 1–17.

Yuan, F. (2019). The one belt one road initiative and China's multi-layered multilateralism. In Xing, L. (Eds.), *Mapping China's 'One Belt One Road' initiative*, Palgrave Macmillan, Cham. pp. 91–116.

Yue, Y. & Fujian, L. (2019). ASEAN-China cooperation under the framework of the Belt and Road initiative: A comparative study on the perspectives of China and ASEAN. In Yue, Y. & Fujian, L. (Eds.), *The Belt and Road initiative: ASEAN countries' perspectives*, World Scientific, London. pp. 1–58.

Yunker, J. (2014). *Global Marshall Plan: Theory and evidence*, Lexington, London.

Yuzhu, W. (2020). New regional cooperation and integration strategy and the 21st century maritime Silk Road initiative. In Jianglin, Z. (Ed.), *21st century Maritime Silk Road initiative, aims and objectives, implementation strategies and policy recommendations*, World Scientific, London. pp. 211–225.

Zhang, J. (2015). China's new foreign policy under Xi Jinping: Towards peaceful rise 2.0? *Global Change, Peace & Security*, 27, 1: 5–19.

Zhengqi, P. (2020). Strategic linkages: China's Belt and Road initiative and power through global value chain. In Wah, C.Y., Menkhoff, T. & Low, L. (Eds.), *China's Belt and Road initiative: Understanding the dynamics of a global transformation*, World Scientific, London. pp. 221–241.

Zhongyuan, Z. (2020). Microeconomic basis for the 21st-century maritime Silk Road initiative: from the perspective of a value chain. In Jianglin, Z. (Ed.), *21st century maritime Silk Road initiative, aims and objectives, implementation strategies and policy recommendations*, World Scientific, London. pp. 101–154.

Zou, L. (2018). *The political economy of China's Belt and Road initiative*, World Scientific, London.

Index

Page numbers in *italics* refer to figures.